Guncrank Diaries

The Collected Works
as originally published in

americanhandgunner.com

Guncrank Diaries

The Collected Works
November/December 2003 through January/February 2018

By John Connor

Published By
FMG Publications
A Division Of
Publishers' Development Corporation
© All Rights 2021

ISBN: 978-1-7366727-1-6

FMG Publications
13741 Danielson Street, Suite A, Poway, CA 92064
fmgpubs.com

YOU'LL BE GLAD YOU HAVE THIS BOOK ...

John Connor is a soldier, cop, father, lover of dogs, protector of the defenseless, guardian of what's right — and a fierce foe of what's wrong. He's fought evil, brutality and tyranny in the jungles of Vietnam, as a cop on the city streets of a major Southern California city, and in a host of god-forsaken places around the world.

His friends often have very unusual names, and all remain fiercely loyal — and for very good reasons.

He refuses to stand by while evil does what it tends to do. Chances are very good, if you hear the crunch of a boot on gravel and a quiet voice saying, "Let her go…" — it's likely John.

This book isn't about what you think, either. Not at all. It's not just simply a series of columns John wrote for the pages of American Handgunner Magazine. They're stories, yes, but each has a meaning stronger than the words on the paper convey. Each one — I promise you — will drag deep-rooted, powerful memories from deep within you about things that were, or might have been. You'll be surprised by how a simple story of a hungry soldier in a communist border guard unit will become part of your everyday thoughts for days — even years.

And Little Lizzie? Don't get me started on that one. Why do we carry guns? Why, to protect Little Lizzie, that's why. John explains it powerfully, and it's sure to stick in your thoughts, playing on a continuous loop tape — pretty much forever.

I promise you won't be able to resist sharing John's narrations of life. His thoughts, memories, wishes — and just plain good writing — demand sharing. I encourage you to do just that.

The amazing thing is most everything you read is true — or at least based on the real story. The reason I know is because I've been John's friend for almost 40 years — and I was there when some of what he writes about darkened the streets. Experiencing what John later writes about is as if I suddenly had someone explain what happened to me, to us, that day — and why.

The effect this modest book will have on you won't buff out easily.

Be prepared to be changed.

Roy Huntington
Editor, American Handgunner Magazine
Retired

Get More Guncrank Every Week!

Subscribe to the Guncrank Chronicles e-newsletter
and get new crank content every Friday.
Visit:
americanhandgunner.com/guncrank

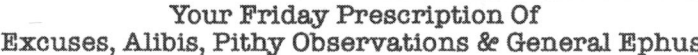 

You guys need to keep digging up ol J. Conner, just don't get the same laughs from anybody else, and I love the looks my wife gives me when I'm giggling and blowin snot on my smart phone.
~ Lucas D

Darn it Connor, stop it-stop it-stop it... my old eyes are not as tough as they used to be. Your story of the custom colt was just wonderful.. I forwarded it to my wife... now her eyes are leaking too.. so just stop it!
~ Gary M

I have been a fan of John Conner for longer than I can remember. His recent story-telling pieces are awesome! I truly look forward each week to see what literary mayhem he has wrought.
~ Curt B

Connor knows how to get to us and especially those that have experienced the brotherhood of the military.
~ Sam A

I love John Conner's stories and articles. I'm sad to see our country in such bad shape. Who could believe it? We need more John Conners on the front line.
~ Robert M

I don't give a damn if the writer of Guncrank is or was a super secret special forces tacti-cool bad ass or if he was a truck driver or a mess sergeant. I like what he writes. I enjoy it because it is entertaining. And its usually just plain funny.
So whoever you are thanks, I appreciate what your do or did.
~ Just an Army Guy.

Like fine wine, Connors insights age well and remain cogent. More please.
~ Doc H

It used to be I loved Friday's because it was the end of the work week. Now I love 'em because of Guncrank Chronicles! Keep up the great work!!
~ Gary

CONTENTS

GLOCK WINS OVER GUCCI
— This Time, Anyway

NOVEMBER/DECEMBER 2003

I muttered, "Okay, okay," giving it my best dejected-hangdog look. I would have shuffled my feet, too, but doing the ten-year-old-kid foot-shuffle would be way over the top. I said, "I'll give up desserts."

I couldn't see her eyes — mine were still downcast — but I know she didn't even blink as she batted that one back over the net, hard! All right, I don't know squat about tennis, but I know about gettin' the ball whacked back at you at 152 mph, straight for your throat.

"Yeah, right," she snapped. "How often do we even *have* desserts?" I saw a faint glimmer of hope; a chance to derail the topic.

"Not often enough!" I lobbed back, but no dice. She switched to her backhand and whopped that one.

"Off the subject, dear." Damn. She said "dear." She only says "dear" when it's a substitute for "jackass."

The subject was — my guns. Specifically, that I sorta semi-collect guns. I mean, nothing big-time; no Janet Reno "arsenal," or an open account at Bob's House of Thunder-Sticks. I just have some guns stuck in a nice closet gunsafe. No fully-engraved jobs, no gold inlays, no ivory grips. Just good quality, solid, durable, okay — beautiful — guns. They're all shooters, not "collector pieces." Okay, a half-dozen are mint, unfired, but they're still shooters, and that only makes sense. Guns are like gold coins you can shoot; like multi-purpose ingots, or investor-quality gems you can also mow the lawn with. I have kids, and they might go to college, see? Sure, I have college savings funds for them too, but … guns are better, safer, a surer value, and — just better. Because they're guns, you know? Of course you do. And, maybe the kids won't go to college, in which case, I have those guns. Nothing wrong with that.

Her objection to my gun-gathering thing, which she calls my "personal perversion," seems to come on like a rogue tsunami on a cyclical basis. Like those wet tsunamis, they seem to come 'outta nowhere, threatening to wipe out the placid beachfront of my gun-sorta-collection for no good reason at all. None I can see, anyway.

It's not like I'm taking food out of the kiddies' mouths or swapping the family silver for an 1873 Colt. About 20 years ago I started my "gun fund" with $500, and since then I've wheeled, traded and bargained for about 90 percent of my guns, ammo and peripheral gun-junk. Hey, the mortgage gets paid, I got the pinks to the truck and the Outback, and the kids' teeth are straight, so put that pointy-finger of irresponsibility away. That ain't me.

She knows all this. At least, on some level of Vulcan logic, she knows this. And it's not like she's against guns. She's married to me, after all. She just has these fits where she believes one or two guns ought to do me. I think these episodes probably have more to do with her unrequited desire to throttle a certain soccer referee, or that Wendy's employee who screwed up her order at the drive-thru. But still, the tsunami rolls in.

I had only one more move. I knew it was dangerous — perhaps lethal — but it was all I had left. I pointed to The Sacred Shrine — her shoe closet. "Shall we compare," I drawled, "My personal perversion to your private passion?"

Gotcha! I saw a half-tremble, a microsecond of doubt, a paper-thin slice of primal fear glimmering before she raised her arms, slapped 'em together across her chest, and tiger-smiled, "Okay, yes, lets."

She opened the Shrine. You know how railroad tracks seem to converge to a point as they disappear into the distance? That's what her shoe racks do in that long, long closet. I had never gone there, literally or figuratively. Mentally, I think my head might explode. Physically, I think it might be mined; booby-trapped. Claymores, at the least.

"First," she said, "I think we can agree that a woman can never have too many shoes." I squinted. Her eyes flickered. "And a man can never…" I said gently — and she wavered. I pounced. "No, first, let's ask, who has more? Pairs of shoes — or guns?" Point! "Ummm … how many pairs you got in there, honey?" I don't know for sure. Heck, I don't want to know! But my gunsafe is one-quarter the size of her shoe closet. I know I scored a point there.

Thud! Bang! Whop!

"But," she parried, "I only wear one pair at a time!" Whop! "And I only wear one gun at a time!" Another eye-flicker, but I parried, "Okay, sometimes two … Sometimes. That's like a pair. Sorta."

"How about all that other gun stuff, besides the guns?" This serve was weak, weak …

"Oh, you mean accessories," I asked, "Like holsters and ammo and magazines …" Her head was bobbing like the back-window doggie in a Chevy Vega — "Accessories like somebody's matching belts and purses?" The bobbing stopped. Dead. She recovers! What a save! Whop!

"When's the last time I spent $600 on shoes?" Backhand, bang! I pointed to a pair of wine-red kid leather Dolce & Gabbana pumps. "Those?" I didn't touch them — I knew better. The blow was effective enough without that. The angry orange lights faded from her eyes, and I knew she was mine, fini. Shaken, she drifted into dreamy-eyed somnolence, reaching out and stroking shoe after shoe …

"But," she murmured, "My shoes are beautiful… and well-made, and they're Zanotti's, and Versace, and Gucci, and I just love touching them, handling them, and…" Her eyes glistened. Tears? Of what? Joy, tenderness, passion? I lowered my voice to a whisper.

"And my guns," I murmured, "The Smiths, the Colts, the Glocks and the Rugers … They're so beautiful, and well-made, and I just like … You know …" If I'da had an onion in my pocket, I woulda used it, you bet, but I think I got a little honestly misty-eyed anyway. Hey, they are pretty dang beautiful, right?

"And my guns," still tenderly, gently now, "They increase in value every day … I appreciate them, and they appreciate for me — for us … for us …"

I didn't have to point out there ain't a single pair of heels, flats, pumps, or slingbacks in that cavernous closet-of-dreams that would fetch back ten percent of their original cost. I didn't have to. As long as I didn't rub it in.

There was something else I didn't say, but I thunk it: "Point, set, and MATCH, dear!" I also refrained from any kind of football "victory" dance as I stood, with just the right big, brown, Golden Retriever-type eyes I could muster, toes just touching the tiles at the entrance to the sacred closet. Discretion is, indeed, the better part of valor.

WHAT'S THIS "ESSENCE" CRAP?

JANUARY/FEBRUARY 2004

There was silence. Then the editor says, "Write me an intro. You know, for your column." I thought for a second. "Whaddaya mean?" I asked. Sometimes I'm so intuitive and articulate it's scary, huh?

He got that kind of indulgent, I'm dealing with a large, slow child here look on his face, and leaned over the desk. "You're a columnist now, John. It's different from just being a gunwriter. The readers need to know about you, your family, your background. You need to give them your philosophy, your flavor, your essence."

"Too late," I said, "I already wrote that first piece. They know me." I would have said more, but I was still amazed he could say that flavor an' essence stuff with a straight face.

"No," he says, "Not enough. They know you've got a wife, and she has shoes. They need more. Here," he says, shoving some paper at me, "This will help. You've got mail from that first column."

Mrs. C.

Okay, that helped. Some of you guys wrote asking how I could be married to someone who hates guns, why I don't just "put her in her place;" that kinda crap.

First, she doesn't hate guns. She just thinks a brace of Les Baer Premier II Super-Tac .45's, a Ruger M-77 in 30-06, and a Remington 870 12-gauge ought to be enough guns for any woman. Maybe a man should also own a nice .22. She carries. She shoots. Really well.

As for this "putting her in her place" stuff, maybe you guys are married to women. I'm married to a Force of Nature. Take a six-foot billet of steel and hammer-forge it

into a woman, mostly legs. Attach flaming red hair, big blue eyes, and a tuned .45. As for attitude, meteorologists in Bangladesh hate it when she gets torqued. They pick it up on their Cyclone Early Warning System.

Here's a CAT-Scan slice of Mrs. C: Some years ago, my uncle, Commander Gilmore, let us tag along on a Cape buffalo hunt in Africa. I was disappointed that he used a big double rifle. I thought he was just gonna fistfight 'em. Anyway, Mrs. C contented herself with nature photography, wallopin' camp meat, and practicing her draw-and-pop on the occasional overly-curious or aggressive hyena. This happened mostly about twilight or in the dark, around camp, and without warning. This "impressed" the hired hands, you might say.

One evening I was walking past their cookfire with the headman, and we saw they had caught some kinda big long-tailed rat-lookin' critter, and one of the guys was crouched, swingin' it by the tail and whacking it on the ground. They were all laughing, and I caught something about "simba" and "Memsaab Helen-ah." Then they saw us, and snickered, kinda embarrassed, behind their hands. The headman explained.

"They say," he laughed, "That your wife, the Memsaab Helen-ah, she need no rifle to hunt the lion. She will take him by the tail," he chopped his arm down, "And beat him on the dirt."

Got the picture? Personally, I think it's just fine havin' a wife who can carry you out of a burning building. The other side of that coin is, she could also toss you into a burning building. Or just grab you by the tail an' whack you on the ground until you squeak. Or stop squeakin'.

Otherwise, I am owned and operated by a teenage daughter, and if you don't know what I mean, you don't have one. When her lower lip sticks out in a pout, my brain shrinks. Dazed, I unconsciously reach for my wallet and empty it into her hands. I see the right side of her face from time to time. The left side has a phone growing out of it.

I am also engaged in feeding and training her older brother and his pals, the Refrigerator Raiders. Being 17-ish, their language skills are limited to things like "Good grub, woof-woof!" and "Go play ball, woof-woof!" Put any one of 'em in a padded cell with a bowling ball, and they'll eat the padding and break the ball. At any moment I expect Dian Fossey to show up at the door with a film crew, wanting to study them for "Gorillas In The Mist, Part II."

Tilting Windmills

As for me and my dog, Sancho Panza, we hang around, oversee this circus, and write about guns and stuff. I used to run around the world in a variety of uniforms chasing bad guys, and fixing problems with liberal applications of small-arms fire. Now I just run amok, and fix problems with duct tape.

As for that flavor and essence and philosophy stuff, my flavor is Dreyer's Grand Vanilla Bean ice cream. I checked the dictionary, and essence seems to be what would squeeze out of you if you got squoze hard enough. That would be a mix of Hoppe's Number Nine, RemOil, and Wild Turkey. My philosophy is, "The pen may be mightier than the sword, but a good Glock beats the heck out of a gross of the finest pens."

Your next couple questions were, "How do you get to be a gunwriter," and "What the heck is a gunwriter?" I'll give you a clue on the first: The same way you get a busted leg. Think about it, and I'll explain next time, okay?

ALL ABOUT GUN WRITING, PART I

MARCH/APRIL 2004

Okay, we got all that philosophy and flavor and essence crap outta the way in the last issue, so I can get down to your piercing, semi-intelligent questions. First, you ask, "How do you get to be a gunwriter?"

The same way you get a busted leg. You start out doing something else that's interesting and a lot of fun, and then you screw up. If you're not dead, sometimes you then become a gunwriter. Try this: First, become a weapons operator. Then, go operate 'em in jungles, deserts, mountains, streets and alleys. Do silly stuff like jump out of airplanes, dangle from ropes, an' kick in doors. Get shot at a lot and hit a little. Then get bent, folded, spindled an' mutilated, preferably without becoming null and void. Worked for me.

I don't think you can just like guns, start writing, and become a gunwriter. I think you have to be lookin' the other way and get blindsided by it, like getting hit by a bus.

Next question: What the heck is a "gunwriter"? Is that different from being a "writer"? Oh, yeah … See, a "writer" would write something like this:

The telephone dangled and then fell from Derek's trembling hand, clattering among the Hummel figurines on his French Provincial sidetable. Drawing in a shuddering breath, his mind reeled with the crude and violent threat of that, that … that horrid person! A mounting swell of emotion crested in his soul, then broke like a storm-tossed wave on the shore of his heart, and he wept, silvery tears tracing down his pale cheeks.

"Oh, my poor, dear, dear Derek," Abigail whispered, touching her delicate hand to her alabaster breast, which fluttered like a frightened dove. There was only one thing to do: Flee to Scones-on-Avon, the family lodge at Buttersby Hill! There, on the lonely windswept moors, perhaps the demons could not find them!

Now, a "gunwriter" would write it like this:

This wimpy dude, see, he's in a jam, and he don't even plant his feet or nothin'. He just goes all gutless, throws his sucker in the dirt, an' busts out cryin' like a little girl with a skint knee. Meantime, the babe, get this, she thinks it's cool that the dude's blubberin', like he's so-o-o sensitive or something, and she's soppin' this up like country gravy, okay? Here comes trouble, see? — and not a roscoe between 'em!

Action Gun'riters

Maybe someday I'll become an "Action Gunwriter," and I'll write stuff like this:

Derek slammed the phone down, crackin' it like an egg. Never telegraph your punch, sucker! He grinned to himself. Now that he knew the What's-Up, he'd dictate the Where and When. Jamming his Springfield 1911A1 into a Galco Fed Paddle, he then slipped its little cousin, a Micro-Compact, into the Yaqui Slide at his back. With two stuffed mags already on his belt, he hesitated, then dumped two more in his jacket pockets. Somebody serves you a hot cuppa trouble, he chuckled, You bring 'em a chilled bucket of ice-cold Whup-Ass. He turned to Abby.

"Anything but me comes through this door, kid," he told her, "You light 'em up."

Biting her lip, fighting tears of rage, she tapped the barrel of her .40-cal Glock 23 on the hated white cast that ran from her ankle to the curve of her hip. Damn that Harley! she thought, And double-damn that loose gravel! She should be there, she knew, back-to-back with Big D when the BrownStuff hits the fan.

"None of these 155-grain Gold Dots have your name on 'em, sweetie," she pouted bravely, "They're all addressed To Whom It May Concern." He grinned wolf-like from the door.

"Who's your daddy, baby?" — and he was gone.

Abby absent-mindedly danced the beam of her LaserMax sight on the darkening door. She knew even if Satan himself showed up and wanted to waltz, Big D would return with the devil's tail, whacked off neatly at the base. Then he'd want to skin it out and wear it as a gunbelt. But still, she thought, and choked back another angry tear.

"Cocked, locked, and ready to rock, baby," she breathed.

> **Somebody serves you a hot cuppa trouble, he chuckled, You bring 'em a chilled bucket of ice[coldWhup-Ass.**

Trade Secrets

See what I mean? Now, you notice the "gunwriter" writin' didn't really say much about guns? That's one of the trade secrets of gunwriting. Basically, what you do is take some opinions and observations, wrap 'em around a firearms-related fragment, and bury that ball in some word-salad. I obeyed a couple rules of the trade there.

First, I inserted a "key word" to get your attention: babe. At that point, the male readers' pupils dilated and their brains went into reptile-mode. Female readers' pupils constricted, and they kept reading to see if there was gonna be something stupidly sexist to write in and complain to the editor about. Both ways, it keeps 'em reading. Next, I "painted a word picture." That was the "soppin' this up like country gravy" part. You didn't know it, but I was subtly tappin' into your subconscious to create "comfort imagery." Tricky, huh?

Then I used a non-gun word to describe a gun: roscoe. This is a ReallyBigDeal part of gunwriting. I'm not sure why, but you're not supposed to use "gun" more than once in four paragraphs. I think it's part of the "mystique" business. Beats me. Note: Do NOT attempt these gunwriting techniques at home, kids. I'm a professional, workin' on a closed course.

Next, you have to learn "gunwriter's terminology." That's next time, maybe.

• • • •

Editor's note: If you want to contact Connor, you can find him on his e-mail at: thatgunwriterguy@aol.com, although for the life of us, we can't imagine why you'd want to. We're not even sure why we do.

ON GUN SHOWS

MAY/JUNE 2004

For some men it's junk food. For others, it's power tools, jet-skis, four-wheelers, fine cognac, or whatever. For me it's … GUN SHOWS. God help me, I can't stay away from 'em. Oh, man, they say crack is addicting, but how many crackheads drive 400 miles out of their way on a 1,000-mile business trip to try another variety of crack? Dang! And it's not like I even get a "high" out of it. Nine times out of ten, all I come away with is a sore crotch. But I gotta go — just gotta.

And I never seem to learn. I don't care if they're in Bangor, Biloxi, or Broken Pelvis, Montana, there are some things about gun shows — both features and weird people — that never change. In fact, I suspect a lot of these folks just travel from one gun show to another, all conspiring to stand between me and that one great gun, that one spectacular "find" that keeps pulling me back like iron filings to a magnet.

The Personalities

First, there's the Wildebeest People. You know, the graduates of Gnu U. They move down the aisles like a single giant gelatinous many-headed organism, oozing right, then left, then inexplicably reversing course, anything possible to keep you away from The Great Gun Deal! Try to squirt past 'em, and without responding to any detectable signal, the whole mass will shift subtly, implacably, to block you. Personally, I think it's some kinda CIA experiment in mindless mind control. And none of 'em use deodorant. They might be French.

At least six percent of the crowd will be Ice Cream Commandos. These wannabe-warriors attend decked out from bandanna-top to combat-boot bottom in nine kinds of camouflage, all of which stands out like an Abrams tank on the Interstate. Usually, there's not a square yard of terrain within 52 miles where their camouflage might "blend in." If they wanted to melt into the surroundings, they'd be wearing outfits painted to look like rusty old Colts, oddly-angled sheets of plywood, ammo boxes, and sawhorses. Tricky pattern, but it could work.

Maybe I've just got an archaic view of wearing camouflage. See, I used to wear it in forests and jungles to make it harder for people to shoot me to death. It worked okay. Not once was I shot to death. I usually wear khakis and a sport shirt to gun shows, and I blend in pretty well. I can't quite become one with the wall, but close.

There will be at least four tables occupied by guys trying to sell sixguns chambered for a 20mm cannon shell necked down to shoot carbide phonograph needles at 84,000 feet per second. "This sucker'll smoke a bull bumblebee at a thousand yards!" Yeah, that's what I need. Probably spoils the meat though.

Six tables will be devoted to prototype handguns incorporating some kinda techno-crap to identify the authorized shooter before it will allow itself to be fired. One of 'em sticks a needle into your hand when you grasp the grip, confirming your identity by blood-gas spectrochromatograph. Soon as they get the five-shot .22 model down under 56 pounds, I'll check it out again. Another one looks pretty much like a regular chubby revolver. You swing out the cylinder, spit into one of the chambers, and get ID' by DNA analysis. Personally, I see a problem with this. In emergency situations, I tend to run a little short of spit.

My favorite was a pistol incorporating a retinal scan. All you do is peer directly down the barrel with your Mark I Eyeball, and squeeze the trigger half-way — gently. The instructions are specific about that: "And only half way! NO MORE!" I think the technology needs work.

Organ Donating

There's always this huge, fat guy in greasy bib overalls — the one with a grizzled gray two-foot ponytail dangling from his bald noggin. You know him. He carries an unidentifiable rust-bucket rifle slung muzzle-down, with a tattered price tag hangin' from its 2" tall razor-sharp front sight. At least once at every gun show, he cruises silently up behind me, hooks that front sight between my legs, and then … turns briskly away to look at something! I'm okay with being an organ donor. Just not those organs. Not yet.

Some of the regulars are entertaining, at least. There's the skinny little dude with the Boston Blackie moustache who poses himself as a firearms expert, then asks questions like, "So, what kinda bullets does this one shoot?" or, "Is this the kind that goes pop-pop-pop, or the kind that goes BaddaBaddaBaddaBadda!?"

But the big problem with all gun shows is this: There are 312 guys there who are near-clones of me. Our gun-buying budgets are all within about seven bucks of each other, and we're all looking for the same gun, that one Super Deal that exists, and is available, for one brief and shining moment at every gun show.

And at that moment, I'm in the men's room, in pain, checking to see if I left something precious on a rusty front sight. But, honest, somebody said there was a mint condition S&W Heavy Duty with original box and the guy was only askin $300 for it. Now, if I can just beat out those 311 other guys and find it. Yeah. Right. But it could happen. Poop.

NINJA-FIED

JULY/AUGUST 2004

And this is our new Ninja Warrior model," the factory rep burbled. It looked like a black 1911A1 to me. I started pickin' around the grips and magazine well with my fingernails. "Uh, Mr. Connor," he asked, "What are you looking for?" "Where've you got the little throwy-stars an' numchucks an' pointy-stabby-things hidden? Ain't any? So, what makes it a Ninja gun? Does it disappear in a puff 'a purple smoke or something?" Undeterred — and not gettin' it at all — he bumbled on.

"Well, it's all kinda matte black, and see?" — he pointed proudly — "See the little ninja-guy stamped on the slide?" I looked down. There was a tiny hooded figure in a robe etched in the steel. I frowned. He looked confused. But he turned on a dime, whipped out another pistol and shoved it at me.

"Where've you got the little throwy-stars an' num-chucks an' pointy-stabby-things hidden?"

"Now this I know you're gonna like! It's our Tactical Operator model!" Looked just like the other gun, only this was a two-tone job in flat olive drab and black, sporting these raised kinda ditz an' warts on the grips and front strap. No little ninja-dude on the slide. Same gun. Things went downhill from there. The Stealth model wore a gray phosphate, but the guy finally admitted there was no button to push to put it into "stealth mode," and no, it probably couldn't disappear off radar or anything.

This happened in February at the 2004 SHOT Show in Las Vegas.

Bad start to the show. At a dozen other booths the result was the same. As far as I could see, a handgun is ninja-fied if it's black; tactical if it's black an' green; stealthy if it's gray and if it has any combination of the above plus little ditz an' warts on the grippy-surfaces, it's a Professional Operator model. And 92.8% of 'em claimed their guns were high-velocity low-drag. They couldn't define it, but they claimed it.

The jury's still out on Extreme or X-Treme or EXX-TREME! models. I think if they're photographed with muddy leaves an' raindrops on 'em, they're "Extreme." By the time I got to the last poor puny polyestered little factory rep, I was crackin' my knuckles real loud, givin' him the Mark II Hairy Red Eyeball, and barkin', "Put that crap away! I wanta see your Lance Corporal In A Mudhole model! Oh, got none of those? How 'bout your Guy Who Runs A Pizza Place In Detroit model! Got any models called, Shoots Good & Holds Up Okay? Huh?"

My daughter stopped it. She went an' grabbed Mrs. C. "Mom, better come," she said, "Daddy's goin' all Baghdad on some skinny gun-guy." Helena led me away. Okay, dragged.

The question is, who says this gear is stealth-ninja-tacticalpro-extreme-hi-vel/low-drag, huh? Now, if a gun is stamped somethin' like "Thunder Ranch," I know Clint Smith has thundered it, ranched it mercilessly and it didn't break much. If Les Baer says it's "Premier," then bet it's pretty-dang-prime, and if Bill Wilson stamped a crowbar "Combat," I'd count on it in a fight. But this other stuff? Well, who the heck SAYS? Some guy in the marketing department?

Now — drum roll — I do. As of last month, I am legally the Connor Institute for the Certification of GunStuff (CICGS). Send me your NinjaStealthProTacticalOperat orExtremeHigh-Vel/Low-Drag gear and we'll see what's-what, guys. I have designed a number of real-world tests, and if your stuff passes, you get certified. If not, well ...

Testing Ephus

For a full listing of test criteria, see my CICGS website, soon as it's running, but here's a sampling:

For Ninja testing, I lean a pistol up against the baseboard in my office, turn out the lights, an' leave the room for 30 minutes. If I come back and can't find it 'cause it has become one with the wall, that's ten points. If it slithers out and attacks me in the kitchen while I'm makin' a sandwich, that's 25. If it can Disappear in the Dirt or Pass for Puckerbrush, that's extra points.

"High-Velocity Low-Drag" testing compares a weapon's performance against known scientific standards. Hooked up to a surf-casting outfit, I heave a pair of rusty Florida license plates, loosely attached with baling wire, into the lagoon south of the docks. I then reel it back in as fast as I can crank the handle, noting rate-of-retrieve an' drag-resistance factors. That's the low end. High-end comparison is made by hookin' a recently-deceased three-pound mackerel through the lips and repeating the cast-an'-retrieve regimen. On a scale of 100, weapons are rated according to their Plate-Like Performance or Fish Fluidity Factor.

Oh, man, the "Extreme" testing is fun! For a high school science project, my son and his pals built a 16-foot tall medieval siege catapult. Dang thing cost me a small fortune in lumber, rope, watermelons and damage claims. I'll stick your gun in a sack with a coffee-can load of nuts and bolts, three pounds of gravel and a frozen chicken. Then we launch it 400 feet in the air on an 800-yard parabolic arc, terminating in impact in the parkin' lot of the football stadium across the canyon from my place. Ratings range from "Whoa, dude! Insta-Junk!" to "Huh! Still works! Cool!"

"Stealth" is tested simultaneously, with traffic officer Bobby LaChaise sittin' on his cop-cycle in the parking lot, pointing his radar gun at the incoming object, and trying not to get boinked-an'-blotted in the process. Starting right now, we're gonna check the lot for parked cars before each launch. Sorry, Pete. We didn't know you go there late to run your little remote-control cars. Keep the chicken, pal — it's already tenderized.

> **'Mom, better come,' she said, 'Daddy's goin' all Baghdad on some skinny gun-guy.'**

For stuff claiming to be EXXTREME! I've got another test involving mud, blood, my boy wielding a 22-ounce ball peen hammer, and — can I say "peepee" in this column?

At the end of testing, your gear either gets stamped with my Good2Go Gear™ mark, or one of the following: Great Paperweight, SissyGear, or "HGD" for Hammered Goat Dung. Bring it on.

IT'S TIME FOR SOME GUN-RICH ZONES

SEPTEMBER/OCTOBER 2004

I've just about had it with this "Gun-Free Zone" crap, you know? True, I live in a fairly sissy-rich environment but, usually, the only visible effects are too many restaurants with "Chez" in their names, dogs with designer haircuts and guys wearing magenta polo shirts. I'm not sure what magenta looks like, really, but I'd bet some of those shirts are it. Mauve, too. But lately I've noticed an even more troubling trend. You've seen these little round signs with a gun in a circle and a diagonal line through it and it says "This Is A Gun-Free Zone"? And it's like they're proud of that or something! I'm seein' more and more of those and it's bothering me.

They've also got these little huggie-children signs proclaiming that it's a "Child-Safe Place," where kids in trouble can run to and get help. Now, guess what? I'm seein' places with both those kinda signs! What in heck is that about? A "Child-Safe Place" in a "Gun-Free Zone"?

Real Safe Havens

When my kids were little, I taught 'em the two best places to run for help were police stations and gun shops. If the trouble they were running from was Large & Lethal, I knew either of those places were full of folks who'd be armed, alert and prepared to go to General Quarters to protect a child from any harm. What kinda help do you think they could get in a Gun-Free Child-Safe Place?

"Ooohh, come hide with me in the corner, dearie! We'll weep uncontrollably together and if necessary, we'll grovel and beg for mercy!" Yeah, that's where I want my kid going. Mahatma Gandhi was a really nice guy, okay, but not my first choice for my kids' bodyguard. If my stand-in has to be a guy in sandals, I'd prefer it was Spartacus. At least he had a sword and an attitude.

Not so long ago, you could even tell your kid to run into a bar if somebody mean was after 'em. You were virtually assured there would be at least a couple of men in there quaffing boilermakers who would be just tickled purple to defend a scared kid. In fact, there was a guaranteed butt-whuppin' involved, generally happening to the next dude who came through the door. Might be the wrong guy. Might even be several wrong guys. But there would be two absolute results: (1) buttwhuppin'(s), and (2), a safe, happy child sittin' on the bar enjoying a frosty 7-Up.

Re-Zoning

In my experience, these "Gun-Free Zones" are usually freely roamed by dopers, carjackers, gangbangers and assorted thugs, all armed to the teeth, plus mass-murderers creepin' around lookin' for masses to murder. They know where the easy prey is. After all, those gun-free signs even have graphics to accommodate illiterate crooks. The only folks unarmed are the law-abiding types.

In fact, when you look at the mass shootings occurring in the U.S. over the past several years, just about all of 'em have happened in supposedly gun-free areas. That's just wrong, guys.

I think what we need are some "Gun-Rich Zones."

Like, wouldn't you really rather do your grocery shopping in a supermarket with a big sign saying "This Is A Gun-Rich Zone! Legal Concealed-Carry Customers Welcome!"? Maybe another sign below it could read, "Notice To Scumbags: Every Employee, From The Manager To The Kid Who Mops Up The Mess In Aisle 14, Is Armed And A Cum Laude Graduate Of the FunThunder Academy Of Crook-Capping."

Bowling alleys that are posted Gun-Rich Zones could actively cater to the Carry-Crowd. I can see gun-oriented bowling teams like the Kimber Kidz, the Springfield Sillies, the Les Huggy-Baers, the Rockin' Glocksters an' SIG-Piggies and Colt Ponies and ... Okay, smart guys, you dream up some names. I don't even bowl. Even when I do, it ain't really "bowling," you know? But if I could carry openly and not have to hide my Roscoe under a bowling shirt, I'd take up the sport.

How 'bout a "Gun-Rich Zone" restaurant? Wouldn't you be comfy eatin' at the Smith & Wesson Supper Club, "Armed Citizens Always Welcome"? The Ruger Rangehouse Restaurant? I'd even try the CZ BBQ, featuring fine ribs and chops with a European flair. Well, maybe not. But you get the idea. Bet you one thing, folks: There'd be no snail-like service and NO snotty waiters. Customer service always seems to improve when there's ordnance on your hip.

If I owned a bar — maybe the Beretta Bar & Grille — I'd love to post a sign outside for crooks reading, "Everybody In This Place Is Presumed Heavily Armed & Drinking. One In Every Four Is Having Ginger Ale, Because They're Our Designated Hitters. You Guess Which Ones." For the first time, you'd have pals volunteering to abstain, just on the off-chance ...

Lotsa' Shots

Oh, sure, there would be press. Oh, yeah, and it would be bad. I can see the headlines full of dire predictions like, "Slaughter While Shopping!" and "Mayhem At The Mall!" and crap like that. And just like all those rivers-of blood-in-the-streets predictions when the concealed-carry wave washed over most of the U.S., they'd be wrong.

We — the Gun-Rich Zone movement — would just have to explain that it's a bold social experiment, just like "Gun-Free Zones" were a bold social experiment. They failed, so why can't we give it a shot? Or lotsa shots?

One thing we need is the right graphic for our signs. I'm sure there's some graphic artists out there among our readers. Shoot your best to me at ThatGunWriterGuy@ aol.com and I'll check 'em out. Meantime, if you see me on the street, just presume that I'm a Mobile Gun-Rich Zone, okay?

LETTERS FROM YOU LOONS

Jeff Johnson

NOVEMBER/DECEMBER 2004

I got three baskets on my desk. They're marked "IN," "OUT," and "WEIRD & WHATNOT." Some of your recent mail has kinda found a home in the W&W bin, you know? I see a chance for a triple here: Answer you guys, avoid finishing "All About Gunwriting Part II," and get outta here for a wild pig hunt, followed by some tasty barbecue. Here goes!

"Mr. C: What's up between you and the editor, Roy Huntington? Seems like you drive him nuts!"
Hey, that's a short drive ... more like a "putt." His Editorship's job is to rattle my cage and slash up my writing. My mission is to comfort the afflicted and afflict the comfortable. Sometimes he gets too comfy.
PS: We're bestest pals everywhere it counts.

"Connor! I got this great idea for a new pistol cartridge! I took a .357 SIG and blew the bottleneck out to .40 cal. I call it the .40 SIG. I bet it'll push a 180-grain slug at better'n 1,100 feet per second! Whattaya think?"
Um ... yeah, cool. You might wanta check with Smith & Wesson. They've got this cartridge-thingy called ".40 S&W" that's kinda similar. Got rifles? You could try takin' a .25-'06 and blowing the bottleneck out to .30 caliber and see what you get. Let me know how it goes, okay?

"Why is your wife called 'Memsaab Helena,' and why don't we ever see your family?"
I 'splained how she got that handle back in the Jan-Feb 2004 issue. When we got back from Africa, it kinda stuck. It became permanent when we returned a few years later, two countries and several hundred miles from our previous visit. We arrived in camp late, and the instant Helena stepped outta the Rover and unfolded her six feet of red hair and legs, The World's Oldest Dude came shuffling up with this wide-eyed, "The Prophecy Is Fulfilled!" look on his topo-map face. I mean, this guy was like the Methusaleh of the Masai Mara, you know?

He bowed slightly, like he couldn't look directly into her Big Blues, splayed his hands, and murmured, "You are ... the Memsaab Helen-ah!" Done deal. He became her shadow, him and his slitty eyes and that big hooky knife in his sash.

He didn't like people getting near her, including me. He let me, but kept his hand on that knife. I asked the headman what Methusaleh's job was supposed to be, and he said, "Attending the Memsaab Helen-ah, yes?" That's when I found out he didn't work for our guide. He just showed up in camp that day, announced, "The Memsaab Helen-ah comes," an' hunkered down.

When we left, she gave him a Polaroid photo of herself. He touched it to his forehead, turned, and disappeared into the bush. Spooky. Since then, Wendy's drivethru kids, supermarket cashiers, the mailman, everybody's called her Memsaab Helena, and she never mentions it. Not wanting to seem any dumber than I am, I don't either.

I tried to get you a photo of my son, but his head and shoulders are perpetually stuck two feet into the refrigerator, so that ain't happening. Our daughter, Little Red, is in this issue somewhere in an article on hunting accessories. It's okay to call her "a pretty girl," by the way.

"Mr. Connor: One year ago I took up competitive shooting, first, to gain weapons skills, and secondly, I had hoped for some pleasant social contact. But no matter what I do, others seem to avoid me. I don't know why this is happening. Can you help me?"
Whoa! Look at this return address! Dude, I know you! You're the reason I wear body armor to IDPA matches now! Next time you sweep me with your muzzle, there's gonna be distinctly unpleasant social contact! That could contribute to your problem. Also, I know you're new to the game, and you really want that vest you're always wearin' to "look salty," but ... Either launder it, or hang some of those car-deodorizin' pinetree thingies from the pits, okay?

"I understand you've been in gunfights. Besides a good pistol, what do I need?"
Easy: 1. Distance, lots, with big solid objects in between. 2. An automatic rifle. 3. Pals with automatic rifles. 4. Adult diapers, for the "after-action" work. My best advice — don't get into gunfights. If you must, try to make them "shootings" instead, with yourself positioned as the "shooter." "Gunfights" involve incoming as well as outgoing rounds. Avoid this whenever possible.

"Dude! I got this neighbor who's a rabid anti-gun freak. He says if nobody had guns there would be no violent crime. He says the thought of me possibly using violence, even on his behalf, sickens him. I gotta live in this neighborhood. What can I do?"
Dude! You must respect your neighbor's beliefs, no matter how lame they are. I suggest you post an eight by ten foot sign on your lawn saying, "My neighbor's house is completely unarmed, and he's a gentle, non-violent soul. He abhors guns and I respect his right to his own opinion. I pledge not to protect him with my guns, or to interfere at all. Just make sure you get the right place, 'cause I've got an arsenal and an attitude." That should do it. Be sure there's an arrow on the sign pointing to his house.

WE ALL KNOW WHAT SISSIES ARE, RIGHT?

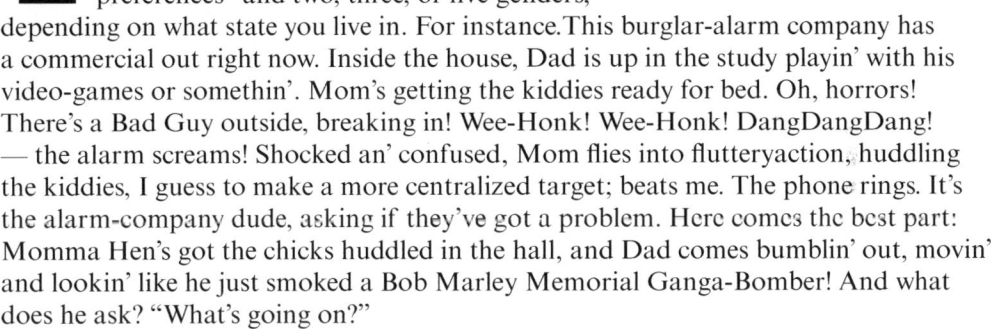

JANUARY/FEBRUARY 2005

You know what I mean. They're like Idjits and Morons, comin' in all colors, flavors, "life-style preferences" and two, three, or five genders, depending on what state you live in. For instance.This burglar-alarm company has a commercial out right now. Inside the house, Dad is up in the study playin' with his video-games or somethin'. Mom's getting the kiddies ready for bed. Oh, horrors! There's a Bad Guy outside, breaking in! Wee-Honk! Wee-Honk! DangDangDang! — the alarm screams! Shocked an' confused, Mom flies into flutteryaction, huddling the kiddies, I guess to make a more centralized target; beats me. The phone rings. It's the alarm-company dude, asking if they've got a problem. Here comes the best part: Momma Hen's got the chicks huddled in the hall, and Dad comes bumblin' out, movin' and lookin' like he just smoked a Bob Marley Memorial Ganga-Bomber! And what does he ask? "What's going on?"

What's wrong with this picture, folks? It's fulla Simpering Sissies, Insipid Idjits, an' Mutant Morons! Oh, this is so wrong on so many levels! Where's your Immediate Action drill? Got a plan to repel boarders? Why were you surprised the alarm went off? Ain't that what it's for? Don't the RugRatz already know what to do? NO? Whose fault is that? Where the HECK is your Duty 870? Oh, man!

Then there's "the Dad-person." What does it mean when you're in a house and the burglar alarm goes off? Get the door, it's Domino's Pizza? These people don't need an alarm system, they need adult supervision, like a Sissy-Sitter. I've done some of that kinda work, but the subjects were mostly elected officials.

Sissies, Idjits, Morons, & The Memsaab Mug-Wipe

Dudes, I'm disappointed. Remember that thing I wrote on "Gun-Rich Zones"? Hey, it's cool that so many of you liked it, but outta all those responses, we only got ONE professing to be deeply offended? Are you kiddin' me? ONE? What's wrong with you people?

If my "Deeply-Offended Response Rate" falls below 17.3-percent, it means (a) I'm not doin'my job, and (b) I got trouble with His Imperial Editoriality, Roy-Boy. He starts avoiding me, snappin' at me, makin' comments like, "Yeah, Connor, you served up some real vanilla pudding that time. Oooh, tasty. Bet you play softball, don'tcha?"

He's much nicer — sorta — when lots of readers are offended by me. Then he can play his favorite game. He asks if he can see my company credit card, like, "Hey, I just wanta check it out; just touch it, y'know? Is it the same color as mine?" Yeah, right. I let him "just touch it" once, and didn't get it back for three months. His is Platinum. I didn't even know they made a "Tin Card." Limit's 39 bucks. Big whoop.

Anyway, this one dude complained I was "gaybashing" an' he called me a "brutish Neanderthal." Gay-bashing? Onliest thing I can figure is he's talkin' about my reference to living in "a sissy-rich environment." And the word "gay" never entered my mind — I was talkin' about SISSIES!

"Little Red" demos Mom's "Mug-wipe" move.

The Patented Memsaab Mug-Wipe

Now, not all sissies are professional victims. Some of 'em are predators. They just tend to prey on weaker sissies. And sometimes, they get their "victim selection" criteria wrong — like, really, really wrong. Here's a good example, and I also get to tell you about this tactical technique the Memsaab Helena pioneered, called The Memsaab Mug-Wipe. To read about the most recent time she used it, you'll have to read my stuff under The Odd Angry Shot in the January issue of GUNS Magazine, okay? But let me tell you about the first time.

> With gun hand at the ready, she plucked the right front hem of that blouse and raised it, dabbing daintily at her chin and lips ...

She was drivin' the High Lonely across Nevada, an' ducked into a deserted rest stop to use the facilities. There was just one other car, a Dirtbag Special, kinda semi-abandoned off to one side. When she came out, that car's occupants had come outta hiding and planted themselves against her fender, leerin' and gawkin' and engaging in "attempted recreational intimidation." Who knows what they had on their teensy minds? Robbery, rape, murder, carjackin' and tomfoolery? It didn't matter. She knew it wasn't gonna happen.

They probably got a peek at her when she arrived, and all they saw was this gorgeous redhead, all alone, in her khaki bush shorts, sandals and wispy blouse. What they couldn't see was the Les Baer 1911 stuffed into an IWB rig just right of frontand-center down her shorts. Oh, it musta been inviting at a distance. As she strode closer, though, I'll bet some bells went off, like, "Dang, that's one big woman, and whoa, she walks like she means business, and why's she smilin' like that?"

That's when she did the Memsaab Mug-Wipe. She stopped. Reaching across her body with her left hand with gun hand at the ready, she plucked the right front hem of that blouse and raised it, dabbing daintily at her chin and lips. This exposed a lovely bit of midriff — and a cockedand-locked cannon — a sight sure to mesmerize, terrorize, and sometimes do both simultaneously. I'm thinkin' both.

Here's the very bestest part: They couldn't bail out to their DirtbagMobile without moving toward her, so — they ran off into the desert! When the Memsaab called, she was laughing a lot and shakin' a little, and she couldn't quite remember exactly what she yelled after 'em, but it included something about "Don't you wanta dance?" and "Ya big sissies!"

I told her about that "brutish Neanderthal" stuff. She just batted her Big-Blues, tossed me a little hip-check, and breathed, "He's right — An' that's why I love ya, baby." Me happy caveman. Go drag knuckles on pavement now. Bye-bye.

THIS LOVE-HATE THING
WITH S.H.O.T. SHOW

MARCH/APRIL 2005

They say dogs can predict when an earthquake's coming, you know? Out in the Pacific, some seabirds know when a typhoon's building before a single blip shows on the radar. There's lots of critters who seem to be able to detect any number of phenomena long before humans or the fanciest electro-techno-junk pick it up. I get the same semi-spooky feeling before SHOT Show.

Yeah, I know, I got the notice in the mail, and the date was on the calendar, but I didn't need that. My BS-meter was already twitchin'. Oh, the aroma of intestinally-processed cow-fodder is definitely in the air, albeit in minute, almost untraceable amounts. And I know that as SHOT draws nearer, the odor will build to the point where it seems like I'm buried up to my neck in Bandini Mountain.

Don't get me wrong — I love SHOT Show. It's one of my few opportunities in life to actually be among the least freakyobsessive GunKnutz in a 50-square mile area. And to spend four days in The World's Biggest Temporary Small Arms Armory? Oh, bliss! Yo, Paradise found! I'd sleep there if they'd let me. I just wish they'd make a few changes.

Sales-Speak Translated

You guys already know how I feel about "painton- performance," right? That's like putting a mattegray finish on a pistol, calling it the "Stealth Operator Model," then bumpin' the price four hundred bucks. But beyond ninja-fied and tactical-ized gun-junk, there's a whole 'nother spectrum of semantic silliness always goin' on at SHOT.

New! means either it's a different color than it was last year, or it now comes in a plastic locking case rather than a cardboard carton, or, they're really hoping you've got a short memory. All New! means it's the same product, but none of the interior parts from last year's model will quite fit this year's and they're not sure why. Their new sub-contractor in Waziristan or Fresno doesn't speak English very well, and just gets frustrated and hangs up when they ask questions about quality control. Improved! translates to, "We think we solved that problem where it might go boom when it's not s'posed to."

You gotta watch for claims like, Foolproof Operation! which generally means you can't adjust it. However it works or doesn't work, that's what you're stuck with, and any attempt on your part to fix it will void the warranty, or cause teensy springs to fly across the room and hide under a bookcase. Even worse is stuff like Unitized Trigger Group — Maintenance-Free!. This means, "Don't come near it with a tool or it'll self-destruct. We tried glue and duct-tape, then gave up and welded it." Read, Years In Development! as, "We had 'way too much money into this pig to drop it, and we finally got one to cycle through a full highcap magazine."

Oh, I just love seeing Improved Balance And Handling! which means it now swings and points like a length of plumbing pipe bolted at an odd angle to a piece of two-by-four, whereas the old model swung and pointed as gracefully as a $5.99 KMart folding lawn chair in a gusting wind. I've found that manufacturers get really upset when you "swing an' point" their new XS-911-GruntFire Magnum and parts come flying off it, sail across the aisle, an' smack the lady at the MilSpecTechLube display upside the head. At least, I heard that's what happened.

Let's Get Real, Okay?

You could wallpaper the New Orleans SuperDome with the posters an' banners at SHOT Show, and some of 'em are pretty nice, okay? But why do so many of 'em have to feature these dudes so covered in explosive-entry SWAT gear that they look like Mutant Ninja Tactical Turtles? And they're so clean! Hey, I was one of those guys, and I never looked like that! I always looked more like a heavily-armed chimney sweep who just competed in the Convenience Store Dumpster-Diving Semi-Finals.

Those posters might appeal to some weekend-TV-rerun Rambo-Commandos, or

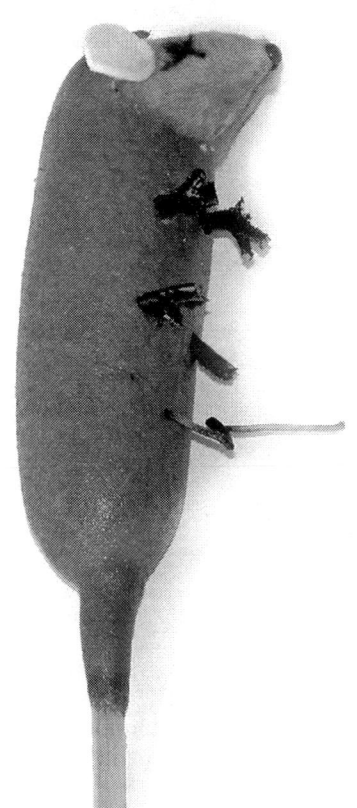

guys who currently serve in the Recliner Battalion of the 93rd Chairborne Brigade, but I'd like to see some real-world graphics like, (1) A skinny Portland insurance salesman facing off two scumbags at an ATM, (2) some balding hefty dude in plaid flannel 'jammies takin' down a crack-freak burglar in his living room, or (3) A single mom in front of her '95 minivan — with her two little kiddies inside — bustin' a cap on a creepy armed carjacker. Folks, that's just Truth In Advertising.

Food?

And finally, there's the alleged "food" available at SHOT Show. Yeah, yeah, there's a "dining pavilion." But I ain't losing two hours of gun-sniffing time to stand in line for a $12 sandwich composed of mystery-meat and "cheese" with the appearance of a melted day-glo orange Frisbee. There are vendor carts, but ... Guys, if I have to eat a corn dog, I'd prefer it didn't have little burnt feet and the charred remains of a rodent tail stickin' outta the dough. So, am I goin' to SHOT Show? Oh, yeah — but I'm packin' my own lunch.

SETTING THE RECORD STRAIGHT

Let's get this perfectly clear, okay? I'm not an expert. I'm just sorta "experienced." They're not the same thing at all. After telling you guys about "The Memsaab Mug-Wipe" in the Jan-Feb 2005 Handgunner, I got lotsa mail on it. Most of you were entertained, some were info-tained, but a couple of readers took me to the woodshed. They found an easy half-dozen tactical errors in the maneuver; things no "expert" on gunfighting would ever endorse, like revealing the presence of a gun before launching a drawing stroke.

They're probably right, but I'm not an expert, remember? Heck, I think she shoulda called in an air strike on those dirtbags from two kilometers away. That woulda been "expert" in my book. I bet Clint Smith would agree. But instead, the Memsaab just had an "experience" and it worked. That's kinda been the story of my life: gathering experiences, not expertise.

Mostly, I've just shuffled around the world learning simple things like "avoid trip-wires," bushes that move against the wind could be getting pushed, and never let little people with guns take cover behind you in a firefight — they draw fire, and dang near blow your eardrums out when they shoot over your shoulder 'n stuff like that. It's useful, but not "expert."

In fact, I think some of the best things I've learned about gunfighting aren't about hardware or tactics at all. They're more like "peripheral considerations," both for those whose job it is to seek out gunfights, and for those who try to avoid 'em if at all possible, and win 'em when they can't. One of them is the fundamental importance of being silent, whether you're sneakin' up on trouble or tiptoeing away from it. Here's my non-expert feelings on that and a couple more.

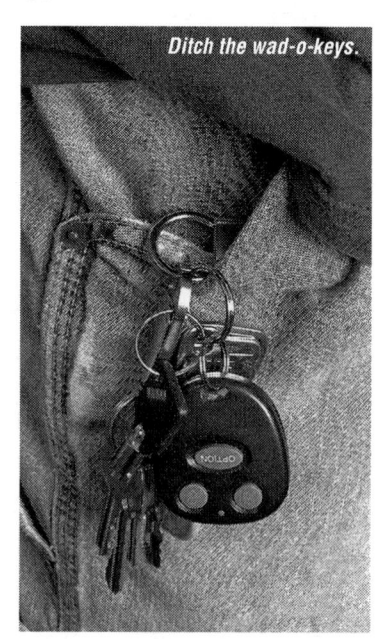

Ditch the wad-o-keys.

SHAKE, RATTLE AND ROLL

Rattles: If you're gonna make noise, make it "Bang!" It doesn't matter whether you're wearing puckerbrush-camo in Whatzistan, dutyblue in Boston or aloha-casual in Honolulu, if you go about armed, you shouldn't tromp around soundin' like Homeless Harry's junk-laden shopping cart. Frankly, some of you have the noise signature of ceremonial Zulu dancers, complete with ankle bells and wrist-rattles.

Ditch that 42-piece key-and-trinket collection, and dump the loose change before it gets you dumped. I personally insist on silent footwear as well, eschewing hobnail boots, dancing taps and skinny-soled loafers that squeak like frightened mice. Get fully kitted out for your daily drudge, and then conduct a "shake & rattle test." If there comes only one moment in your life when you desperately need to sound more like fog than like a dropped tray of silverware, you'll be tickled silly you made the effort. If that moment never comes, then just drift around smug and silent. Rivets: Rivet your Roscoe, Rambo. The finest ordnance and the best ammo ain't gonna help if you reach for Roscoe and he ain't there. No matter what position you wear your piece in, in what kinda scabbard, it ain't certified for emergency use until you've subjected it to simulated fights, fits, falls and butt-whuppins. One pal of mine was almost killed with his own backup gun — a .38 snubbie in an ankle holster — while in foot pursuit of a fleeing felon. My buddy was gaining on the dirtbag when suddenly one leg felt a bit lighter, he kicked something, and then saw a familiar-looking dark object skittering down the sidewalk in front of him. Yeah; his trusty two-inch. It actually passed the suspect, who gleefully scooped it up. The encounter produced two results: First, an interesting game of "mine's bigger than yours," which fortunately ended well for my pal, and second, a new ankle holster acquisition, this one rigorously tested for tenacity.

Please note, this ain't about the merits of ankle holsters, it's about torture-testing and securing your rig. Hip holsters are subject to the same kinda slippage, especially if mated with a too-narrow belt. However you pack it, tack it down tight, folks. Piece Petting: Never pet your piece in public. Off-duty cops and on-duty crooks are the worst about this, but concealedcarry citizens are a close second. Bluntly put, you guys pet, pat, fondle and grope your concealed roscoes in subways, supermarkets, bars and banks like you're checking on a frisky pet weasel. Yeah, I know, it's

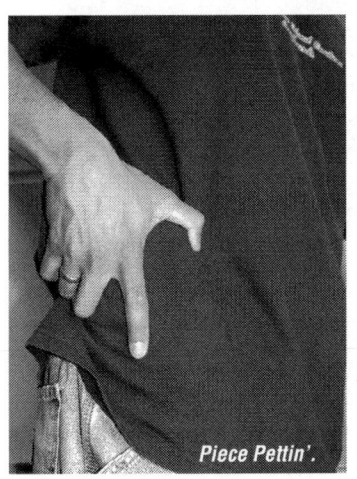

Piece Pettin'.

subconscious, and it's comforting to just give Roscoe a little stroke to reassure yourself he's there at your side. Don't do it. I see it, and the wrong kinda folks see it too.

I see it mostly when people are getting outta cars or trucks, when they've just gotten up from a seated position, hustled across a street, climbed or descended stairs, all kinds of activities, but most notably in these two instances: First, when a uniformed cop appears, and second, when some dude suddenly materializes who looks like trouble — both of 'em being prime times you shouldn't be petting your piece.

See? If you're looking for expert advice, don't look at me — I'll be out getting more "experience." And avoiding trip-wires.

"WHY DO YOU CARRY A GUN?"

JULY/AUGUST 2005

If I had a nickel for every time I've been asked that question, I'd have, uh … as many guns as his firearm-festooned Editorial Immenseness, Roy-Boy. It's been asked of me by all flavors of folks in all slices of society, with attitudes and expressions ranging from angry-arrogant to curtly-contemptuous, to brainless an' befuddled. My answers to it have sorta formed three phases in my professional gun-carrying life. During that first and longest phase, I answered all of 'em sincerely and articulately, often following up with stacks of historic and legal documents. After many years, I concluded only a semi-significant sliver of people even heard what I was sayin'. The rest had already made up their muddled minds.

Finally, I just got sick of it, and moved on to Phase 2. If those asking seemed to have teensy open spaces in their minds, I gave 'em S & A: "Sincere & Articulate." The more harshly-bleating sheep, however, often got exchanges like this:

"So," queried Snidely Snotworth III, lookin' down his unbusted but needed-bustin' nose, "Why do you think you have to carry a gun?"

"Well," bellowed the Brutish Neanderthal (that would be me): "Because you're not QUALIFIED to carry one. You haven't got the skills, the judgment, the sense of responsibility, or the courage for it."

This answer often popped out after I'd just returned from some Heart-Of-Darkness where every living soul knew that the difference between slaves and free people is having the means and determination to defend their lives, property and liberties. That meant having guns and guts and God-given rights. Most of those people would quite literally die fighting for the freedoms so many Americans casually give away, and proudly bear social responsibilities those sheeple* won't even recognize.

*Sheeple: Sheep-like people, many of whom deny the existence of wolves, and vote to pull the teeth of the sheepdogs who protect the flock.

The Voices

Then I matriculated to Phase 3, where I started having some fun with the Snidely Snotworth types. When they asked the Big Question, I'd go all hunchy-shouldered an' secretive, then lean in close and mutter, "Because of the voices, ya know?" "The VOICES?" sniveled the Snidelies, suddenly scaredy-cattish. "Oh, yeah, the voices … They told me to be, you know, prepared for when the killer clowns come … " I'd furtively goggle around. "The voices say the killer clowns are comin' … They're cannibals, some of 'em, and … "

About that time the Snidelies would be skitterin' away like mice on polished marble.

Yeah, I know, the "killer clowns" answer might not have been "helpful," but it did just as much good as giving S&A answers to the sheeple, and it was a lot more fun for me. I know you already know why we carry these cannons. But sometimes, just sometimes, we all need a little reminder. That includes me, and I've got one share with you. One that got me where I live.

The Connor Clan has been nomadic, and we've lived in a number of places. In one of 'em, we shared a side yard and friendship with a young woman we'll call Miss Maine, and her knee-high daughter, Little Lizzie. Miss Maine quickly bonded with the Memsaab Helena. Clearly, Helena's Amazon-warrior spirit and skill with arms impressed Miss Maine mightily, and much of their time and talk revolved around that fierce self-confidence — and guns.

As for Little Lizzie, the munchkin almost duct-taped herself to the Mem's leg. She followed Helena everywhere, but always, always, kept glancing back to check on her momma, as though she were the worried parent.

There was something guarded, something hurt and defensive about both of them, and that fearfulness extended to me for a while. They got over it, thank God. Then I sorta became a moving bunker for 'em, representing cover and protection. Finally, we learned the story.

Miss Maine had been attacked — brutally and viciously. You don't wanta know the details. As with so many such crimes, it wasn't really about sex. It was about hate and domination, cowardice and cruelty. And an even younger Little Lizzie had witnessed it. I like to think the Memsaab and I helped them to recover emotionally.

Then one day Lizzie came and snuggled into my shadow, visibly disturbed. That morning her kindergarten had put on "Frighten The Munchkins Day." Some schools do a pretty good job of alerting children to predators — don't go with strangers and that kinda thing — but others do more harm than good. All they do is terrify the tots and give 'em no operating options. Lizzie already had twin tears glistening, ready to fall when she grabbed a tiny fistful of my trouser-leg and asked, "Connor-Sir, will you a'ways be here? Wouldja be here … When the bad mens come?"

My knees cracked on the sidewalk as she slammed into my shoulder, shaking with sobs as the hot tears came, splashing my neck and searing into my soul. " 'Cause I'm a-scared!" she choked, and clutched me tighter.

Oh, GOD! Who would not — who could not — fight without fear, suffer without sense of sacrifice, and kill or die deliberately, using the most effective means available — to protect life, liberty and a Little Lizzie? For God's sake, who?

Those who would not are no better than the predators.

Maybe in Phase 4, when somebody pops The Big Question I'll just smile and say, "For life, liberty and Little Lizzie." You guys can fill in the details.

THE WIDE WORLD OF WHACKY

GUN LAWS

SEPTEMBER/OCTOBER 2005

Until recent years I haven't had much interest in gun laws, mostly because they didn't apply to me. The political kind, anyway. My personal gun laws went like: 1. Have guns. 2. Be good with 'em. I was either wearing a badge or otherwise employed in the field of shooting bad guys who had guns. Passing over invisible political lines with guns was no problem either. When the helo went "feet dry" over the surf line or across the river, you just loaded and locked an' got ready to rock.

I learned some interesting things about gun laws in other countries, like the many places south of the Ditch where civilians can legally cap crooks with .32s, .380s, .38 Specials, .40s and .44s — but punchin' a scumbag's scorecard with a 9mm or .45 ACP would get you thrown in prison because those are "military calibers."

> You have the state bans on "Like, scary-looking guns, those black ones with the banana-thingies and sticky-out parts, and *definitely* those ones that go *bang-bang-bang!* really fast, like, you know?

In Africa, you can just about divide the continent into three kinds of places. In the first, the local authorities will shoot you dead on sight if you appear packin'. In the second, the local lunatics will shoot you dead on sight if you appear NOT packin'. In the third, both apply simultaneously. If you lose, the only difference is whether the guys rifling through your pockets are wearing rag-tag uniforms or not.

Politicians And Peasants

Everywhere I went, the one thing holding true was the wisdom of my favorite bumper sticker: "Politicians Prefer Unarmed Peasants." And everywhere the politicians had succeeded in achieving that to any degree, they learned the wisdom of Robert Heinlein's statement: "An armed society is a polite society." And an unarmed one isn't very. Polite, that is.

Europe's gun laws are loony, Asia's are largely nonexistent and unenforceable anyway and Britain and Australia? Theirs are just sadly, suicidally stupid. The only thing they have goin' for 'em is they're pretty much the same from border to border, unlike our own homegrown flavor of foolishness. On one recent road trip, I did some legal research and found thanks to local gun laws, I could go from "Welcome Fella" to "Wanted Felon" six times in two hours without even slowing down, much less gettin' out of my truck.

The Lunacy

Since I got semi-civilianized, I've learned a little and picked up a few observations about different areas of the U.S. of A. — gunlaw-wise.

Our Nation's Capitol: In Washington D.C., the cradle of freedom, you are allowed to own plugged muzzleloaders, fake flintlocks and dismantled cap-and-ball revolvers if the caps and balls are stashed in other jurisdictions. You're also allowed to carry cash, credit cards and emergency medical information for the paramedics who'll pick up your post-robbery remains. These gun laws are for your safety, to protect you from "gun violence." How well have they worked? For the past two years, residents of D.C. stood a greater chance per capita of being shot than our GI's serving in Iraq.

> **Great-Granddaddy's horse pistol hangs over the mantle — loaded. Git over it, Yankees.**

Vermont: Breathe free, walk tall and be polite. The Freedom & Unity state has a radical approach to concealed carry laws. Namely, there ain't any. As a result, lots of people pack pistols, nobody knows who is or is not for sure, and Vermont enjoys the lowest rates of gun crime in America. Vermont is believed to possess 92.6-percent of the "common sense" in the Northeast U.S.

New York State: At some point in the dim and musty past, New Yorkers traded their Second Amendment rights for an assortment of spring flower festivals, tasteless public art and mediocre Finger Lakes wines. Now, should you have the temerity to want to touch a handgun, you are allowed to beg permission from a minor local bureaucrat. The "six month process" averages 12 to 18 months, and can be lengthened or aborted by asking where the heck your permit is. If denied a permit, you are allowed to ask why. The answers may range from "None of your business," to "You're ugly," or from some judges, "I don't think you need one." Instead of an appeal process, you have the right to emigrate to "The Free-Zone America" for now, anyway.

New Yorkers can take comfort in the thoughts that (a) their "rights" are protected by such stalwarts as Chuckie Schumer and Hilary Clinton, and (b) things are worse in Massachusetts.

Massachusetts: Some other states are all about limiting gun rights. Massachusetts prides itself on multiplying gun wrongs. Our best advice is to avoid it, but if you find yourself in Mass., just remember if you're attacked — even in your own home — you are required by law to retreat to the maximum extent possible. That "extent possible" will be calmly decided at a later date by somebody in a quiet walnut-paneled office. You do have the right to run, weep and bleed.

The South In General: Handguns are commonly found in glove compartments, tackle boxes and the chest pockets of bib overalls. The cleaning of long-barreled revolvers is an accepted early-evening front-porch activity. Great-Granddaddy's horse pistol hangs over the mantle — loaded. Git over it, Yankees.

The Republic of Texas: Texans tried that gun-control crap, an' that dog just wouldn't hunt. They spat in the dust and strapped on their hoglegs. Case closed.

Idaho & Wyoming: If a lawman stops you and you don't have guns showing, he might get suspicious and ask, "You're not from around here, are you?" Guns are tools. They protect your women, whiskey and water rights.

The Left Coast: California, known as The Schizophrenic State, has no idea in hell what their gun laws are, or ought to be. In some counties, shiny single-actions are considered costume jewelry and in other counties qualify for designation as arsenals. In the Bay Area, certain guns might be allowed, but only if they are modified to propel "gummy-worms" and pass a feng shui test of their karma.

Then you have the state bans on "Like, scary-looking guns, those black ones with the banana-thingies and stickyout parts, and definitely those ones that go bang-bang-bang! really fast, like, you know?" The governor owns his own rotary cannon, but both U.S. senators want to register and confiscate sharpened pencils. If some dude fatally whacked somebody with a frozen fish, the legislature would enact an emergency ban on chilled seafood, calling it the Assault Mackerel Act.

Oh, there's lots more and the research goes on. Meantime, be careful when tap dancing through mine fields, or when considering changes of residence.

THE MEMSAAB SPEAKS

It's second-cuppa coffee time here at home, so if my time zone calculations are accurate, that man is probably crouched by a tiny spark-spitting fire, looking like a bear dressed in dirty bed linens, surrounded by similarly attired tribesmen

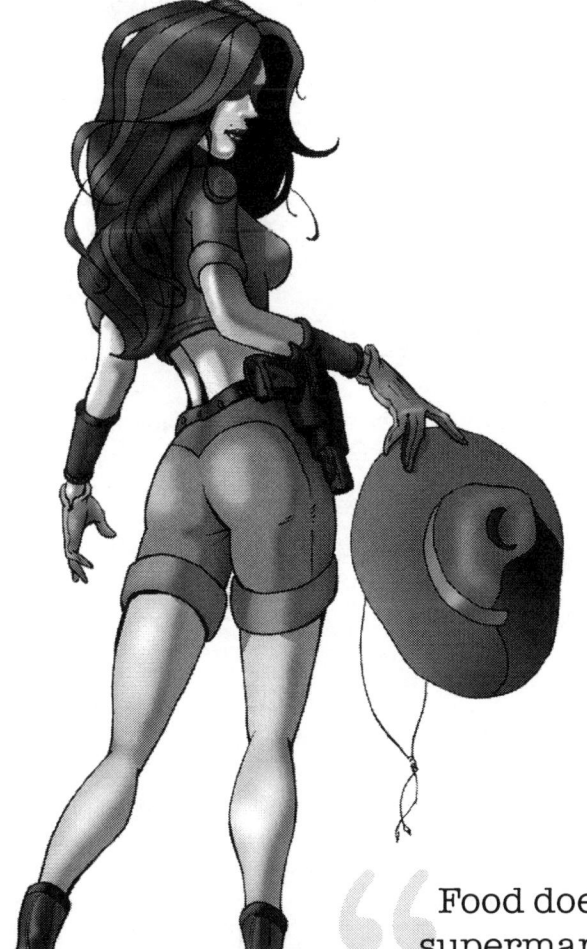

averaging four shades darker, 10" shorter and 80 pounds lighter. I know in my heart who "the life of the party" is, flailing his arms and filling in his gaps in the local language with wild gestures, donkey-laughs, grunts, hoots and whistles. He's cracking them up, whether they understand him or not. I've seen it; I know. And that's especially true if shots have been fired. I know my man. When it became obvious he couldn't file his column from West WhereZitStan or whatever, His Editorship Roy suggested I write it, by answering some emails from you folks, asking questions about me. I've turned down Roy's requests for photos so often, I couldn't refuse this, so — here goes:

First, my name — Helena — is pronounced Hell-eh-nuh, not Heh-LEEna. As my five brothers point out, "The emphasis is on Hell." And I wasn't named for

Sequoia Blankenship

> **Food doesn't come from supermarkets, nor justice from courts, and safety doesn't pour from police stations.**

any Greek goddess, but rather for a wind-scoured high plains town near which my parents raised rangy half-wild beef cattle, hard red winter wheat and rangy, half-wild red-headed kids.

As for the "memsaab" title, well, Connor (yes; that's what I call him, too, except in very private moments) explained all that in the January/February and November/December 2004 issues of Handgunner. Since I'm as mystified by it as anyone else, I won't try to explain it any further. Some say I "brought it home from Africa," like some kind of souvenir. That's wrong. It feels more like Africa laid it on me, like a tribal mark; like a symbol of possession. If that's true, well — it worked. Africa forever owns a piece of me.

Some people go to Africa and look at it. Others go, and Africa looks at them; washes over them; breathes light and dust, smoke and shrieks and sun-baked silence into them; then whispers, "Welcome home, child. This is the tree where man was born. Go run now, and take care — there is beauty and danger everywhere."

For me, Africa is central Wyoming with wildebeest; eastern Idaho with elephants; Nevada's Great Basin with nomads and gazelle. Home.

Guns, Tools & Attitudes

You've asked about my attitudes on guns and self-defense, and it's like this: I grew up knowing guns are tools, and just like a band saw, block-and-tackle, or a quarter-million dollar combine, you must recognize and respect their place in life, their potential for damage — and be skilled with them. If my kids or my mate are ever hurt, it won't be because of my failure to act, period. Besides, I just love a good gun, simple as that.

I shoot a lot of guns, but I train hard with only two; identical 1911's. Like Connor says, "The best spare part is a spare piece," and I figure, the fewer kinks and loops between brain, sights and index finger, the better. On self-defense? It's a God-given right that man has no business legislating against. Clear?

I never knew adults played "let's pretend" until I went off to college in the city. You can't pretend the wheat doesn't have head blight, a cow doesn't have blackleg, or that predators — two-legged or four — don't prey. You can maneuver away from some trouble, but threats have to be dealt with head-on. The Rockies, reinforced by Africa, taught me food doesn't come from supermarkets, nor justice from courts and safety doesn't pour from police stations. These are "follow-ons to fundamentals." You, your values, your skills, courage and tools — those are the fundamentals.

Honor, Humor & History

Several of you have asked — kiddingly, I presume — how I could love that man Connor. Simple: He's a man of honor, a child of humor and a student of history. He lives by six simple rules, which he'll die before violating. I know them by heart; he lives them by deeds. They have nothing to do with lawbooks and everything to do with responsibility and integrity. Sometimes they're inconvenient, sometimes harshly demanding. It doesn't matter — he follows them. Maybe he'll share them with you someday.

The child of humor can — and will — find something to laugh about in any situation, and he won't stop until you're laughing too — especially if things are deep, dark and serious. You've read his stuff, right? Here's a CAT-scan slice of how his demented mind works: He seriously wanted to give our kids the middle names "Danger" and "Trouble." That way, all their lives, when faced with tough, even grave times, they could stiffen their spines, twist a crooked smile, and say, "Danger? Danger's my middle name!" or, "Trouble? My middle name is Trouble, mister!"

His mom and I overruled him, and sometimes we're sorry about that. The kids say it anyway, so he really won, didn't he?

He studies history constantly — ancient, modern, and as-it's-happening, and he examines it on a global, societal and very personal level. He points out that for the first 80-percent of world history, life on earth was dominated by weird, icky, sometimes toxic pond scum — then adds, "That's still the case today in a lotta places, only the pond scum wears Armani suits." I know of two times his life was saved by remembering Napoleon's quote, "Never interrupt your enemy when he's making a mistake." In the here-and-now, he often stops me when my steam valve is about to blow, and gently, firmly reminds me, "Baby, we're writing our history today — How do you want it to read?" Every true redhead needs a John Connor around, I think.

So — let's say your mate is a self-described shaved ape; an admitted "brutish Neanderthal" — but you know exactly where he stands in his head and heart, 24/7, and that's right beside you; what his rules are; the duties he will always carry out, and the lines he will never, ever cross, regardless of cost or sacrifice; who honestly believes his ancestors are looking down on everything he does — and judging him as a man — and then, he can make you laugh?

What more could you ask? I'll tell you. A hammering at the door, followed by a turn of the deadbolt, and a deep voice bellowing something like, "Baby! Don't pay the ransom! I escaped from the killer Gypsies!" He cracks himself up, too. That's my man.

THE (UNWRITTEN) RANGE RULES

JANUARY/FEBRUARY 2006

"**D**angull-ektrix!" the RangeMonster bellowed, squinting at a twisty-wisp of black smoke curling upward from the rocker switch on his plywood control console. "Loo-KEY! Yahl FAHR-opp attair gice jinni naow, hyahr?"

Others less dialectically gifted than I may not have understood what the RangeMonster — that title was `blazoned on his sweatshirt — was saying, but fortunately, I knew something of his language. It's called Jaw-Juh Muh-Zurran; a patois spoken by a small handful of nomadic peoples originating in the state of Georgia, and later migrating to Missouri. A loose translation of his outburst would be, "These darned electrical devices! Lucas! Would you please start the gasoline-powered generator now? Do you hear me?"

The RangeMonster dearly wanted to show off his motorized target-return system to "thet citti feller" — me — and was most upset when the controls shorted out. Judging from the inky smoke smudges and burns around the switch, this wasn't the first time. He had taken a wheeled irrigation line, welded on some target frames, and rigged it to roll out to the 100-yard line and back. It looked like some kinda bizarre crossover from Star Wars to The Dukes of Hazzard, but, I was assured, it worked "lak a summa-gun."

Then Lucas — "Lukey" — ambled out. Construct a roughly humanoid figure from six and a half feet of cables and angle iron, wrap it in bib overalls, top it with a shock of yellow wheat straw, insert sugar cubes for teeth, and you've got Lukey. He tore a tarp off an ancient generator, spit on his right thumb and forefinger and smiled. The RangeMonster smiled, too. "Yawl watch 'issere," he drawled. "Itta be goo-o-o-o-o-d."

Ridin' The Lightning

Over the next coupla minutes, I learned that in order for "jinni" to run, a spring-loaded bridging device had to make contact with two different voltage widgets. The spring, however, appeared to have sprung sometime during the Spanish-American War, and just sorta laid

there, occasionally jumping out of place when Jinni hacked up a hairball.

That's when Lukey would crane his body out gingerly like a crippled stork, grab that "sparkin' rod" with his spit-wetted fingers, press it down, and ride the lightnin'! until Jinni settled down again to a guttural rumble.

Each time this happened, Lukey's body shook like a sack `a crazed weasels, his yellow thatch spiked straight up and his eyes popped bigger, taking on the appearance of fried blue cat's-eye marbles. Once, when he appeared about to involuntarily scratch his left ear with his right hind foot, I moved to grab him.

"Lee-vim be, Connor," the RangeMonster warned. He advised me if I were to grab Lukey "whilst he's got a-holt a' that sparkin' rod," I'd be doin' Saint Vitus's Dance an' drooling down to my socks. "Besides," he said, "Lukey likes it!" I hastily jotted down, "UN-Written Range Rule #29: Don't Grab Lukey When He's Grabbin' Jinni."

Chapter In My Pretend Book

I've shot at a lot of ranges, and learned lots of rules you'll never see posted on signboards. Like, "Never say the words cheese or mother to the range tech wearing the aluminum-foil hat." At another, "If the range-resident raccoon takes an interest in your lunch, just back away and don't whistle!" They're the kind of rules all the locals know — and visitors learn the hard way.

I have a certain history with snakes, spiders, centipedes and other creepy-crawlies. I've spent a chunk of my life lyin' doggo in situations where I had to let 'em slither & skitter over my camo-clad self in strict silence, and I did not get used to it. Instead, I developed a barely-controllable case of the Extreme Heebie-Jeebies. When I saw the men's room at one particular range, my first, second and third inclinations were to tiptoe into the dank-drippy swamp beyond and take my chances with the copperheads and cottonmouths. But others were going in, and I had urgent business to conduct, so…

It was a "basement" facility, though it looked like it had possibly been built above ground, and then submerged into the muck on its own, like a mossy, stone submarine. The first three warped, wafer-thin plywood stalls looked bad enough, but the last one on the right, butted against the mud-weeping rock wall was, well … foreboding. I noted that men were waiting to use the other stalls; not the fourth. It wasn't just the shoulder-squeezing width, the fine patina of dust on the toilet lid, or the strangely yellowed, unused appearance of the toilet paper that disturbed me. After re-conning the seat and taking the throne, I realized what it was: the eerie feeling of — you ain't alone, dude. I finished hurriedly, and reached for the TP.

Rotating the roll brought the owner of that paper up into fighting position — a fist-sized spider, straight outta science fiction. I recoiled left, rubbin' the rock wall and instantly felt something scurry onto my shoulder. Have you any idea how huge a 5" centipede looks when he's reared up on his back fifty legs, wavin' the front 50 at you, 3" from your nose?

I paid for damages to those fragile stalls — the ones which had stood — past tense — between me and the stairway. I apologized to all and sundry for the deafening screams. One fellow who had been severely constipated thanked me. He was cured. And I wrote in my book: "UN-Written Range Rule #30: The far right stall is unused for a reason. Try the swamp."

WHAT WASN'T UNDER MY CHRISTMAS TREE

MARCH/APRIL 2006

O h, man! I thought as my tires crunched the gravel of the Rat Canyon Range parking lot, What a sweet morning for shootin'! It was crisp and cold, the pre-dawn winds had died to a flat calm, and the visibility was what highdesert dwellers call "severe clear." Oh, yeah; sweet!

I slipped on my Walker's "Quad" power range muffs before I even got outta the truck. Having had my hearing damaged enough by our artillery, their mortars, and friends' small-arms fire, I'm kinda sensitive about hearing protection. It can be a blessing, not bein' able to hear Little Red's stereo blaring until it rattles the silverware, but I don't wanta miss any gentle murmured messages from the Memsaab, like, "Join me in a bubblebath, big boy?" Hearing loss is a double-edged sword, dudes.

Note: Never let four small "allies" take cover behind YOU in a firefight. Three of their rifle muzzles were about six inches from my ears as they peeked out and shot around me. I was in a bowlegged half-crouch position, and the fourth munchkin was kneeling between my legs, pretendin' they were tree trunks. Ever wondered what muzzle-blast effect is like, spewing upward from a flash suppressor about four inches below your crotch? Imagine having screwdrivers jammed into your ears while simultaneously, a Green Bay Packers place-kicker repeatedly punts your privates. I couldn't sit for a week, and I still can't hear certain high notes.

"You bettah cover dan a wattah-boo*, Connah-man!" their captain later screamed into my chime-ringin' ears. Hey, glad to be of service, pal.

Anyway, these Quads are great. They amplify normal sounds while suppressing gunshots to a dull thump. I could clearly hear dry grass cracklin' underfoot as I strolled past the "openaction" bay where my pal, Joe Gleason, was practicing his draw-an'-double-tap on some silhouettes. I even heard his whispered "shooting mantra," muttered under his breath just before each draw.

"Excuse me," he breathed, "But that's my Harley, pal!" (draw — pop-pop — on-safe, reholster.)

"Dude! Back away from that Harley! It's mine!" (draw — pop-pop.)

Hey, whatever floats your boat, Joe. I walked on, got settled into a 50-yard range, and I had just taken up trigger slack on round number five of a potential "personal best" group, when …

"YO, CONNOR! WHATCHA DOIN', BUDDY?" Bang!!!

I didn't even bother lookin' for that round I jerked. I think it landed somewhere on the eastern slope of Cabeza Raton Mountain. My "surprise guest" was another guy I know — let's call him "Jack Cass," okay? Besides the fact he apparently learned to whisper in a sawmill, he's got one of those voices that sounds like a jackass braying about a bellyache. Not only did he ruin my great group, he also plunged me into depression, because it reminded me again of what I wanted — but DIDN'T get — for Christmas …

What Does CONNOR Want?

Some will say what I want is impossible, but I don't believe it. With all this nano-techno an' genetic-engineering and quarktransmogrifying research going on, I think it's simply a matter of (a) recognizing what I want is of paramount importance, and (b) gettin' busy grappling genes, souping up subatomic stuff, and nattering with nano-bits or whatever the heck the inventor-geeks do.

I want Quad muffs with a "Braying Jackass Suppression" setting, okay? Besides dampening the decibel levels of gunshots, you should be able to isolate an' identify the audio frequencies generated by Jack Cass-type jackasses, and muffle those too. Hey, Bob Walker! I know you can do it, buddy! Get with it!

Pucker Up

Next, I want group tightener. We've all had those moments when we're staring at a pistol target and wishin' that group was just a teensy bit tighter, right? Like, when maybe there's a sixpack or a lunch at Lonely Louie's ridin' on the outcome? I'm

envisioning a spray-on solution in a little pump bottle that you just spritz on that poorly-punctured paper target, then wait 60 seconds while your group puckers up by, say, 30 percent … Call it something like "Groop-Tyte," and mail me a cut of the profits, okay?

One thing I could really use when traveling is a range-finder. No, not a "rangefinder;" a range-finder! This would be a device like a GPS, only you turn it on, dial in desired features like "covered shooting positions," "good clubhouse coffee," and "seven to 50-yard ranges," then hit Find! — and you get directions to the nearest range. Cool, huh?

Now, you know what a range bag is — and you know what a "bag lady" is, right? So here's a challenge for you genetic engineers: I want a "range bag lady;" a cloned specimen who would delight in hauling my guns and assorted range gear, following me around from one shooting station to another, then pickin' up the empty brass and cleaning weapons when I'm done for the day. She could even use my RemOil on the squeaky wheels of her shopping cart.

I want mine cloned to look like Hilary Clinton. The shock value on the range would be hilarious — and the Memsaab Helena would never get jealous. How many days 'til next Christmas? Better get on it, people …

*Wattah-Boo:" his pronunciation of "water-bull," a male water buffalo, or sometimes, a handy, large American..

MEMSAAB'S AMIGOS

The image contains handwritten annotations: "Wrong!", "NO WAY!", "NOPE", "I DON'T THINK SO"

MAY/JUNE 2006

Ok, ok, all right! I GET it! You like her better than you like me. Ever since the Memsaab Helena filled in for me in the Nov/Dec 2005 issue, I've been opening my e-mail box to find eleventy-one messages for her, and two SPAM mails for me. Hey, I don't blame you — I like her better than I like me, too. But if you're gonna keep writing those thinly veiled love letters, guys, send 'em direct to her new address at TheMemsaabHelena@yahoo.com, okay? My bruised ego is so fragile ….

You haven't heard her voice or met her in person, but you've read her words and seen that drawing, so now you might understand why I can't write about my life without writin' about my wife, and that gets kinda scented with a certain "sensual undercurrent." That's 'cause she's sorta soaked in sensual undercurrent. Overcurrent, too — an' some rip currents. Okay, she's more like a Sensual Tsunami. See, it's less like I'm "married" to a "spouse" than like I'm "hard-wired" to a six-foot, redheaded, babyblue-eyed "Source of Primal Energy." She's my rudder and my running lights, folks, and you got a glimpse of why.

I haven't been reading your e-mails to her, but my eyes have fallen across a few — (dozen) — and I can answer some of your most frequent questions. Like, NO , she does NOT have an unmarried sister — twin, older, younger, whatever, and if you'd read her article instead of staring at the artwork, you'd know that. Yes , our marriage is doin' just fine, thank you; yes , I'm in good health and not expectin' to become null and void anytime soon, nor likely to walk in front of any speeding busses, and now I'm gonna be watching for guys like you trying to shove me in front of one … I'm not angry about that, like I said, I understand. But here's something you really should know about her.

Accurate? Hah! No Way!

So, hordes of you have asked, "How accurate is Sequoia Blankenship's drawing of The Memsaab?" I gotta tell you guys, it's not accurate at all . First, she has never, to my knowledge, worn gauntlets above her gloves. Second, she favors ankle-height boots. Third, she never has rolled cuffs on her hiking shorts. Finally, that 1911 clearly looks disproportionately large on her almost two-meter frame, and … Her hair usually has

45

a little more wave and curl to it. Umm … Other than that, well, yeah, it's … pretty accurate. The relative tightness of those shorts is questionable too, but she's got this one pair that — well, skip it. All right, she's smart, tough, an' gorgeous, now drop it, okay? Man, this "refutation and rebuttal" thing didn't go quite the way I intended.

And another thing: Despite your ardent requests, she still refuses to consider allowing photos of herself in magazines. She has changed her position though, from "When pigs take wing and Roy-Boy starts dancing at Chippendales," to a wink and a "Maybe … Someday." She sends her regrets and fond regards, and … this.

Bein' the woman she is, and travelin' in the circles she does, The Memsaab makes some "unusual" lady friends, and Galina — "Gala" to her hand-picked pals — certainly qualifies as "different." Let's just say, she used to work for The Wrong Guys, and now she teaches our guys how their worst nightmares operate.

Last time we discussed the photo question, Galina was visiting, showin' off a new IR aiming/illumination device, if that gives you some clues. Gala listened to Helena's refusal, smiled, twinkled her hazel 20-13 sniper-eyes, and said, "Kah-norr, EH wull eh-pirr en zhoor megguh-zinns, weh-rink eh mesk!" Translated from her butter-thick ex-Soviet commie skull-shooter accent, that means, "Connor, I will appear in your magazines, wearing a mask!"

With Helena's nod, I took Galina up on it. You'll be seeing more of her here and in GUNS Magazine. I'm forever faithfully wedded to The Memsaab's big blues, but ya gotta admit, a man could fall into Gala's eyes and drown, huh? Now, can I get back to some regular gunwritin'? Gee, thanks.

The Memsaab's AMAZON ARMY

Whenever The Memsaab hooks up with a new gal-pal, we just sit back and watch the transformation. It's sometimes subtle, sometimes not, but usually it goes somethin' like this: No matter what they were like before they met her, they start wearin' bush shorts, desert boots and wispy-silky blouses; packin' guns, or if they did already, packin' bigger guns or more of 'em; pumping iron at the gym; placing makeup-coupon bets on what they can hit at what range with one shot; spicing their speech with Swahili and dealing with condescending dipsticks at the auto-parts store with statements like, "Oh dear, I can tell from your attitude that you haven't had a good butt-whuppin' in far too long! Care for one, sweetie?"

Our daughter watches this, rolls her eyes, and sighs, "Another innocent human is assimilated by the Red Borg! Jeez-Louise!" Our son the Refrigerator Raider asks, "What's the cult count on the Amazon Army up to now, Dad?" Me and the dog, Sancho Panza, just stay outta the way, police up brass and line up for chow-call. Got the picture?

ABOUT THAT FOUR-LETTER WORD

JULY/AUGUST 2006

Over 500 of you wrote in with responses to "Why Do You Carry A Gun?" (July/August 2005). If you missed it, or need a refresher, it's posted on the Web site at www.americanhandgunner.com. We'll wait. Done? Good. I carried Little Lizzie and her mom, Miss Maine, around in my head and heart for several years, waiting for the right audience to share them with. I guess I found it.

Numbers-geeks who study these things tell me that 500 write-ins means your feelings were shared by somewhere between 50,000 and 100,000 readers. That article has spread to chat rooms, BLOGs, gun forums, lunchrooms and bulletin boards, with copies scattered in some very unusual places across the country. I was overwhelmed with its impact — and struck with some unsettling themes in your responses. First, the ferocity and determination you expressed were stunning.

Virtually every one of you spoke of your willingness to kill or die to protect Little Lizzie — any "Little Lizzie." Second, so many of you were confused or surprised with the depth of your own reactions, saying you had never really examined — not deep in your guts — this very primal and central dynamic, which drives all of your more intellectual and super-conscious reasons for being armed, for asserting your right to self-defense, and to intervene to protect the lives of others. Third, those of you who have not been tested under fire wondered — How would I do? Could I cut it? — if you had to stand and deliver, at grave risk, as a human barrier between "the bad men" and a Little Lizzie. Folks, we need to talk.

SO LET'S TALK

These are three same-and-separate issues, as tangled and twisted as human emotions can be. I can only try to answer them in an equally tangled way, using slices of my past.

When I was a small boy, a great-uncle, a 48-year British Army veteran, told me about our family history, laying out that long, unbroken line of lifelong warriors. "We fight, boy," he growled. "We lose and die sometimes, yes, but we always fight." I asked him, "Why do we fight, sir?" He laughed, harshly, and pointed to the puppies rolling in the yard. "Why do they hunt, boy? Why do those dogs point? Born to it, bred for it, they are, same's us. And because we will not be trod on." I accepted that explanation for a long time. Later I learned he had it halfright, and nine-tenths wrong.

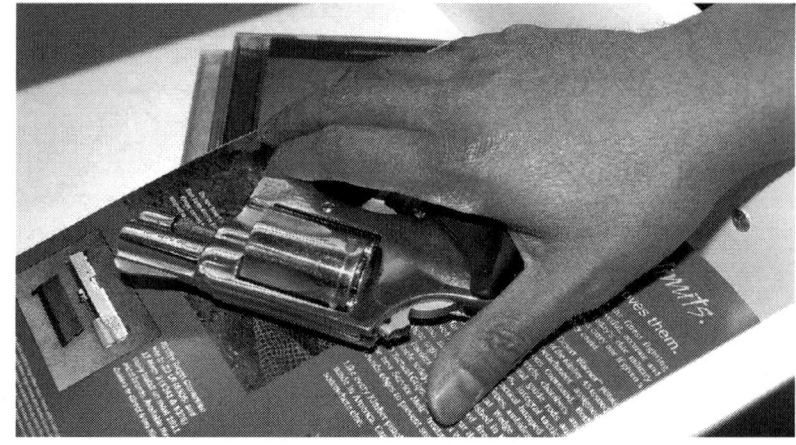

There had been some ugly incidents involving other teams. Men, some living and some dead, had been left behind, both due to "combat circumstances," and to orders. We could not live with that. Before each mission, my and I began joining hands and swearing that we would never each other behind; the mission, pain and fear and wounds be damned, orders be double-damned; if it came down to it, we would all go down together. Together.

On a pitchy night in another world, five good men and I violated orders. We ferried nine small children across a murky, shallow river because other men wanted them dead. It took a twelve-eternity hour to cover 100 meters of dark water into darker trees, and we fought for every child and every meter. Two of my mates and one of the kids didn't make it. I remember that night with a piercing sweet sadness — and an immense, soul-filling, self-defining pride. I never knew those children's names, and I never saw them again.

There is no bloodline so thick with history, so red with ancient battles, as to render anyone into an unfaltering warrior by birthright. There must be something more. There is no acceptance of duty ; no oaths, no allegiances ever sworn so binding that they have not been thereafter cast aside and forgotten under fire — when men had nothing more to hold them than the memory of those pledges. I've seen it. There must be something more.

You have not armed and oriented yourself for fighting, in defense of yourself and others, just because you are fearful of attack by predators, have you? No. Because you are blessed with natural bravery and it's just the "right thing to do?" No. There must be something more. And there is.

That Four-Letter Word

It is love. Perhaps not the kind of love that first springs to your mind, but love, yes. None of you ever met Little Lizzie, so you couldn't love her. Why risk death to fight for her? I have served with many men whom I would willingly fight and die with, but in truth, I loved only one. When the Memsaab Helena and I first got together, we discussed what I did for a living and how I felt about it; my best and worst times, my motivators and morale busters. I talked about duty and promises. I didn't know I was shotgunning around the center, fooling myself, until she put one dead in the 10-ring.

"Bullshit, Connor," she said, "It's about love, ya goof. Admit it; get over it." She was right.

Unless that gun on your hip or in your nightstand exists only to protect your own hairy hide, and if it extends beyond your own mate and offspring, then it's about love; another kind of love, but love nonetheless, ya goofs!

It is about a nameless thing — call it "honor" if you will — that is the finest, purest shred of yourself and all humankind. It's a love you only feel when you face the ultimate self-sacrifice — for the life of another; even a stranger; no, especially a stranger. In a way it is a love of self, even if it is only a love of the smallest, least recognized, most rarely exposed slice of your self.

We talk about it so little its unbidden emergence surprises many of us. That's because in this weirdly warped "modern society," its presence strangely embarrasses us, and its absence shames us. So we avoid it altogether. That's a pity. Only by bringing it out in the open and knowing it can we lean on it; live by it.

90 Percent

Without knowing what you'll kill or die for, how can you know what you really live for? In the end, it's about love — and in the end, love is all you have, and all you ever really had to begin with. And as for whether or not you'll stand and deliver if and when the time comes? Ten percent will depend on how you've trained. Ninety percent will hinge on what you love.

Now I'll go back to being the capering clown of the gunwriting circus, and you can forget I ever said these things, okay? Good luck to both of us.

STONES, STYLE AND DOOR STOPS

SEPTEMBER/OCTOBER 2006

Opening my e-mail these days is a double-edged sword, folks. It's great so many of you are comfortable writing and askin' me just about anything. On the other hand, the sheer numbers are gettin' staggering, and all you guys want to know is everything! My policy is to answer every e-mail, but this month, I'm gonna try to whack a flock of birds with a single stone, okay? Each line or phrase here answers multiple inquiries by multiple mobs of you.

"Who are you? What are you? John Connor is a nom de plume, and you got it from those Terminator movies, right?" Nope. De plume, de guerre, whatever. I was writing and fighting under John Connor long before Ahnold's movies, and I can sign certain checks and pass through certain doors with it. All else must remain as it is, shrouded in legend, myth and mystery. (I just love that line — ain't it cool?)

What am I? I'm a warrior, and I say that with no embarrassment, hesitation, or any particular pride. Pride or shame should hinge on the morality and ethics of how you think and act, not on titles, position or appellation. My life has been devoted to the art and science of defeating domestic predators and foreign enemies by force of arms, strength of will, distraction and stealth. I've done okay at that, and some scribbling.

My favorite titles are "faithful husband" and "Dad." There are lots of warriors out there titled "insurance broker," "diesel mechanic," and "high school teacher." They're just not working full-time at the warrior gig. Neither am I anymore. The Memsaab prefers a shift in the balance of "Scribbler-Soldier" to more of the "scribbler" role — I presume, because she likes me home to take out the kitchen trash. That, and my dog, Sancho Panza, gives me this look like, "Hey, this ball ain't gonna throw itself, dummy! Where you goin'?"

Ain't Exactly "Writing"

Which sorta leads to my "writing style" — or lack of it. Yeah, I know some people are offended when I drop a "g," invent a contraction Webster never heard of, or dangle a participle. But I don't "write articles and columns." I just talk to you guys on

paper, see? I've written reams of info-crap — both government and commercial flavors — in slavish obedience to Strunk & White and the AP Style Guide, then submitted it to hyper-critical horse's patoots who knew all about grammar and syntax, and nothing about weapons, tactics, history, humor or human communication. I'll never do that again.

That sucked. The result was dry as bones in the Ténéré, and about as appetizing. I didn't even like reading it myself. The response I've had from you folks has been one of the biggest, most pleasant surprises of my life. Which segues into ...

What kinda guy are you personally? What's your temperament and tick-offs? If something ain't heart-attack serious, fall-down funny, or relaxed-tothe- max, I get bored easily. I'm prone to stand up from circular conversations, banal dinners and mindless meetings, and just wander away. Life's too short for that crap. I do the "Queen Elizabeth wave," say, "All done now, bye-bye, Connor out," and I'm gone. I'm short on social skills but long on loyalty to friends, so maybe that's the trade-off, okay?

I'd say I'm a happy guy who knows how lucky he is; simple by nature and inclination, and I work at keeping things that way. I've fought for a living, so I don't go looking for trouble unless I'm getting paid to do just that. I tend to tell people exactly what I'm thinking — if they ask, or if I think they really need to hear it. And I figure if they're over 15 in years or five feet in height, they should be able to take it straightup, no soda, no ice.

In some circles I'm considered a crass, insensitive boor. A gentleman I respect once told me, "Connor, you may not be seen as a very nice guy, but you're a good man." I'll gladly settle for that.

Guns & Door Stops

On my tastes in guns: I'm a big admirer of plain, cheap, black rubber door stops. When they're new and shiny with crisp sharp edges, they perform their function beautifully — they stop doors. When they're old, worn, dull and dinged up, they still stop doors reliably. There are more expensive, elegant and high-tech ways to do the job, but none work appreciably better. I admire the same quality in people, by the way.

I'm not a gunsmith or a gun connoisseur, and I'm far from being a gun expert. I do love guns and shooting — it's been a big chunk of my life — and I appreciate guns as tools. My personal battery clearly reflects this; my guns are the ordnance-equivalents of rubber door stops. I know enough about 'em to use and maintain them. I'm fascinated with function, not finery and fancy finish.

I think tactics more than I think about tools, because I've rarely had much choice in the guns I've carried "on business." Frankly, if I were issued a bumbershoot and a brick, I'd be concentrating on tactics which allow me to up under the concealment

51

of the deployed umbrella, then leap out and deliver multiple brick-bonkin's on my opposition's noggin.

Now I'm outta "word count" and I have to bail. If there's a next time, we'll go down & dirty on competition, "combat accuracy," and gunfighting, okay?

KWAHERI!BLASPHEMY & HERESY
Or How I Became A Heretic

November/December 2006

Lots of you have written asking what handgunning "discipline du jour," signature school of shooting, trademarked technique, or method-of-the-month I subscribe to. I don't. I have what I call "evolved practices," and they're still evolving. It's kinda hard to explain, but imagine most, but not all of your "mechanical firearm handling, feeding and functioning" details being derived from training here, there, and everywhere, military and police, and then, your "engagement processes and procedures" being built like the layers of a monster sub sandwich, as you learn just exactly how you — and others — tend to react under fire, fear, fatigue, pain and anger; what sticks with you and what doesn't.

What you wind up with is, "Here's How I Fight — Generally — Today. It may differ somewhat tomorrow, and I'm sure I'll make some stuff up as I go along." These "evolved practices" are the result of my experiences and I've bet my life on 'em, so they're sorta the Ultimate Empirical Experiment, you know? They principally spring from three episodes in my life, supplemented by scads of fill-in slices from other scenarios. We'll call 'em The Two Dudes, The Greyhound Rules, and The Shoot-Down Drill. You may not understand until I've explained all three and then wrapped 'em up for you.

The Two Dudes

My first two engagements with handguns occurred in the three months before my twentieth birthday. In both cases I was moving, pistol in hand on rough ground, with my off-hand "occupied," in the first instance with a jammed long gun, and in the second, I was half-carrying half-dragging a wounded comrade, with our two rifles slung. Both took place in heavy foliage and in both cases I suddenly came up against lone enemy troops.

I had just turned a blind hook to the left on a moderate downhill grade when the first dude appeared at about 20 feet. He was holding a rifle in his right hand at the receiver. Still running, I shot him twice at about ten feet. In the second, I was struggling on a steep, heavily-jungled trail when up popped Dude #2 at about 15 feet. He was rising from a crouch and reaching for a rifle leaning against growth to his right. He looked shocked and confused. Without breaking forward movement, I shot him twice.

Only in retrospect was I surprised at the similarities of these events. At the time they seemed like "business as usual." There were other similarities, and some differences which may only seem significant to other people — not to me. Results and reactions were the same in both cases. They sat down hard and fell over. In neither case did I stick around. Their side of the fight was over, and that's all I cared about.

Both were hit solid twice in the torso. I was conscious of a firm grip and trigger control. I didn't glimpse my sights. I was only aware of forcefully extending my right arm and pointing. I had not been taught "double-taps" — that wasn't included in Marine Corps training. I just shot 'em twice. In one case my sidearm was an issue 1911; a well-worn warrior that rattled like your Uncle Fred's flat-bed farm truck. Ammo was issue 230-grain round nose ball. In the other, I was carrying the standard sidearm of the unit I was working with — an equally experienced Hi-Power — and ammo was standard NATO 124- grain round nose ball.

Tremblin' Trepidation?

If I had been reading and accepting the writings of many handgunning gurus of the time, I might have gone into those encounters trembling with trepidation, thinking I was seriously ill-equipped. Old, clunky, issue pistols? Plain-Jane round-nose ball ammo? Horrors! Instead, in my ignorance, I thought I was a well-trained warrior with reasonably reliable roscoes. Keep in mind I was painfully young, and didn't know any better. I only learned what worked for me. Yes, I'm being sarcastic.

Lessons learned? A working gun in the hand is worth more than two premium pistols in holsters, four rifles slung, or 40 fine firearms stored, stacked, or leaning against trees.

Caliber and ammo ain't as important as being first, and hitting. If you can get better guns and more effective ammo, fine. If not, you dance with him who brung you, in the outfit you got on. If that means your footwear is brogans instead of tap shoes, just dance better and faster.

I had been religiously practicing the combat rule, "shoot 'em where they're biggest, and do it more than once." That wisdom was reinforced. Combatants, crooks, cops and crazies all make fatal mistakes, and most of 'em involve HESITATION; disbelieving your own ears and eyes, and failing to trust your own survival instinct.

Disciplines are fine, but they have to be Gumby-flexible. If I had skidded to a halt, assumed a two-hand hold and gone for a sight picture, I'd have been half-past dead.

Okay, that's kinda "chapter one." Think it over, and if you've got the patience, meet me here next issue for The Greyhound Rules.

MY GUNS & GEAR DU JOUR

JANUARY/FEBRUARY 2007

You guys routinely pack my e-mail box with questions about what guns & gear I like, play with, carry and covet, so we'll take a break and answer about 412 of those, okay?

Between two articles — "Rockin' Glocks — Beyond Basic Black" in the March 2005 issue of GUNS, and "Who Uses What? Guns of the Masthead Guys," in the Nov-Dec 2005 Handgunner, you know I shoot a buncha Black Guns (Glocks) and why. Those who read the GUNS article know four of mine aren't black "Black Guns" anymore, nor do they have those humped backstraps, overdone finger-grooves, square-hooked triggerguards or stock sights, not since Master Gunsmith (or GlockSmith?) Frank Duren did surgery on 'em at DG Custom in Nixa, Missouri.

We're showing this pic of Leigh because we wanted you to see the HK P7 her husband built for her. Okay, now look at the gun.

Still a solid shooter, "Foul Fritz," an HK P7, was pretty road-worn and dull.

From that litter, my favorite "Pocket Mamba" is still the little ghosty-gray single-stack .45 ACP Glock 36. With about 4,000 rounds digested, she's only burped up twice; both times with featherweight "eco-friendly green loads," with slugs apparently made of compressed horse dung, my fault. Baby, sorry.

After scribbling my piece of that "Who Uses What?" article I neglected to mention my most-carried, totally trusted, world-traveled handgun of the previous 15-plus years: an HK P7 "squeeze-cocker" 9mm, the PSP variant. About the same time, I noticed that Frank's wife, Leigh, was carrying the American variant, the P7 M8, but except for the distinctive silhouette, it was unrecognizable and drop-dead beautiful. Frank 'splained since he is in fact an HK factory-trained "squeezer-'smith" (another surprise for me) he had done some magic on that one to protect his number-one sweetie.

I showed him my beat-up, double-dinged PSP. He made what five-year old Little Lizzie woulda called " a uggyface," grabbed the gun and disappeared. It finally flew home, and I'm glad my eyes are wired to their sockets with them squiggly stringy things. That made it easier to poke 'em back in. I'll share a "before" photo with you, then write it up an' photo it for GUNS or Handgunner. I've bet my life on Foul Fritz before; I'll geqladly bet it on Handsome Hans again.

The $4.95 .45

If e-mails had mass, I couldn't lift your letters asking about a bargain-priced carry-quality 1911A1, specifically, something like "a tricky-tactical high-speed low-drag melty-cornered custom 1911 for under $500" I don't own a rabbit, dudes. No top hat, cape or baton, either. Got the picture? Not a magician.

But if you can ante-up another hundred bucks, take a look at Springfield Armory's plain-Jane "GI .45" — a faithful recreation of the World War II-issue U.S. 1911A1. I've found as long as you hold her firm and feed her hardball, she'll probably shoot straighter than you can, and more reliably.

The sights though, are squinty, teensy and terrible. If, like me, you don't wanta permanently alter the GI, some "no- 'smithing" group-tighteners include Chip McCormick's contoured drop-in rear sight, and/or, installation of a LaserMax or Crimson Trace Laser laser sight.

If you're gonna get Socially Serious, add quality magazines like ACT-MAGS from Precision Sights International or McCormick's eight or 10-round Power Mags. The best part? Parkerized or OD, the GI .45 lists at $587, and stainless goes for $632.

The Mudhole Model

I've told several 1911 makers I'm not interested in "Lieutenant Colonel at Camp Perry" models, but rather, a Lance Corporal in a Mudhole model. First, that's just my nature — I'm a "service-issue" guy. Second, I live under the rule of "Kidz Insteada Kash." Hashin' it over with the guys at Rock River Arms, they handed me a "Basic Carry" model. Check the Sept-Oct '06 Handgunner, top right on page 46. You'll see two "plain black door stops." One is rubber, and the other is that Rock River pistol.

I've petted, popped caps and played with it, and here's my verdict: This pistol is dangerous! I wanta keep it, and can't afford it! $1,555 ain't a ton of money, but it's a tuition payment (remember "Kidz vs. Kash"?). Go check it out at www.rockriverarms. com. I admit I have limited "Luxury Limo-Class Pistol" experience, but in my opinion this piece is the easy equal of some 1911's at twice the price. Dang! Outta space!

THE GREYHOUND RULES

MARCH/APRIL 2007

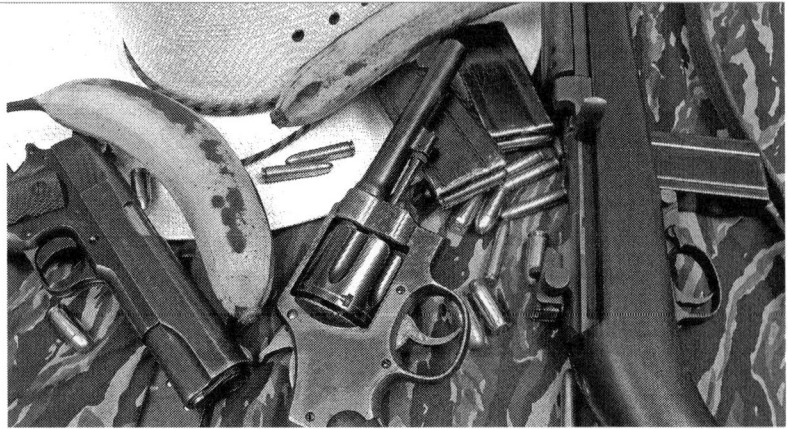

Okay, now you folks remember which page we're on, right? If not, go back to the last two issues, then rejoin us. This is the only way I can tell this, so get yourself a refreshing beverage, relax, and we'll play "let's pretend," okay?

Long, long ago in a galaxy far, far away, there was a fair and fertile land festooned with lotsa bananas, bunches of Bad Guys, and some buses. The bananas grew mostly out in the countryside, and the Bad Guys did too. These Bad Guys used to be armed, funded an' fed by an Evil Empire, but when its wheels fell off like a flattened Flexy Flyer, the Bad Guys just dropped their political pretensions and became freelance murderers, bandits and killerkidnappers. They 'specially liked killing and kidnapping BananaLand's judges, mayors and Deputy Assistant Ministers of Thus-and-So, because it was both entertaining and profitable.

A group of "Hard Hombres" was formed to protect these officials. About half of 'em came from the state police, a quarter from BananaLand's army, and the rest were just really tough dudes with shiny hair and shinier pistols. All of the Hombres could shoot, though they tended to get kinda festive with the fireworks, and all were either very brave or too proud to ever back down from a fight, which is almost the same thing. What they didn't have was "consistent tactics," so they couldn't dance well together while fightin' BadGuys.

Far to the North, a country called YanquiLand heard about this and offered to help. YanquiLand sent four guys to teach the Hombres how to fight BadGuys, and how not to shoot innocent bystanders. This training would happen at The Big Bus Farm, upcountry from the capitol, Santa Mañana, on the edge of a dark, damp forest called The Yongle.

The Big Bus Farm

The buses — lots of 'em! — and some assorted trucks lived on a not quite- flat crazy-quilt expanse of asphalt, grass and concrete patches behind some charm-free but roomrich government buildings. The buildings housed a vehicle maintenance facility, some s'posed-to-be-secret treasury offices and not enough bathrooms.

Training was fun, though some Hombres questioned the value of learning to fight as "fire teams." Everybody played nice, and the coffee was excellent and plentiful. So, during a break, the whole happy group kinda wandered out amongst the buses an' trucks, to go pee on the bushes at the edge of The Yongle. As the Hombres and YanquiDudes wandered out, they encountered some other dudes wandering in, like maybe they'd hadda go pee too, you know? But they didn't.

They were BadGuys, and they had picked the wrong day for whatever mischief they had planned. Actually, they looked kinda like the Hombres, except not so clean and neat, and they had pistols like the Hombres, and some rifles, too! Everybody sorta looked funny at each other, an' then some eyes got really big and others got really squinty, and then there were some shots, and then things got really weird.

Everybody scattered like a good break on a pool table, scrambling in and around an' over those big buses an' trucks, all the while shooting at each other. One Yanqui described it as "a disorganized, chaotic, drawn-out string of vicious firefights involving two, three, up to 10 participants, which would then break up and form different firefights — a helluva mess."

Window-Weirdness

Several BGs clambered aboard buses, and that was dumb. They trapped themselves. Most of the bus windows were two-piece, so they could be opened from top or bottom. One BG stood up and fired over a window's lowered panes, as though the glass was "cover." It wasn't even concealment. He was shot lotsa times. Another stood up at a closed window, holding a pistol in one hand and fumbling to lower the top pane with the other. He got punctured plenty, too. Another fired at some Hombres and then just ducked down below the window. Bus skin didn't stop bullets. Neither did bus seats.

Some guys on both sides stood and fired over the decks of flat-bed trucks and semi-trailers. They got shot a lot in their hips, groins and legs. About a dozen guys from both sides fell flat on their beaks or butts while traversing the uneven seams of those asphalt, earth and concrete sections. Some of 'em didn't get up. It's like they were only thinking and fighting from their belts up.

At one point, a glass-rattling godlike voice commanded Stop shooting! — and amazingly, everybody did. Then the voice went on, Stop! You're shooting my buses! PLEASE stop! It was the motor pool manager, screaming over a PA system. Firing resumed.

The BGs, who had some rifles, began fighting in cells, while the Hombres, with only handguns, fought as individuals, pairs and amoebae. The BGs started winning. Then some Hombres returned from their vehicles with M-1 carbines and Thompson submachine guns, and the tide turned — hard.

Pistol ammo ran low fast. A teenager wearing a Chicago Cubs cap appeared outta nowhere, passing out loaded Glock-17 and 1911 .45 magazines from cardboard boxes. That was nice. Afterward, nobody seemed to know who he was. Weird. The surviving BGs fled into The Yongle. Many lessons were learned, to be discussed later.

One YanquiDude wrote this in his book of "Evolved Practices": "From touching distance to bus-bumper width, I'm gonna start shooting fast as soon as my muzzle covers meat — kneecaps, elbows, I don't care, and I won't worry about conserving ammo as long as an enemy is armed and upright. From front bumper to rear bumper distance I'm going for a straight point, a flash sight picture, a firm grip and trigger control. From there out to The Yongle, I want a crisp front sight and a rock-steady hold — or I'll move closer, or get further away." He called these "The Greyhound Rules."

THE SHOOTDOWN DRILL:
A Fairy Tale

MAY/JUNE 2007

"It's not enough to shoot a guy until you think he's dead. You gotta shoot him until *he* thinks he's dead."
— *The Tao of Connor* ©

Once upon a time on a faraway world very much like our own, there was a teeny-tiny nation surrounded by bigger, bitter enemies. On one side of it lapped an azure sea, but it otherwise kinda sat there like a chocolate fudge nut brownie on the edge of a ping-pong table. And all the giant Ping-Pongers wanted to smash that brownie an' sweep it off onto the floor.

The Pingers tried to sweep it off with conventional novelties like tanks, artillery and bombs, but they failed. The Pingers had the numbers and the ordnance, but the Brownies had D&D: Determination and Desperation. See, when the Pingers lost, they could go home, award each other shiny medal, and re-equip. If the Brownies lost, they would be exterminated.

Then the Pongers jumped in, and they were less conventional. They selected some less-than-stellar Pongs not noted for their joie de vive, wrapped 'em on the outside with high explosives, and filled 'em on the inside with painkillers, stimulants and some really toxic stuff called "death-dogma." Then they'd send these Pong-Bombs out among the Brownies, to their bus stations, grocery stores, schools and movie theaters — even their weddings — to blast as many Brownies as they could.

These Pongs were told to look and act inconspicuous — to move within crowds, and whenever possible, to stick to older, even ancient areas where passageways were narrow and numerous, so they could slip along to their targets like fishies in weedy waters. Then all the Pongs had to do was pull a loop, punch a button or squeeze a little squeezie-thingie, and Bang! — their job was done. Detecting, closing with, and intercepting the Pongs was a really tough job, but there were some really smart, tough nuts in that brownie.

Tough Job Toughnutz

The TufNutz had to spot the Pongs by such miniscule clues as head and eye movement, subliminal behaviors, a neck and jaw that wasn't quite fleshy enough to match a Pong's waistline, compulsively touching the same place on their clothing and stuff like that. Then they had to move in, locking on their targets like heat-seeking missiles, never losin' sight of 'em for a second or they might escape — and "escape" wouldn't mean escape — it would just mean moving a mass murder to another location. Pong-Bombs could not be allowed to get away.

All of this had to be done while moving around obstacles, threading through swirling throngs of people, hustling over cobbly, uneven surfaces, not shooting if it could be avoided at all, absolutely controlling every shot, and — neutralizing a Pong who might be soaked in a painkilling chemical cocktail. Too, as soon as the TufNutz engaged, people would do crazy stuff like freeze, scream, fall down, run the wrong direction and even reach out and grab at the TufNutz, like "Save me!" — makin' it much harder to save 'em. Easy, huh?

TufNutz were mostly commandos, intelligence wizards and cop-types. But this job wasn't much like regular soldiering, or regular police work, or even like tactical counterterrorist team operations. It was more like plainclothes execution of high-risk felony fugitive warrants on armed and dangerous psycho druggie-crooks in a metropolitan environment. So, they got some help from cop-friends called "Yanx" in a far-off country who had sorta "been there and done that," and were combat vets besides.

The TufNutz had to suppress a lot they'd been taught, like fire-and-maneuver doctrine and classical shooting positions, and learn things like tuckin' their weapons, arms and elbows in close and centered, adopting an "agile crab" rapid but stable scuttle, hip-checking an' stiffarming people outta the way; hearing, seeing, and feeling peripheral dangers and interference without reacting to them unless they threatened loss of focus on that one monstrously dangerous, all-important Pong target — and lots more; too much to tell here. And there was another problem to deal with.

The Shoot-Down Drill

Even if a Pong — especially a "medicated" one — took a solid hit, after a few seconds, he could frequently recover enough control and dexterity to "punch his button." Two Yanx and some TufNutz had even seen guys take wounds that good sense and medical experts would term fatal, but they remained briefly functional, as though "science says he's dead, but he didn't get the message."

One of the Yanx observed that the TufNutz were shooting tightly controlled single shots and some doubletaps. He had been taught to "shoot 'em where they're biggest, and do it more than once," and his own "evolved practice" had become "shoot 'em where they're biggest lots and lotsa times, until there ain't no threat anymore."

Several who had observed this phenomenon agreed a man who is receiving a steady, unrelenting series of impacts, spaced, let's say, a tad less than a second apart, will be

virtually unable to do anything but involuntarily react to those continuing impacts. Man being essentially a big wet sack of electrical connections, the response is like timed low-voltage shocks, or mechanically, like a boxer taking a rapid volley of punches: The first couple of blows may only stun and shock him, but he is prevented from coordinated reaction, and the disabling effect only increases and deepens as he is hammered all the way to the canvas and into oblivion.

> He had been taught to 'shoot 'em where they're biggest, and do it more than once.'

The TufNutz technique changed: No more single shots; no more double-taps — just absolute focus on timed, continuous, accurate fire; and it wasn't at all about "shooting to kill," but about "shooting to zero-threat." It worked.

The Yanx went home, and one scribbled a new chapter in his little book of "Evolved Practices." He called it, The Shoot- Down Drill.

THE DEVIL'S IN THE DIGIT
... And The Gremlin's In The Grip

JULY/AUGUST 2007

I have created a monster — a "serial saga" which I'm now obligated to complete. A bunch of you wanted to know which School of Shootery I subscribe to, or the Temple of Tactical Technique in which I kneel. A wise parable says, "Never miss an opportunity to shut up," and maybe I shoulda. Instead, in the Nov/Dec 2006 issue, I explained I have what I call "evolved practices," and then wrote about the first of three epiphanic and evolutionary episodes in my handgunning life.

That was "The Two Dudes." I had to take a break in the series in the Jan/Feb 2007 issue, so that "The Greyhound Rules" and "The Shoot-Down Drill" could be run through a final legal rinse cycle in the word-washer. That was necessary to avoid violations of non-disclosure agreements, classified-materials restrictions and stomping on some tender international toes. So, those episodes appeared in fairy-tale form in the March/April and May/June 2007 issues. Reviewing those stories might be helpful in understanding the rest of this mess. Go ahead; I'll wait. Done? Good.

I've seen a lot of men die for two reasons: First, because they failed to do what they were trained to do. Second, because they did exactly as they were trained to do. For example, "The Two Dudes" told of my first two lethal handgun engagements. If I had obeyed my training to that point, in both cases I would have skidded to a

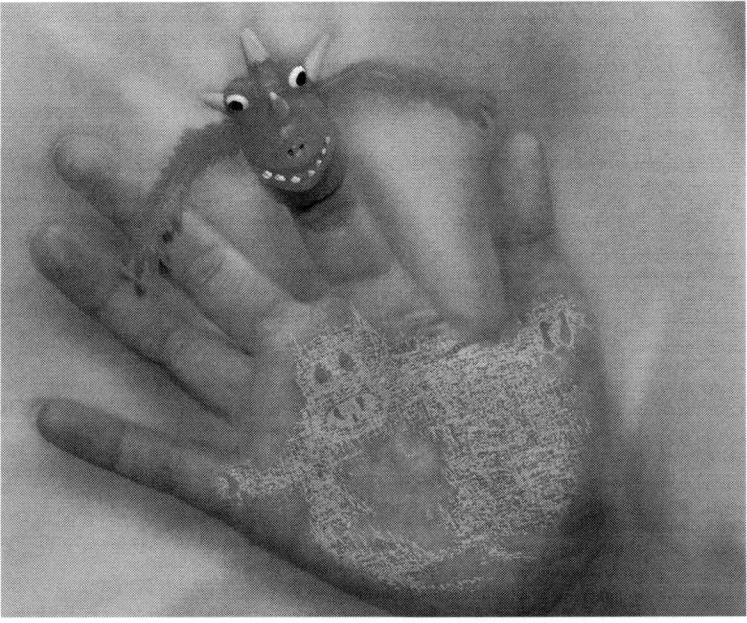

stop and assumed the Classic Pistol Position. Had I done so, I would have then assumed the "Permanent Prone Position," and shortly ceased breathing due to ballistic perforation by my opponents. Instead, I violated that training and won those gunfights. Hence, my "evolved practices;" some derived from training, some from the University of Hard Knocks.

You asked for more details, so I'll start from a weird place: the beginning.

DANCING WITH THE DEVIL

One of the first things I learned about shooting was I'm not a naturally gifted shooter. I've known some, and I'm not one of 'em. Nevertheless, I've always shot "Expert" in military qualifications, and taken some gongs and trinkets in cop-competitions. More importantly, I've acquitted myself honorably, survived and won when shooting for my life. I give a big chunk of credit for those accomplishments to this warrior-wizardry from my Dad.

As a pup out in the Pacific, I had minimal small-bore pistol-poppin' instruction when Dad presented me with my first "very own" handgun — a S&W 1917 .45 ACP revolver. Even with the forked stick he gave me to rest the barrel of that hand-howitzer on, I was an enthusiastic but imprecise "area-wide artillery threat." Forget "groups;" my CPE — Circular Probability of Error — was about the size of a Navy-issue trash can lid. I wondered why he chose that huge gun for me. There was, as always, a method to his madness.

He introduced me to two friends. One was a crude, fierce-looking little native-made finger puppet, which he slipped on his index finger. He waggled the digital-demon and then opened his hand. He had drawn a gray, shadowy spirit on his palm. I can still hear that deep, oil-tank voice rumbling, "The devil's in this digit, son, and the gremlin's in the grip. They can be your worst enemies or your best friends."

I think you can guess what he was talking about, and he hammered the lesson home. If all the other tools in your handgunning haversack are at least nominal, your grip and trigger control are the most important factors determining whether you score or suck, hit or miss, win or lose, live or die. Concentrating on a solid, stable grip and smooth, purposeful trigger control as only a little boy or an idiot can, I became the "Scourge of Small Scuttlers" — the crabs around our lagoon.

Time after time in training and competition, I shot up to or surpassed superior shooters because when the pressure was on, they squared their stances — and jerked their triggers; they moved faster — and fumbled their grips, foulballing their shots. There were 'bout 19 factors that caused them to shoot below their capabilities, and just two that kept this caveman competitive: The Devil & the Gremlin.

All Roads Lead To Battle

But for me, all roads lead to battle, and when it comes to fighting, the Devil & the Gremlin are the king and queen of combat. Think about it: With all other factors favorable, an unstable grip is likely to throw off your first shot, and certain to doom those that should follow, fast! With a poor grip, that sidearm can even squirt right outta your hand. And the sharpest, clearest sight picture possible is lost the instant you jerk or stutter on the trigger. Conversely, if your bleary front sight seems to be circling your aiming point and won't hold still, a smooth, even trigger pull will at least give you a hit — maybe the one that saves your life.

You shoot under, over and around what you have to, in whatever position you're mooshed or crunched into. Mud, blood, sand, smoke and snow; adrenaline, exhaustion and pain are often present and problematic. "The fog of war" is both figurative and literal, and when you can't even see your sights, that devil-digit and gremlin-grip are all you've got, and sometimes all you need. They have saved my life.

Next time, we'll talk about things like Terminal Hesitation, "A bird in the hand," how surviving got me in trouble and OtherStuff. Kwaheri!

BIGGER BLASPHEMY, HAIRIER HERESY

SEPTEMBER/OCTOBER 2007

After that last column, I can hear the cries of the Mad Mullahs of Marksmanship all the way from the bazaar: "Blasphemy! He places grip and trigger control above The Front Sight! Heresy! He speaketh of point shooting when all know it is an abomination! Did not the prophet Jeff Cooper say, "Blessed are they who, in the face of death, think only about the front sight?" Do we not chant 'FrontSightFrontSight-FRONTSIGHT?' Stone the blasphemer! Smite him about the neck with knives! Burn him!"

Yeah, and I sometimes eat with my left hand, too — if it's clean. No undue offense to front sight zealots, but reading Colonel Cooper in context, he was talking about a lot more than sight picture, including the reduction of weaponcraft to second nature. That way,

Little Red's personal version of "Ready" — politically incorrect, but pretty dang survivable.

when you're engaged in a fight you don't have to think much about the mechanical minutiae of runnin' the gun, and having achieved a proper mindset about the use of lethal force long before a lethal condition developed — all this so the shooter could concentrate with absolute focus on the task of hitting his target, period.

I fully suspect the good Colonel, while concentrating his training on a solid two-handed Weaver stance and a front sight focus that would melt mild steel, also paid more than passing attention to snapping off point shots from port and starboard. Even more than "front sight X3," he was all about "fundamentalsfundamentalsFUNDAMENTALS" — all of 'em. Without a granite grip and tight trigger control, your front sight better be really big and sharp, so you can use it like a hatchet at kissing distance.

And Also Blessed

I believe they are also blessed who can plant rounds roughly in the boiler room at 11 paces without that front sight. Blessings too for those who remember their sidearm is a hand-gun, not a "handgun;" who practice popping with either paw because, while recognizing two hands are superior, conditions may dictate one mitt is occupied with chores like carrying a comrade, stiff-arming some sucker, throttling a throat or even twisting a tourniquet.

Consider the circumstances of my first two handgun engagements — see "The Two Dudes", Nov/Dec 2006 — and this: One of my best pals on my old PD commenced a gunfight by taking the first round into his right wrist, exiting under his elbow. This had a profound impact on the incident, and on our future self-directed training. We also started carrying two guns at all times, both accessible with either hand.

I see lots of handgunners who avoid training with their "weak hand" simply because they suck at it, and that makes it no fun. Hey, I'm a terrible left-handed shooter, and I see no signs of a big breakthrough. My best efforts have elevated me from JustBloodyAwful to "terrible." But my realistic goal is to be the best Terrible Left-Handed Shooter I can be. Why? Because someday, like my old partner, I may be tryin' to fly with a single wing and — "terrible but determined" just might be enough. When it comes to survival, "just barely" beats the heck outta "not quite good enough."

The Two Dudes: Silenced But Still Speaking

Lessons learned from "The Two Dudes" have become even clearer to me with the passage of time. They taught me weapon and caliber mean less than hitting first and hitting decisively; that is, sufficient to end the fight. In both cases, mine was the inferior weapon and caliber, but mine was also the only weapon "up" and ready to engage, when clearly, theirs should have been as well.

That personal penchant for having the weapon at the ready when my judgment said it ought to be, got me in trouble a couple of times as a cop.

In interrogations reminiscent of the Spanish Inquisition, I was fortunately able to successfully articulate the wisdom of being ready to shoot, rather than waiting to be shot to my inquisitors. I emerged with scorched tailfeathers, but my tail was fairly intact. As a soldier, cop or citizen you may be similarly scourged for having the temerity to be prepared when the curtain goes up. Despite the downsides, I'll still opt for winning. The winner is the one who lives to be questioned and criticized.

Overwhelmingly, the factor that made The Big Difference with The Two Dudes was "terminal hesitation." Both of them were armed soldiers, not just in a combat zone, but in the midst of an engagement. Lotsa shots had already been fired within their hearing. At the instant of revelation, they shoulda been on me like sharks on a wounded tuna. Instead, their responses were exactly as I've seen repeated many times since: They were visibly shocked at being suddenly confronted with precisely the kind of scenario they were presumably trained to deal with; stunned into momentary — and then permanent — shut-down of their systems.

I've discussed this phenomenon with a wide range of people, including a lion hunter and a fighter pilot who survived such "fighting-freeze" lapses, and they all said essentially the same thing: "I was armed, I was trained, and I was there for that purpose. I guess I just hadn't thought about it enough." Now go back and re-read Colonel Cooper's "front sight" comment, okay?

And that might give you something to think about until next time, huh?

BULLETS FROM BANANALAND

NOVEMBER/DECEMBER 2007

Re-read that piece and you'll note both sides screwed up before the first shot was fired. The Good Guys, lulled by a bright warm morning and pleasant company, were mentally in "training mode," not possible-threat mode. I'm convinced the Bad Guys had reconned the site, and didn't expect any interference until they approached the building complex where the small "organic security" detail hung out. As a result, neither side anticipated what they ran into where and when they stumbled into it. Upon confrontation there was a mental stutter-step or two. Fortunately, "Mutual Stupid" affected both sides for a couple of seconds.

Bullet #1: If you live with a gun, be ready to engage anytime, anywhere. If that training had occurred in the US, I know we would have been wandering out to the bushes for that potty-call with empty sidearms. The thought gives me chills.

Lots of poor choices were made about position and "cover." Some Bad Guys fled into vehicles, where they were trapped. The BG's really blew the whole concept of "cover," with deadly results: glass and thin sheet metal won't stop rounds. Good Guys who should have known better stood up to fire over chest-high flatbed trailers, leaving their lower bodies exposed. Both sides occasionally left feet, hands, knees and elbows stickin' out from cover, and a few paid dearly for that.

Bullets #2, 3, and 4: Ordinarily, distance is your friend, but the urge to put distance between yourself and muzzle blast can override your good sense. "Know cover," or it's no cover. Most walls ain't cover a'tall. If you have any doubt that what you're hunkering behind will stop slugs, it prob'ly won't. Be as aware as any human experiencing "Pucker Factor 9.7" can be of exposing stray parts of your body. One of my standing rules is, "If all you see is a piece of your target, shoot the piece! Shoot it to pieces. Then shoot the pieces to pieces." Your opponent might have the same policy. Don't show him your elbow — or even an earlobe. He might be good.

Crabs & Gazelles

The Bus Farm Fight occurred on crazy-quilted uneven ground — basically flat, but cut with abrupt minor changes in height from asphalt to earth to old, tilted sections of concrete. Stumbling while running, scanning for targets and shooting cost a few lives. Mixing movement and shooting can be disastrous unless that movement is very deliberate — or charmed.

Bullet #5: If you feel that shooting during movement is a viable option for you, first work hard on your "combat shuffle" and your "agile crab sideways scuttle," or, just hold onto your piece with your finger outta the triggerguard and take off like a cheetah-chased gazelle. I've found I can shuffle straight ahead and deliver semi-accurate fire without trippin' much, but that's it. Simulations can tell you what you're capable of, and I recommend you find out before you try any ballet moves or "sprint'-n'-spray" techniques under fire. Falling and shooting yourself or a comrade can ruin more than your day.

In the midst of a vicious gunfight, nobody expected a glass-rattling voice to command "stop shooting!" – so everybody did. When you're low on ammo and a sweaty, a smiling teenager in a Chicago Cubs baseball cap suddenly appears, dashing from bus to bulldozer passing out loaded magazines, you first wonder if you've gone completely nuts — and then you grab some.

Bullet #6: Weird things happen in gunfights. Expect an Albanian satellite to fall on your head, or a gopher the size of a grizzly to erupt from the ground at your feet. It will happen during a gunfight. Believe your eyes, shrug off bizarre twists, and stay focused on the threat.

Combat Cool & The Samurai Class

The most striking thing about the Bus Farm Fight was the "combat cool" exhibited by the Hard Hombres. I had seen veteran fighters engaged all over the world, and few had the uniform cool of this thrown-together group. Wounds were expected; death was casually considered. Should they be maimed or crippled, they would be respectfully cared for — even lauded — by extended families and their villages or towns. They knew and embraced how they would live and quite possibly die.

An absolute of their lives was that they would fight well and never yield — never. More than anything else, it was this cool and this refusal to yield that won the Bus Farm Fight.

If not born to it, they had become a Samurai class. I learned something about it, and that's a tale for another time. But let's close with this: the Hard Hombres' combat cool had less to do with how much actual fighting experience they had, and more with how much time they had been tumbling "fighting" around between their ears.

I'M NOT RUNNIN'
So Forget About It, Okay?

JANUARY/FEBRUARY 2008

If His Editorial Immenseness Roy-Boy prints one or more of the letters — I asked him semi-nicely not to, so I'm sure he will — you'll see why I'm upset. It's happening again: A buncha you guys want me to run for president. Here's the news flash: I ain't runnin', and you can't make me!

Let's nip this right in the bud. You might think I'm takin' this too seriously much too soon, but consider this: Even if only 19 people wanta draft me for the presidency right now, at the rate the major candidates are shootin' themselves in the feet, trippin' over their lips and stabbing each other in the back, I could be the Last Man Standing! If I don't kill this grass-roots movement quick, I could wind up in the White House. With all due respect for the office, bein' the Chief Executive comes with too many restrictions for me...

First, there are these insurmountable problems with the Secret Service protection detail. I've worked with those folks and admire them, but I have the clear impression that POTUS* ain't s'posed to PACK! — and that won't work for me. In fact, I'd be shoppin' for a third daily-carry Roscoe instead of givin' up two. And what if, as Little Lizzie would say, "the bad mens come" and the stuff hits the fan? The Pres is supposed to pucker up and hunker down, while highly-motivated dudes in dark glasses with dreams of "takin' a bullet for the boss" fling themselves over his body and jump in front of him. Not for me, folks.

Yeah, I could just see bein' pinned down in a gunfight with some altruistic agent in my line of fire, tryin' to pull a machine pistol outta his underwear with one hand and pushing my head down with the other. "Hey!" I'd ask, "How many times have you shot for your life?" Most likely, the answer would be, "Umm… None, sir." My response would have to be, "Well, I've done it plenty and I'm pretty good at it, so move over, willya?"

The "First Memsaab"?

Oh, man … I just had a flash sight-picture of a buncha death-wishful armed idiots attacking First Lady Helena (the "First Memsaab"?) with the kids in harm's way! The best and most survivable course of action for the members of her protection detail would be to run and hide behind one a' those armored limos and stay put until they heard her whistlin' merrily and policing up her brass. In the aftermath, I can see Secret Service agents with bumper stickers on their private rides reading "Our First Lady Can Whip Yours! (and your First Dude, too!)"

We wouldn't need the Secret Service for vetting visitors to the West Wing, either. Our dog, Sancho Panza, would gladly be on-duty 24/7 as he is now, standing by to sniff any stranger's pants. I guarantee his nose, whether applied in the area of the zipper or the seat, will yield more and better character references and "intentions analysis" than any skilled senior agent backed by unlimited intelligence files. The Service would be wise to wire the White House so that if Sancho growls, the whole place goes "Condition Red," and if he bites, you can bet that whomever's been bitten probably needs shootin' as well.

There would have to be some changes in transportation, too. Air Force One could be something a little zippier, like say, a tandem-seat F/A-18D. That way, I could not only leave the entourage and Press Corps behind, but leave 'em 'way behind in seconds. The current "Marine One" helo could be replaced with a gunship, and I wouldn't mind riding sittin' on the deck in the open hatch with my feet on the skids and a rifle on my knees. Been there, done that. Otherwise, this business of limousines and being driven everywhere would have to cease.

I don't like ridin' in the back of limo's, and the only time I want somebody else driving is when I'm in an LAV— the view from the gunner's position is superior. And, there ain't no such thing as a "stretch limo diesel dually truck." We'd need one to pull "Ground Force One," a 30-foot fifth-wheel incorporating a parking deck for two ATV's and a big barbecue grill. What the heck's the use of being president if you can't enjoy an all-American family trip now and then?

Presidential Perks

I guess there could be some perks to bein' president. I've seen that huge hallway in the upper deck, and it's got plenty of room to put in a seven, ten, and 15-yard combat range, at least. That could really help me unwind after a long, frustrating day of not bombing people who truly deserve bombing. For the first time in our history, nighttime passersby on Pennsylvania Avenue could see tactical lights and lasers flashin' and hear gunshots comin' from the West Wing, nod to each other and say, "All's well; the President's home and enjoying himself."

And there is that superb Jamaican Blue Mountain coffee they serve in the White House galley. All right; I'll think it over and get back to you. Meantime, think "campaign funds," okay?

GUNS & MEN:
Metal Vs. Mettle The Memsaab Speaks

MARCH/APRIL 2008

These boys think they're so sly, but I read them like books; kindergarten books; three words to a page, with big bright pictures in primary colors. I'm talking about our Uncle John and Uncle G (the latter, some of you old-time Handgunner readers will remember as Commander Gilmore). Every time that Connor-man is gone too long, especially if we're not that sure where he is or what he's doing, they gravitate to me like 10-year olds who smell cookies baking. They may be twice my age, but when they come tip-toeing around like bashful buffalo, they're just boys.

Oh, I know their game. They arrive simultaneously from different states and then pretend it's a coincidence, all frozen smiles and warm but stiff greetings, and they won't mention Connor at all for at least 24 hours. Then the vigil begins. I can't complain; I enjoy their company, and every hinge in the place gets oiled and a mountain of firewood split while they putter around pointedly not talking about Connor. I only get concerned if they wash and wax my truck. That means they know or suspect something I don't, and it could mean trouble. This time they put on two coats of Carnauba wax.

They think I'm worried about Connor — and I am; but in a way that's been refined over the years. I call it the "Truck Tire Analogy." Imagine a big truck tire, like the kind on 18-wheel semis. Now visualize one, untied and unsecured, bouncing off the rear trailer of a semi while it's rolling down the highway. It could be due to a pothole in the road, a collision, or even an IED. The speeding truck is life; at least, the way Connor lives it. Connor? Well, he's that big, resilient truck tire.

The truck might keep rolling unfazed, or it might be destroyed, but that big tire takes its own course. Oh, it might be destroyed too, for sure. But most likely it will hit the road rolling, and come to rest in a ditch or out in a field, maybe smacked up against a tree or just losing speed and falling over in a pile of litter; a little dirty and banged up, but fine and fit for duty. It could be hit, but whatever hits it is probably going to suffer more damage than that tire will. It may be chewed up, gouged and scarred, but if any single thing survives, it will be that truck tire. That's my man. Yep; I'm married to a loose truck tire.

The Touchstone .45

That first evening, after feeding the boys about half a grilled steer, I cleared the table, got out a counter mat and cleaning gear, and began taking down a certain .45 pistol; a hard-used veteran marked "UNITED STATES PROPERTY M1911 A1 US ARMY" on the right side of its worn-shiny frame. It was the first gun Connor ever gave me, and though it had already seen God-only-knows what kind of use, it meant almost as much to me as the little gold band that followed soon after. Oily rag in hand, I began a routine I've done countless times, and never really thought about why until Uncle John's dammed-up reservoir of nervous tension cracked wide open and he spilled:

"Dangle-blaggit, Helena!" he exploded (something like that, anyway) "You only pull out that old clunker when you're worried about him, and then you polish it like Aladdin's lamp, girl! What the hell's up with that?" He was embarrassed and subdued

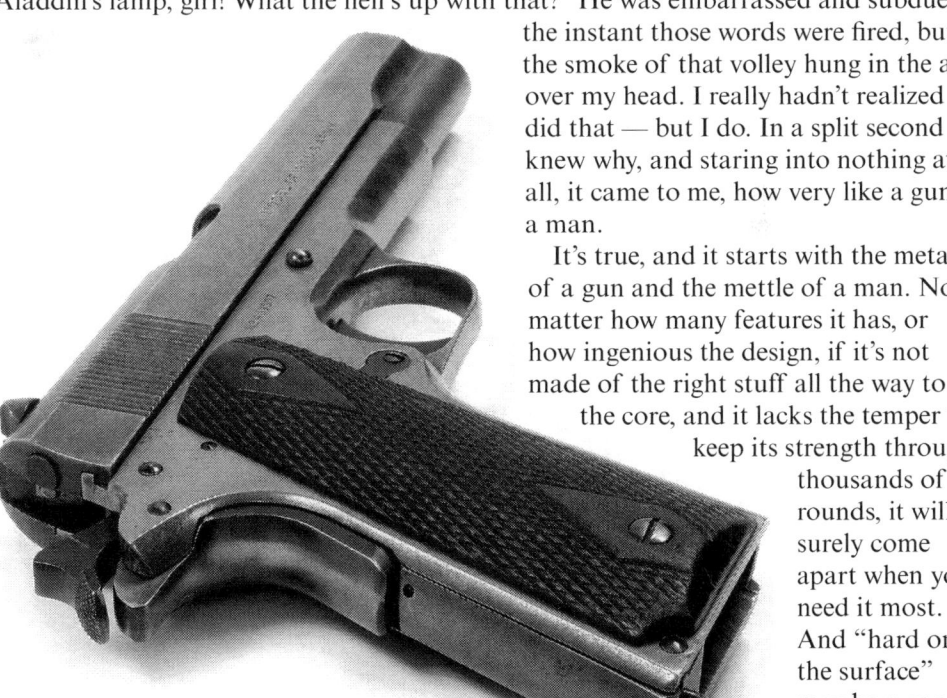

the instant those words were fired, but the smoke of that volley hung in the air over my head. I really hadn't realized I did that — but I do. In a split second I knew why, and staring into nothing at all, it came to me, how very like a gun is a man.

It's true, and it starts with the metal of a gun and the mettle of a man. No matter how many features it has, or how ingenious the design, if it's not made of the right stuff all the way to the core, and it lacks the temper to keep its strength through thousands of rounds, it will surely come apart when you need it most. And "hard on the surface" may be a good thing, but if it's hardened and unyielding all the way through, the more prone it is to crack and fracture all the way through. Better that a gun — and a man — should be just hard enough to shrug off the occasional ding and dent, but be tough where it counts, and have just enough flex to deal with heat and cold, but always retain its essential shape and character.

In college I dated a brilliant guy; a genuine genius in his field; a man with an astronomical IQ and a blazing-bright future. He charmed me with his intelligence and articulation, his refined manners and social graces. Besides that, he could dance and he knew how to dress! Oh, he was a custom-crafted "race gun"! Connor on the other hand, well, let's just cut to the chase and say he couldn't dance if you shot at his feet, and his idea of "dressy casual" is clean bush shorts and stomping the mud off his boots. He's definitely a "service issue" gun.

I dropped the race gun and picked up the service .45 for a simple reason: The genius was a moral coward. Picking his "positions" from whichever view or attitude was popular at the moment, and plucking his "ethics" from whatever stood to benefit him, he simply lacked the mettle.

Saucer-Sized Groups

A handgun capable of shooting the tightest one-hole group imaginable just "ain't worth shucks" as my gramma would say, if it's not consistent. I'll take this old "Touchstone .45," with its day-in year-out saucersized groups over an erratic dinger every time. A man and a gun have to be above all else trustworthy and reliable to their mate or master. What they could do is nothing if you can't count on them all the time in every situation. And a man with a wild hair, an uneven temperament, is kind of like a 1911 that, one out of a hundred times when you flick off the safety, the hammer drops — and you never know when it might happen.

We've all known pistols — and ladies, we've all known men — who were smooth, steady shooters as long as they were sparkling clean, lightly lubed, and you never fed them anything but their favorite fodder, right? That's like a man who handles the humdrum of daily life and muddling in the mainstream well, but he chokes and stovepipes when conditions get gritty and he has to fire for effect with what he's got — not what he wishes he had. One of my favorite "Connor-isms" is, "Don't tell me what's right or what's fair or what we wish it were; just tell me what IS and I'll handle it."

I want a man and a gun that can feed and fire any ammo at hand, no matter how grungy and hard to swallow, and do it in a swirling storm of mud, blood and BS.

Target sights are nice, and they can put you right into the X-ring. But if they tend to come loose and "wander," then ladies, I'll ask you again — you've known men like those roving sights, haven't you? Fancy sights don't mean beans if they won't stay aligned, whether they're in the gunsafe or getting knocked around, out of your sight on another continent. I trust my old blunt, squared off, fixed iron sights to stay on target, and if I couldn't, I wouldn't wear this ring.

Guns and men need regular service and maintenance too, and this is where many mates and masters get it wrong. You can't leave either one lacking lube or love for so long they run dry and gall, and then "fix them" by dunking them in the finest oil. And if you've misused or ignored that man or that gun you can't make it up to them by slapping a set of expensive grips on. Whether they're seeing hard service or just standing by, it's regular attention — handling, inspection, a little loving tightening and tuning — that keeps them running right.

By the time the boys broke through my lost-in-space reverie, I knew exactly why that pistol is and will always be my "Touchstone .45": That gun is Connor with walnut grips.

One Line Says It All

Often, friends and family will ask me — laughingly and joking, I presume — how I could possibly love a man like Connor. Maybe from now on I'll just pull out this old Touchstone .45, show it to them and see if they get it. But something else just occurred to me, and I'll share it with you. Connor is fond of using what he calls "CATscan slices" to illustrate a point. I'm thinking of one particular sentence, one phrase that I've heard him use on three occasions, and it's my CAT-scan slice of Connor.

The first time was at Camp Pendleton, and he was training a really mixed bag of officers and NCOs from several foreign countries at "Combat Town," running them through house-to-house and room-to-room drills. You wouldn't believe the difference in ages, shapes, skin colors and "grooming standards" in that bunch, not to mention many were dressed as "aggressors" or insurgents, and others were in the worst and dirtiest of the uniforms and field gear of their forces. I came by to bring him a big sandwich and a thermos of coffee, about two minutes before a small fleet of official cars pulled up.

It was some kind of visiting general — maybe an Inspector General — and taking just one look at that group, he was inflamed. One looked like Pancho Villa on a train-robbery raid, and — well, use your imagination. The general almost blew a gasket, and loudly demanded to know "Who on God's green earth is in command of this … this … debacle?"

The second time was at a highway diner outside of Amarillo, Texas. We were moving cross-country — again! — and stopped for breakfast. The kids were eight and 10 then, and they'd been cooped up in the car too long. They found the juke box, and started putting on their own "show." They were just being kids, and they were no louder than the music, but this irritated one of several cowboy-types at the counter. It takes a BIG man to cast a shadow over Connor, and this guy looked like somebody had wrapped denim around an arched double church door. Red in the face and working his fists, he got up and barked, "Who do these brats belong to?"

Third Time's A Charm

The third time Connor was kind of "along for the ride" while I was teaching a seminar. He says I "teach mice to roar" — it's more like bringing out the strength and assertiveness people have inside, and they just need counseling in how to let it out appropriately. Sometimes, when teaching this, you have to get "demonstrative," and "walk the walk." I was doing this, demonstrating firm assertiveness when the Big Cheese walked in; the man who owned every stick, stone, out-house and in-box of that company, and a renowned egomaniac.

I think he was PO'ed because I didn't stop the show and genuflect when he slid into the back of the room, where he happened to wind up bumping elbows with Connor. Loud enough for several people in the back rows to hear, he growled, "I see she's wearing a wedding ring. I wonder what poor bastard has to put up with that mouthy broad?"

On all three occasions, Connor did and said exactly the same thing. He strode up to that general, that cow-pie, that up-jumped power-puffin, closed to nose-to-nose range, cocked an eyebrow, and simply intoned, "I have that honor, sir." That Connor — he's my favorite pistol.

FUNNYBONE FRACTURES & CRACKED CONCENTRATION

MAY/JUNE 2008

I've warned you guys. Weird things happen in gunfights. You should expect an Elbonian satellite to fall on your head, or a gopher the size of a grizzly to erupt from the ground at your feet. I've encouraged you to believe your eyes, shrug off bizarre twists, and stay focused on the threat. Some of you shared your own stories of bizarre "moments 'midst mayhem," and a whole bunch of you asked for real-world examples. A few readers were even dubious about the possibility of such strange happenings happenin'. So, for you doubting Thomases, here are some examples from my private stock.

NUCLEAR .38 SPECIAL ROUNDS?

I was a rookie patrolman when my senior partner and I were called to back up a pair of robbery detectives. They planned to kick in a door at a felon-filled flophouse hotel, crunch some cockroaches and yank a sleepy stickup-shooting suspect outta his grimy sheets. His room was on the second floor of this converted century-old residence, and a rickety stairway led directly from his crib down to a garbage-littered lot. That's where Davey and I were posted — just in case Plan A went South when the "dicks" kicked the front door. It did.

We weren't quite "positioned" when multiple muffled gunshots preceded Hairball Harry's rapid exit out onto the landing. There was a flash of light as the door banged hard against the rail, and both Davey and I thought it was a muzzle flash and gunshot. Davey was standing in front of me with his trusty 6" S&W Model 10 aimed at Harry. He squeezed (or jerked) the trigger — and the stairway landing seemed to explode, with a hurricane of splinters and dust billowing out toward us as simultaneously, the entire stairway screeched, groaned, and collapsed to the deck.

I pushed past Davey when a second after that, a ground-floor back door flew open and two skivvie-clad bed-headed dudes with pistols in their mitts staggered outside, blinded by the clouds of dust, shouting stuff like "COPS! They're usin' grenades!" and searching for targets. Using some ungentlemanly language, I convinced 'em of the inferiority of their tactical situation. Good thing they didn't fight — my partner was still standing there, frozen, with his revolver a hand's-breadth from his nose, staring incredulously at the muzzle. He was lost in his own world, wondering how a lead 158 gr. SWC could blow up a stairway and two landings. Finally, I had to grab the gun and gently awaken him.

The gunshots were Hairball Harry's response to his door gettin' kicked. The dicks had sidestepped, and were occupied with straightening out a pair of pucker-factor-induced "wedgies." That flash was the bulb of an outside light's last gasp as its fuse blew out. The once-heavy wooden beams and planks of that stairway were virtually hollow shells filled with a century's worth of termites and wood-powder. It simply imploded under Harry's weight. He was unconscious, suffering multiple injuries, snoozin' in the wreckage.

The Big Diff between me an' Davey was that previous combat experience had taught me stuff blows up and weird things happen in gunfights, and you have to keep your head in the game.

ALLEYWAY ANTICS

A patrolman pal of mine had an armed dope dealer cornered in an inky-black blind alley. They were casually trading occasional shots, waitin' for backup to arrive, when suddenly a huge supernova light came on, a door swung open, and the alley was instantly filled with laughing, leaping, twirling cheerleaders, complete with pompoms, ponytails, big bells on their shoes and those cute little kick-skirts. Dudes! Wanna talk weird here? The entire pep-an'-cheer outfit from a local college had just finished a late photo-session on a theatre stage. The best part? As the cheerleaders danced an' advanced down the alley past my pal, the dope-dealer tried to sneak out with 'em!

"Unbelievable," my buddy told me; "Here's this dreadlocked dude wearing a Rastafarian cap and a filthy M-65 (field jacket), skipping along between cheerleaders, still holding a Beretta 92 in one hand. Skipping!" Rasta-man didn't get away, and nobody got hurt, but my pal said it was an ugly scene. "The shrieking and screaming hurt my ears worse than the gunshots did," he said. "Never jump out from behind a dumpster and point a pistol anywhere near a buncha cheerleaders."

DON'T SHOOT WHITEY: HE'S MINE!

"Tommy D," another badge-wearing brother, is well known for his morbid fear of dogs. They tend to bite him, fiercely and frequently. He had chased a biker bad guy into the back yard and the two were faced off pointing pistols at each other, when outta the shadows waddled an irritated overweight Welsh Corgi, who commenced chewing Tommy's ankle.

Distracted but undaunted, Tommy and Biker Bill continued discussing whom oughtta throw down whose howitzer when suddenly, a little white Pit Bull pup ran between Biker Bill's legs and skidded to a snarling stop in front of Tommy. That's when I arrived — just in time to slap leather and watch in horror as T.D.'s eyes saucered and his shaking gun dropped to point at the Pit Bull!

I was a half-second short of blasting Biker Bill when he flung his gun to the grass and screamed, "Don't shoot Whitey! He's mine!" I'll leave the detailed analysis to you guys. Just watch out for grizzly-gophers and Elbonian satellites, okay?

THE NEXT-TO-LAST
MAN STANDING

JULY/AUGUST 2008

I told you guys to knock it off, didn't I? Go back an' re-read the Jan-Feb 2008 issue — it's right there: I don't wanta be President! Seems like that was your cue to start crankin' out petitions, slappin' on bumper stickers, and jammin' "Connor for President" signs in front yards — including mine!

Respectfully decline to run, and what happens? I've got 312 campaign managers and 1,781 political advisors — all self-appointed and extremely opinionated. The only good things are, they're all Handgunner and GUNS readers, and they're currently serving without pay.

My own predictions are coming true. The more the candidates flap their yaps, the lower their ratings plunge. If present trends continue, they may achieve approval ratings below zero. Certain political analysts

Actual petition at the FMG booth at SHOT Show. Every time I took it down, somebody would replace it. We got tired and left it up. Exactly 2,769 people signed it. Go figger. Editor

are saying at that point the top three candidates will be undeclared, including me, an insurance broker in Kankakee whose mail comes back stamped "DECEASED," and a cab driver in D.C. — but he's not a US citizen, which could lead to constitutional issues with his candidacy — and he only speaks Umfombali. Or that's his name, I forget.

I'm just not a viable candidate for political office, guys. For one thing, I don't believe in leaving problems untreated simply because they have no neat, clean, painless and easy solutions. Do you know how third-degree burns are treated? I do. It's messy and it hurts, but it's better than dying from the inevitable infection. Here's an example:

Go Now, In Peace, Or ...

As President, my stance on immigration would be: Illegal aliens, go now, in peace. There's a subtle message in that phrase, and the comma is important. If you apply for Exfiltration Assistance we may grant and pay it — once. Legal aliens will have firm departure dates, and the "Permanent Resident Alien" status is hereby revoked. You're either a citizen, bustin' your hump to become one, or learning to say "Bye-bye" in English. We have immigration laws; we just haven't used 'em.

The illegal alien problem is "insoluble?" I think not. There are at least a million Americans who would, if empowered to do so, personally remove ten illegal aliens each from within our borders — free. Ten million fewer illegals would be a good start.

The United Nations would be given an eviction notice. My message to them would be: We Americans are far too crude and primitive for you. Judging from your voting record, you don't like us anyway. I would suggest moving UN HQ to Baghdad. Surely your suave sophistication, your fine words, impassioned speeches and diplomatic skills will bring immediate peace to that troubled region. Be careful where you park, dudes.

On Foreign Aid: The gravy train just derailed at 1600 Pennsylvania Avenue. Rule Number One is, Nobody Gets Money! Prove your need for food and medicines due to a calamitous event — not a continuing natural condition or self-created crisis — and we'll send food and medicines, and monitors to see who actually eats the beans and gets the meds. Don't screw with us on this. Your country gets one chance per century.

You owe us on foreign aid loans? Make your payments or we're turning your account over to the Mafia. We'll write off the loss, and their cut will be all they can get. Don't laugh, Mister silk skivvies Prime Minister; the Mob doesn't send carefully-worded letters — they send Vinnie and Paulie with aluminum baseball bats. They know where you live. You'll pay something — count on it. They'll make you an offer you can't refuse.

Career Criminals

Prisons & Felons: All your color TVs, foos-ball games, computers and air conditioners are going to veterans' hospitals. They earned 'em; you can too. Your weights and workout machines are going to police stations nationwide. Yoga classes will be available and literacy classes mandatory. If you want a tattoo showing you're a bad-ass prison inmate, we'll give you one — my own design. If you get an unauthorized tattoo in prison, it will be removed immediately, the hard way.

Prisons won't be comfortable, but they will be safe, for guards, staff and inmates. This will be achieved by medieval means if necessary. Use your imagination; I can. "Three strikes and you're out" laws will be repealed — predatory criminal behavior ain't a ball game. Two strikes, max. "You're out" will take on new meaning. "Recidivism" will become an archaic term. Don't worry about the electric chair. Worry about electric bleachers.

Gangs: Wanta join one? We've got five. We provide "colors," weapons and discipline. We even have cool thrown "hand signs" — they're called salutes. Think you're tough? Hang with the homies of "The Few, The Proud" for a while, then we'll talk.

There's more, but you see why I shouldn't bother running? There is this one presidential announcement I would love to make, though. It is: "Good morning, my fellow Americans! You are all now duly-appointed members of the United States Militia. Under the clear provisions of the Second Amendment, you are invited to enjoy the UN-infringed RIGHT to keep and bear arms."

Hmmm ... Check the polls and get back to me, okay? I might be available after all.

A DIFFERENT TWIST ON TRAINING

SEPTEMBER/OCTOBER 2008

The first of two related themes in dozens of your e-mails goes like, "Wow, do I envy you the training you've had!" Dudes, if you only knew how much I envy the training many of you have received.

See, like many others, I feel like I got shanghaied into being a trainer long before I was sufficiently trained myself, and then my duties became so esoteric and specialized so fast I've never had time to "back up and catch up."

You could divide my working life into roughly four interwoven pieces: Military and law enforcement, with those two split into foreign and domestic. Ninety percent of the training I've done has been either "pre-school rudimentary" for "indigenous personnel," or high-speed low-drag shock & awe stuff. For a while I was even an "appointed expert" on Soviet urban combat tactics. I taught those to both U.S. and foreign troops, adapting some for training American metro SWAT units.

The experience has left me qualified to teach ex-and-future goat herders the basics of sight picture and trigger squeeze, and team tactics on clearing stairways, stairwells and blindwells with smoke, gas, automatic weapons and novelty pyrotechnics.

Folks, this ain't the kind of training you — or I — need for confronting a prowler in your kitchen or surviving an ATM stickup. If you go everywhere with three or five heavily-armed commando pals, I'm your man. If you want to serve bench warrants on felony fugitive gangbangers, I can help. Otherwise, well, read on.

Your second recurring theme tells of your lack of bucks and time to get away from home and business to attend appropriate training at a reputable facility. Many of you, up to your ears in kids, second jobs and coaching Little League can't even get out to the range to pop some caps as much as you'd like. What to do, you ask? First, let me tell you, munchkin-wrangling, paycheck-earning and being a Solid Gold Spouse is the greatest, most honorable calling given by God or man, and then, be glad we're living in the Golden Age of "remote training!"

Books & Movies

Clint Smith and I don't travel in the same circles, but I've come to know and respect his training through both his articles and DVDs. My first "animated" exposure was when I picked up Streamlight's two Thunder Ranch Illumination Systems — the TL-2 based handgun system and TL-3 based Urban Rifle setup. Both come with excellent DVDs on use of tactical lights, and now, his six double-DVD training sets from — guess who? — FMG Magazines, are even better. Find 'em here in this issue or go to www.americanhandgunner.com.

I'll first recommend his Defensive Handgun and Defensive Revolver sets. Then, only after you've soaked and steeped in those, go on to Defensive Tactics. Don't skip; it's important, like learning how to walk before mastering the tango. If all you got out of these DVD's was his "Mental Preparation and Logic" and "Loading, Unloading and Malfunction Clearance," you'd be far better prepared for Socially Serious Situations — but you'll get a lot more, believe me. Don't look for flashy and fancy "experimental" crap here; look for logic — and reasoned, rational, even legally defensible techniques and tactics. I like Clint's style as much as I approve of his substance. In some ways his "one-on- one" manner of on-camera presentation can be better than a course at Thunder Ranch with the distraction of other students and their fragile or frictional egos — or, it will better prepare you for a visit to "Clint's House."

The Other Kinda Cornbread

If Clint Smith is the armed Socrates, the gunners of Gunsite must be the Spartans and Hoplites. Building on the foundation of their iconic founder, Colonel Jeff Cooper, many of the world's most talented and devoted practitioners of pistolcraft have contributed to Gunsite's encyclopedic store of knowledge, mostly centered on what might be termed "The fighting use of the heavy-duty handgun." Go to www.gunsite.com, click on "Training DVD's," and try not to get sidetracked by appealing titles like Defensive Walking Stick and Edged Weapons I, okay? Save those for later.

Tactical Pistol I is a solid starter, accompanied by Tactical Concealed Carry I. My Dad would have loved these guys, because like him, they obviously believe the three most important elements of training are fundamentals, fundamentals, and FUNDAMENTALS! Tactical Pistol I starts so rock-bottom basic you may be tempted to fast-forward. Don't. The more you are reminded of essentials like stance, balance and grip, the better. Then the pace quickens through braced positions, barricades and corners, low light and more.

The differences between the training DVDs from Thunder Ranch and Gunsite are like the difference between sweet yellow and salty white cornbread: texture and the nuances of flavor. You'll note some variation in drawing presentation and a few other details, and absolute consistency in emphasis on safety, accuracy and speed built on

smoothness. I'm comfortable with either, and happier with both.

Note: No book or DVD is a comparable substitute for personal training. But while an entrenching tool ain't a substitute for a pistol, either, it sure beats an empty hand. Wait a minute! Books?

A VETERAN'S STORY

NOVEMBER/DECEMBER 2008

It is the morning of June 6th as I write this — a fitting day to remember an American veteran. He was not a veteran of the landings at Normandy, which occurred on this date 64 years ago, in 1944. Jack Lucas fought in the Pacific, on a tiny volcanic island called Iwo Jima. There he became the youngest Marine ever to win the Medal of Honor. I wrote his story in the July issue of our sister publication, GUNS Magazine.* It hit the newsstands and mailboxes just days before Jack passed away, yesterday at 0020 hours.

The BigBoss Editor, Roy, and I talked about it, and he suggested I write something about Veteran's Day for this issue. I had a story in mind; one never written about before, at the family's request. They said he never sought recognition and wouldn't want it. But they agreed to my telling it without naming him.

The Woodsman's War

News of the Great War in Europe had hardly reached the backwoods hills of western Kentucky. Folks thereabouts tended their own business and paid little attention to the doin's of flatlanders and foreigners. But one day at a trading post an illiterate young hardscrabble farmer and woodsman asked the clerk to read him a page from the newspaper. The headline read "Your Country Calls You," and he said it "struck him like a stone."

His country was calling him? He dearly loved his country — the part and people he knew, anyway — and his country had "never before asked for a red cent nor a drop of sweat." But now she called. That's what he told his family, and announced he was "Goin' for to be a soldier and fight the Hun."

He walked and hitched over 100 miles to enlist in Black Jack Pershing's Army. They made him a machinegunner and sent him to France. There, his unit replaced the decimated wraiths of a battered French regiment in the freezing, shell-blasted mud of the trenches. And there, on one side of the cratered moonscape of No-Man's Land, he and his fellow "doughboys" lived and died and were sometimes buried alive in their collapsing bunkers.

The woodsman's war consisted of keeping his machinegun running amid the muck, sometimes gunning down ghostly gray lines of patrolling Germans caught in flare-light, and once shooting down an enemy observation blimp which had broken its tethers and drifted west. Otherwise, he learned to burrow like a rat when the shells fell — and they did, constantly.

Unable to read or write, he occasionally got another Yank to pencil a brief letter for him. His family said he never complained other than to say "It's hard here; hardest for the city boys and younguns." Then the letters stopped.

The Last Fight

Envision a broad valley — No- Man's Land — between rows of hills, with German trenches on the northeast and American trenches opposite. A reconstituted French force approached from the southwest, coming to relieve the Yanks — and the Germans knew it. They unleashed a hellstorm of artillery rounds on the Americans, blasting them with high explosives and the dreaded mustard gas. Then gas-masked infantry assaulted the Yank trenches, bayoneting survivors and then moving on, sweeping up the northeast-facing slope behind the Americans. Silence settled.

Unknown to the approaching French, the Germans held that high ground, in perfect position to cut them down like wheat as they marched up the treeless southwest slopes. But they had missed a few Yanks — one of them, the woodsman.

Almost blind, blasted full of shrapnel, badly burned both by fire and mustard gas, he crawled to his machinegun. It had been blown into the air and come down on the southwest side, facing the wrong direction — except now, it was the right direction. He opened up on the Germans' backs. Without cover, they scattered — or fell. Alerted by the angry stutter of a Yank machinegun and Germans fleeing over the crest, the French deployed and attacked.

For uncounted months the woodsman lay unidentified in a French hospital, unable to speak more than "croaking like a crow." The Armistice came and went. The French gave him a Croix de Guerre, and finally, America gave him a voyage home.

The Woodsman Returns

Eighteen months after the homecoming parades, the woodsman limped into his family's yard and up the porch, where he dropped into a rocking chair. Pelted with questions, he waved them away.

"That Kaiser Bill," he croaked, "He was a rough 'un" — and he never spoke of the war again. Over decades, family members were able to fill in some details. He lived, raising corn, beans and two sons, who went back to fight the Hun again. The woodsman had his Croix de Guerre made into a watchfob. He died just after V-E Day, 1945, and his dying words were:

"Don't get beat, ever, by anything; anyone. You might get killed, but never get beat. Don't never, ever give up. If your country calls, you answer her! And never ask for nothing but God's light to see by."

On Veteran's Day, November 11th, if you haven't got anyone else to honor, remember the woodsman. I will.

SIGNS OF A GOOD LIFE

January/February 2009

I f your pain is bad enough and the painkillers strong enough, struggling up to consciousness is like swimming desperately for the surface in a sea of thick gravy. It also has a definite effect on your thinking if you're awakened by a telephone. My first thought was, If I hear a phone ringing, it must be ringing in a movie, because I don't spend much time around ringing telephones. But I became aware I was in my own bedroom, and there were no TVs there to be playing movies. Then, again, it must be in a movie, but somehow I'm in that movie, and it's happening to me. Drugs make a lot of people stupid. Me, they make weird and stupid. Groggily, I realized there was no movie, but there was a telephone, and it was ringing right next to me on my bed. I answered, "'Lo?"

"Connor!" I recognized the voice; an old friend. "Man, I heard you were dead or missing! Either way, I wanted to hear it straight from you!" There was a pregnant pause. I allowed it to go to the third trimester, and he finally gave it birth. "Uh," he said, "That was pretty dumb, huh?" Gently, I agreed it was. This is a guy I once told "The word gullible is just slang. It's not even in the dictionary." He found my Webster's and looked it up. Then he came back with a half-grin, half-scowl on his mug, muttering "Hey, I get it, Ya got me, huh?" He is, in fact, a scientist; just not a "rocket scientist," if you get my drift.

BIG HURTZ: I Don't Mess Around

As some of you know — and I don't know how you knew — I recently Zigged when I shoulda Zagged and almost got Tagged & Bagged. Bad, like lots of pain and virtual immobility. The deal is: extended recovery, semi-good prognosis, and I'm home with the world's prettiest redheaded nurse. The worst part is, I'm not a very patient patient, and I hate the whole "recovering" process. I've done too much of it and it sucks.

Not being able to get up, down, outta bed or up the stairs on my own steam is not only frustrating, but depressing. Yeah; I was sinkin' into the dumps, gettin' beat by

the blues. Funny; a while back someone was checkin' me for signs of life, and here I was checking myself for signs of a good life. Then I started opening piled-up letters, some two years delayed, and reading backed-up e-mail.

Got one from a young soldier I once taught a useful knot to. Called a "blind rescue bowline," it's handy for quickly getting yourself and casualties hauled outta trouble. He used it one night under "extreme circumstances" in a

Baghdad slum-burb. He thanked me, said other guys in his unit asked him to teach it to them, and yeah, that ignited a little spark.

One letter came from a young man I had "counseled" at length some years ago. Indulged and abandoned, over-schooled and under-educated, he was a whining, miserable wreck. Just before I moved to another state, I gave him a farewell gift, a wallet-size card. On one side it said, "Read other side aloud 3X daily." On the other I wrote, "Shut The #### Up. Get Over It. Move On." His envelope included a photocopy of the well-worn card — which he still carries — and a snapshot of him, his pretty wife and their little boy. Good job, faithful spouse, good life. At that moment, my life felt a little better too

And The Hits Keep On Rollin'

Three e-mails from Handgunner readers — guys I've never met personally — who offered to be at my door in 48 hours, stand guard duty, fetch and carry, run errands and help me walk, all on their own dimes. Wow. Thanks, Captain Bob, Standing Bear, Ol' Frank — how did you know?

There was a package. It contained a neatly folded U.S. flag, a letter and certificate. Those colors had been flown in my honor over a certain camp in Al Anbar Province. If there is a better painkiller than the regard of fellow warriors, I ain't found it.

Sometimes one small package is worth a pound of painkillers. This one was.

Another call — this one VERY long distance, from an old combat-mentor whose brief bio might read: 40 Years, Four Continents, Fighting Under Four Flags. He hates telephones. We did NOT have a "conversation." He doesn't have conversations — he snarls orders. His call went "I hate tellphonz. You listen. I hear you are fool. Learn from the dog Sancho (my dog, Sancho Panza). Life is hard and fast. You sleep, rest, heal when you may. Do not be fool. I finish now. Fini." (click)

For him, this was an unprecedented emotional outpouring. I suspect a redheaded snitch who has a certain way with warriors.

Finally, when your cool, collected "nurse" suddenly stops massaging and angrily declares, "When you're better I'm gonna beat the crap outta you, Connor! You scared the hell outta me! What would I do without you?" — and the hot tears fall, what does this say about your life? Thank you, God. Thank you, Helena my love. Thank you, friends met and unmet. It's a good life.

NO SODA, NO ICE.
Just Plain, Straight-Up Talk

MARCH/APRIL 2009

One of the benefits of bein' busted up an' crippled is I get to catch up on e-mail from you guys! Usually, given the kinda stuff you write to me about, I can keep answers pretty brief, like, "Dude! Great idea, but don't shoot it in your own gun — borrow someone else's!" or, "Simple. Just have everybody in the club surround him and say, Next time you muzzle-sweep ANY of us, ALL of us are gonna thump you like a tub of butter." Easy. But lots of you have asked for a little straight talk about a big current issue. Okay, you got it. Straight up; no soda, no ice.

Don't Clap Too Loud

Q: What do you think of the Heller decision? We won! That's great, isn't it? Umm … Isn't it?

Lots of folks are high-fivin', back-slapping and celebrating the Supreme Court's 5-4 decision in D.C. v. Heller. People who ought to know better are claiming this decision has, virtually without restriction, affirmed our individual right to keep and bear arms. That bothers me, because it says those folks are lowering their guards and overlooking the purely temporary, snowflake-weight impact of the court's action. To them, I say, "don't clap too loud nor too long, because you might need a free hand to hold onto your gun."

It's just my opinion, but what Heller told me is that four of the nine most powerful jurists in the land knowingly and deliberately ignored the abundant historical record of our founders' meaning and intent when they wrote the Second Amendment. The dissenting justices engaged in social engineering while crouching behind the protection of the bench. The mere fact they did so encourages other judges at the district and appellate levels, and politicians as well, to embrace such contempt for the Constitution and give such acts validity, as though, "Well, we're just arguing the issue from different viewpoints." Yeah right. Insistence that the Second Amendment is somehow overwhelmingly complex and beyond the understanding of mere laymen is a smokescreen and a sham.

Our "Friends" Ain't So Hot

As for those five justices joining in the majority opinion, it seemed to me the lackluster zeal of a few for protecting our rights was less than inspiring. In some ways it seemed the majority's conclusions were grudging and reluctant. And consider these points:

First, there were two dissenting opinions, longer and more wordy than the majority opinion. That's not a surprise; snow jobs typically require a lot of shoveling. The worst part is, they laid considerable groundwork for overturning Heller in a not-too-distant future. Second, the outcome affirmed "reasonable restrictions" — to be crafted and imposed by unreasonable people — and left the door wide open for D.C. and other jurisdictions to use bureaucratic blocks and administrative barriers to render the decision virtually meaningless. They're already doing it.

I ain't clappin'. After one or maybe two octogenarian justices fail the "wake-up test," who will appoint whom to the Supreme Court? Are you ready for a "Justice Charles Schumer," or a "Chief Justice H. Rodham Clinton"? Both? Then watch how fast an anti-Second Amendment "challenge case" rockets through the system.

Fighting On Another Front

Dr. Lawrence Tribe is a professor of constitutional law at Harvard. For many years he has been recognized as a top authority in the field. For almost as long, he had held the Second Amendment addressed a "collective" right, not an individual right, therefore arms could be restricted to government possession and use. Surprisingly, last year he announced he had come to a new conclusion: The Second Amendment is an individual right — just as lots of us grunts and peasants had always asserted.

Given his startling conclusion, however, he opened the door to another avenue to disarmament of us riff-raff: Simply repeal the Second, as we once did the 18th. The Brady Bunch and other gun-grabbers immediately seized on the idea, then apparently agreed to keep it quiet until after the November elections. Repeal The Second? I predict you'll be seeing more of this.

Over The Horizon – Barely

Q: So, do you think another "Assault Weapons Ban" is coming?

A: It's mid-October as I write this, and the coming November election will probably give you not just a clue, but a clear statement wrapped around a brick and hurled through your window. According to the LameStream Media, which is dancing with glee, we are likely to have a White House and a Congress solidly opposed to having armed peasants hangin' around. They make tyrants nervous. Go figure. (Connor was right, of course — Editor)

As for a broad, ridiculously inclusive gun-ban, I'll say this: If you prepare for it and it doesn't happen, you'll be far better off for having prepared. If it does come to pass, you'll be 'way better prepared, and you'll have earned a secretive, smug smile.

Elsewhere in this issue, you'll find my little blurb about handgun ammo. Yeah, it's expensive. But the expense goes beyond mere money when ammo becomes expensive and unavailable, or worse, prohibited. Besides, in good times, ammunition is a terrific commodity investment. In bad times, it's better currency than gold.

As for guns, I'd advise if there is a semiauto defensive firearm you've always wanted but haven't acquired, do it now. Further, analyze what kind of guns you may need, versus those you simply want, write up your acquisition plan, and beat the ban!

Hey, that should keep you busy for the next couple of months, huh?

GO AHEAD — AMAZE YOURSELF
And The Best Thing To Be Amazed With Is — YOU

MAY/JUNE 2009

Lots of you guys wrote and asked about the blind rescue bowline knot I mentioned in the Jan/Feb 2009 issue. Yeah, it's a great knot; one that can save lives, with many other uses too. The ability to quickly throw a secure knot which won't jam, slip or bind can not only make your life easier and impress the heck out of your pals, but you'll amaze yourself with what a smooth line-handlin' rascal you are.

I don't know how many lengths of rope I've cut and then given to "knot-challenged" friends with BRB instructions and a little book on knot-tying. Later, I love it when they say they're amazed at how useful that skill is. But the BRB is just one element in my sinister "Amaze Yourself" program.

Whenever I identify gaps in a friend's skill-sets, I like to give 'em a little gift and comments like, "next time I see you I'm gonna shake you down to make sure you're carryin' this, and test you on its use, okay? If you don't have it, you get an Atomic Wedgie. If you have it but fail my little test, you get a Three Stooges knuckle-noogie on yer gourd." Some folks find this practice strange, but more are pleased and even amazed with the results.

Since I can't give these gifts and instructions to all of you, how 'bout if you give 'em to each other — and yourselves? Go ahead … amaze yourself.

What, Where, How and Wow!

A Teensy Light In The Dark. We all love cool tactical lights, right? But aside from light-freaks like me, how many people carry one 24/7? A pal of mine got a hard jolt and scorched-black burns on his fingers when he stuck his hand into an outlet box he didn't first illuminate. If you start carrying a mini-light and use it every single time illumination is needed, you'll be amazed at how helpful it is. I probably use a mini-light a half-dozen times a day. Check here or on Web Blast at www. americanhandgunner.com for some recommendations.

This ToolLogic mini-light pulls apart and the magnetic swiveling base sticks to any ferrous surface – a really handy feature.

Little-Bitty Duty Cutters. More true confessions: I usually carry four knives on my person at all times, but my LBDC is used more than the others combined. My current favorite weighs 2.5 ounces, has a blade under 2" long, and it's used and abused daily. Get one, use it, and amaze yourself. Note: nobody needs to know what other blade or blades you're packin', pal.

Wow! You could cut through, umm — soft butter with that! Having played with knives around the world, I gotta conclude that Earth is hip-deep in dull, nicked an' dinged blades. The weird thing is, as sharpening technology has improved and great sharpening tools become less expensive, there seem to be fewer and fewer people who know how to keep their blades bright and keen.

Matching Boker SubCom F folders.

First get a good little pocket sharpener like the Lansky Quick Fix, or DMT's DiaFold Sharpener; the FWFC fine and coarse model. Even if you claim you're "edge-challenged," just follow the instructions and you might just be ... amazed. When every blade in your purview is scary-sharp, move up to a real sharpening system and join the "one percenters" who can dress an edge right.

Uh, where am I? Whether you live and work in a metro concrete jungle, the High Lonely or the pool-table plains, you should know your cardinal points all the time. I'm one of those lucky people sorta born with an on-board compass, but even I get turned around, so I always keep a little compass

DMT's DiaFold features coarse and fine diamond sharpening surfaces. Lansky's Quick Fix has V-notches on each side for coarse and fine sharpening.

at hand. Get one, and take readings at every point you routinely travel. I think you'll be surprised at least once, and later, amazed at how "centered" you feel when you've developed your own on-board internal compass.

Bushnell's new BackTrack can tell you where you are, how far you've gone, and how to get back; what we call "a good thing."

Seeing Farther

Enhancing the Mark-II Eyeball. As a police trainer, I used to loan cops a monocular or a set of mini-binocs, and coerce them into using that gear for at least a week, on and off-duty. Every last one reported amazement at how much more activity they saw, and how their overall comprehension of given areas improved. Most people tend to only see what's happening out to about 60'. That's bad — and dangerous. Go ahead; become an amazed peeper.

How far is THAT? Whether it's a peak on the horizon or the phone pole down the block, sad to say, most folks' ability to gauge distances sucks buttermilk. Others just need re-honing of old skills. You might start with a set of pace-counter beads (from many sources including www.brigadeqm.com) and literally pace off some distances around your home and work. You may initially be surprised at how wrong you are — and later, amazed at how accurate your gourd-mounted organic onboard rangefinder has become.

Train More, Bleed Less. Finally, get a target setup, one easily put up and taken down, in your garage or hallway, and resolve to practice handgun "presentation," sighting, reloading and malfunction clearing at least once a week for twenty minutes. Most shooters don't, and even such short sessions will result in some degree of self-amazement, I promise.

If Blade-Tech offers their Training Barrel for your pistol, pop the $13.95 and train safe! Check details at www. blade-tech.com. Revolver shooters can use inert training rounds — try www.stactionpro.com. If you can, put a laser on your roscoe and have an amigo see where that laser-berry wanders or jitters off to when you're slappin' the trigger.

DARK MOON RISING

JULY/AUGUST 2009

I've never paid much attention to astrology; all that business about Venus kissin' Mars an' Jupiter making you walk in front of a bus. But if I were into astrology, I'd tell you this: It seems to me certain pale planets are linin' up like a bad break on a snooker table, and I see a dark moon rising. Check these planets:

Never before in history has the election, succession or appointment of a chief executive triggered as big a nationwide record-smashing run on sales of firearms and ammunition. Notably, the greatest demand has been for defensive — fighting — firearms and ordnance. Clearly, millions of people expect their new government to severely tax, restrict or prohibit such arms and ammunition. Many — again, with good reason — fully expect their government to ultimately, unlawfully and forcefully confiscate those weapons. Yeah, kinda like the British attempted to do at a place called Concord.

The government's declaration — such actions must be taken "for the safety of the people; a crime-reducing measure" — is such a blatant lie only a government could utter it without prompting laughter. Consider this: there has never been a serious, concerted national effort to disarm convicted felons! But they are not a threat to entrenched powers. Armed free peasants are. Rifle-bearing riff-raff are. We are not a "crime problem" — unless we become criminalized by government fiat.

Where are the credible records to indicate, in any way, the past "Assault Weapons Ban" reduced crime? Having failed that challenge, the White House and Congress are now saying weapons sold in America are threatening the government of Mexico! To even suggest this is so stupid I fully expect millions to believe and embrace it … after a media massage. Brainwashing is so much easier when your "clients" only need a light rinse.

The Great Divide

Some share my opinion that Americans today are profoundly polarized, deeply divided politically and philosophically — and perhaps irrevocably. That thought alone should bring chills: irrevocably? In my view, that division essentially exists between self-reliant citizens who cherish freedom above all else; who grudgingly consent to be governed; who believe they are the most effective defenders of their own lives, their loved ones and properties — and those who would freely surrender certain rights in exchange for promises of security from those who cannot provide it, unearned shares from the redistribution of other peoples' assets, and relief from any burden of decision-making, ceding to a presumably wise and kindly government.

Last year, the highest court in the land hesitantly agreed to examine a case requiring interpretation of the Second Amendment. This produced a superficially split ruling which, while salving some proponents of individual rights, allows "interpretation" and bureaucratic blockade to the exercise of that right. It has worked.

Following the Supreme Court's Heller decision, Adam Winkler, a professor at the UCLA School of Law, tracked gun-control law cases being heard in the lower federal courts. As of January 2, 2009, 60 of those cases closed. In all 60 — every last one — those gun-control laws were upheld as though Heller had never happened. "Reasonable restrictions," you know ... by unreasonable people.

Over decades our federal judiciary has become divided between prisoners of precedent, handcuffed by "case law," or radicalized and activist, selected for their social agendas rather than constitutional scholarship. So, if not the federal courts, who will defend and honor the Constitution?

Our Senate? The House? That's laughable, isn't it? One might hope that having just orchestrated the greatest raid on any national treasury in history, seizing fortunes yet unearned by grandchildren unborn, they might fall into a pork-induced food coma, but no; no luck there. Are our founding fathers' greatest fears — of an all-powerful, malignant federal government — being played out?

The Other Side

Interestingly, several states are now considering resolutions to warn Congress they have exceeded their constitutional authority as defined in the Tenth Amendment, to wit: The powers not delegated to the United States by the Constitution, nor prohibited by it to the States, are reserved to the States respectively, or to the people. Congressional excesses — wielding power like a mead-soaked berserker with a broadsword — are nothing new. Congress has shown no reluctance to routinely overstep their authority simply because — who would stop them?

No; this newfound interest in limiting federal power is apparently a wary — if not outright shaken and scared — reaction to the reigning government's plans. Among them, to make the entire country as "safe" as, get this — Chicago?

Even more interesting, some scholarly folks have noted the federal government's authority to enact national firearms laws is enabled by the interstate commerce clause, presuming all firearms and ammo travel in interstate commerce. Well ... not if they are manufactured entirely within a state, and remain within that state. The feds would then have no legal authority to regulate those arms. Hmm ...

Oh, there's a whole 'nother rack of these snooker balls to consider; galaxies of planets lining up, and that foreboding dark moon rising. The question is, where do we stand? I'll get back to you on that. Connor OUT.

KNOWING WHO WE ARE

SEPTEMBER/OCTOBER 2009

I was going to open this with something like, "Now keep an eye out for these tell-tale clues" — but they've already happened, long before you'll read this, and they're "clues" like a blinding, eye-searing flash and a mushroom cloud are a "tip-off" of a thermonuclear detonation. The message from our new administration seems to be that you, me, and people like us are somehow a greater threat to our fellow Americans than a Jihadist with a C-4 cummerbund or Osama bin Laden with his own fleet of nuke-bearing B-52s.

You had to know it was coming. All that campaign hype about "respecting the Second Amendment" was a clearly-marked load of desert sailboat fuel.* The gloves are off, folks, and the new administration is not just demonizing guns, but painting all those who possess them — in fact, all those who might object to or oppose any

Yes, we still exist — and he would be proud.

action by the federal government — with the broad brush of "right-wing extremism" and "domestic terrorism." Imagine pushing a spilled gallon of paint over a postcard with a shop broom. Yeah; that kinda "broad brush."

Just do a 'net search on subjects like "Right Wing Extremism April 7, 2009" and "Missouri The Modern Militia Movement." I recommend reading columnist Michelle Malkin's comments on the former. She calls it an "Obama DHS Hit Job on Conservatives," and that's what it is. Essentially, if you breathe, think, honor the Constitution and own a firearm, you're a suspected or indictable right-wing extremist and an enemy of the state.

The single most repeated word — always in a negative, threatening sense — is "militia." Sure; some truly radical fringy types calling themselves "militiamen" have given it a bad name, but about in the same numbers and percentages as people who rent moving vans have used them to transport illegal explosives. This much is clear: "Militia" is to become the Obama administration buzz-word for anyone owning a gun who is not an Obamaton — and if you own a gun, you can't be one anyway.

It seems that me and everyone I call friend is a threat — and a militiaman. How could it be that an institution so intrinsically American; so valued by our founding fathers they gave it its own amendment in the Bill of Rights; so necessary to the security of a free state, could be a threat?

What IS This "Militia" ?

Increasingly over the past century, latent fuhrers, incipient dictators, paranoid politicians and moral cowards have claimed that first, the Second Amendment applies only to governmentally-operated parties, and second, it's far too complex for mere "lay minds" — dummies like us — to understand. They magnanimously invite us to leave interpretation of it to them, the very people it was written to protect us against. The first is an outright lie, and the second, a cynical and disingenuous lie. Much confusion lies in the Second Amendment's first words: A well regulated militia …

> **Essentially, if you breathe, think, honor the Constitution and own a firearm, you're a suspected or indictable right-wing extremist and an enemy of the state.**

In the language of the time, "regulated" in reference to the citizens' militia, did not mean governed, operated, overseen, armed by or even responsible to government. "Regulated" referred to individual proficiency with individually-owned arms; "well regulated" citizen-militiamen were both knowledgeable and proficient with their personal arms.

The founding fathers and the general populace perceived three kinds of armed forces: a standing army of careerist or long term soldiers employed by and responsible to their commander-in-chief; a "select fyrd" or "select militia" called up by levy or draft by local government to serve during a particular emergency or campaign, again, responsible during that time to their commander-in-chief, who may or not necessarily supplement their arms, victual and supply them.

They understood and envisioned the "great fyrd" or citizens' militia as being composed of the "whole body of the people," in many cases in those times further described as "all men able to bear arms," or able-bodied males aged 16 to 66. The allegiance of the militia was — and is — to the Constitution.

Our founders rightfully feared the abusive potential of standing armies: they had recently suffered terrible atrocities forcing them to go to war with their own sovereign. They also knew the hijacking of lawful government by ill-intentioned men, turning the power of that authority against the people who originally granted it. They knew a free nation could not exist; could not defend itself from dangers within and without, unless the mighty majority of citizens were sufficiently and proficiently armed and determined to defend its ideals to the death, hence the words, "necessary to the security of a free state."

Look around today's world, folks; it's still going on. The militia — the armed, proficient, vigilant and unconquerable body of the people — could, and at least at that time would, stand as a bulwark against such actions.

Now go back and re-read the Second Amendment. All it takes is an appreciation of the language of the times, and what you knew in your heart is borne out.

Yes, We Exist

Some say there is no "citizens' militia"; that it doesn't exist anymore. How many thousands compete in three-gun matches? IDPA? USPSA? How many well regulated law-abiding Americans, proficient with their arms, honor the Constitution? In fact, we outnumber by thousands to one the colonial militiamen who guaranteed our freedoms with their blood.

In my opinion, any genuinely free and democratic government would be gladdened by the existence of such a great Citizens' Militia. Apparently, this government doesn't know us. Maybe a couple million of us should stand up and wave. I'll go first, okay? I am a militiaman.

———•———

*Desert sailboat fuel: (1) Hot, gusty air, bearing grit, trash and small stinging insects. (2) Presidential campaign promises. (3) Congressional speeches.

———•———

Recommended Reading: The Second Amendment Primer, Les Adams, www. palladiumpress.com.

A LITTLE BIT OF LEARNING

November/December 2009

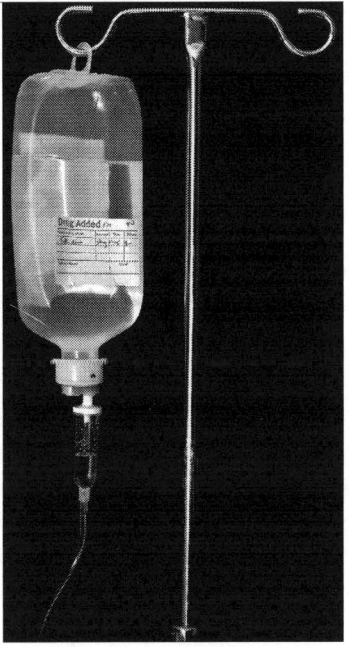

If American nurses are our "Angels of Mercy" — and they are, believe me; especially military nurses — then our candy-striped teenage hospital volunteers must be the cherubim, God bless 'em. They're pretty much restricted to fetch-and-carry work in hospitals today, but still, I think their mere presence has more than a dollop of medicinal benefit. Sometimes, just pulling smiles, even an occasional painful laugh, out of badly hurt patients seems to be their sole duty, and they're certainly good at it!

One such candy-striper we'll call Candy here, almost caused me to split my stitches. I could describe her more, but let's just say with her red hair, freckle-flecked face and baby-blue eyes, I mistook her for one of my own Red Squad girls when I came out of a morphine fog and peeped her for the first time.

On one of Candy's many "hangin' out" visits, my surgeon had left my medical records on a side table in my room. The cherub was leaning on it when she commented that my file was the fattest she'd ever seen. I told her it was sort of a chronicle of "Life's Lessons Learned"; representing the curriculum of the University of Hard Knocks. She smiled impishly, worth sixty mg's of morphine, easy, patted it and said, "Gee, you musta learned a ton, Mister Connor! Can you graduate now?"

I splurted, 'sploded, knocked something over and people came runnin'. Good question, though … can I graduate?

A PhD From The U Of HK

Yeah; I've learned some things, both esoteric and mundane, and the learning, while free of the usual tuition and lab fees, often came at the cost of blood, pain and/or embarrassment. Here's one: If you lose blood an' suffer pain from any given social encounter, at least try not to embarrass yourself too! Not in front of your mates, anyway. That does nothin' but make the sting of a wound worse. The sorta-corollary is, if a deadly incident ends with you bein' deeply embarrassed but not grievously wounded, don't give it a second thought — as long as you learn rom it.

In a fight for your life, You don't shoot a man until you think he's dead — You've got to shoot him until HE thinks he's dead. Please hold any sanctimonious complaints about this one until you have fought men who, despite wounds which ought to drop a grizzly like a box 'o rocks, keep on determinedly killing your comrades and tryin' their dangdest to kill you.

I've learned there are millions of men who are absolutely, crazily willing to shed blood, draw blood and die for their cause, however weird, ridiculous and twisted it is. But thank God, there are very few of them willing to put the necessary effort into the training it takes to be proficient at that enterprise. About training, I've learned that Amateurs train until they get the drill right; professionals train until they can't get it wrong.

I've learned that real fights rarely resemble fighting scenes filmed by Hollywood, but lotsa times you'll wind up fighting guys whose only weapons-handling training apparently came from the movies. If you go up against a guy who shoots using the "Gangsta Grip" — over his head, gun horizontal on its port side, sorta pushing his rounds toward you with jerky arm movements — just thank Hollywood for his poor technique right after you ding him.

I've learned the currency of some countries makes much better toilet paper than their toilet paper, and using it that way actually costs less than buying their toilet paper, if there is any available. Usually, there's not. Continuing on this potty-path, I've also learned that when mortar rounds have you bracketed and the only hole in the pool-table plain you're on is a pit toilet, Yes, you can do it … Just jump in. See "embarrassment" above.

This naturally leads to what I've learned about digging in under fire. Did you know that anytime you think you're excavating at peak efficiency, your digging speed can triple when the first round impacts? Then triple again between the second and third "incomings"?

Bugs & Bolt-Cutters

I've learned satellite intel is good, like, it can read a license plate from space. But only human intel can tell you what the fatcat in the back seat is sayin'. And no satellite can tell a mobile field kitchen from a mobile biological-weapons lab, but a fire team of Marines with a set of bolt-cutters can.

I've learned if you're anywhere roughly between the Tropics of Cancer and Capricorn and you find a natural source of water which appears clean, clear and free of bugs, don't drink from it! If even the bugs won't bathe in it, it'll probably kill you. You're better off with water that looks like bug soup. Here's another piece of wisdom about waterholes which somebody might have chucked a canister of cyanide into: Hoofprints both arriving and departing don't mean squat. Track 'em away from that hole at least 500 meters, 'cause that's where you might find 'em dead. Go thirsty, guys.

And finally, from me, for now: Never be in a shot-up all-concrete building when it falls down.

Hey, Tony! This just needs a little Bundy Rum, eh, mate?

THE BIG GUN GUY GOES "LITE"
New Year, New Dude, New Needs

JANUARY/FEBRUARY 2010

Ijust had my biannual "friendly chat" with His Most DeLuxe Self, Roy-Boy the Publishing Potentate. That's his new title, y'know, though you can still address him as "His Illuminating Immenseness." For about 50 minutes HII glibly gabbed about neat an' nifty new stuff he likes — and it was actually interesting! Occasionally I enjoy learning what potentates possess. A lot of it is like the stuff we have, except it's handmade, 24-K gold plated, Renaissance-engraved, microchip-driven and custom-something. Then it was my turn.

Fifteen seconds later he busted in with, "Yeah; cool. Why don't cha write this up in GunCrank and I'll print it. Maybe."

I've always been a Big Gun Guy:

Big, big on guns, big on big guns. As a neo-Neanderthal, I've customarily packed multiple guns of the hefty-howitzer sort in just about every role of my life, personal and professional. Like, it made perfect sense to me, if my primary piece was a full-size 1911, my backup boomer should be "Commander"-sized, y'know? If my right-hand Roscoe was a Glock 17, easy; just carry two of 'em, plus a Model 26, okay? No problem — back then.

Ain't it funny how all it takes is a measly half-dozen fractured vertebrae, numerous dings an' dents and a monster dose of nerve damage to change your carry-gun tastes? Envision a crippled semi-shaved ape, held precariously upright by a four-toed walker-cane. Shaky at best, he can be blown over by a stiff breeze, is limited to free use of one clutching hand, and the addition of a coupla pounds of unsprung weight causes severe pain. Got that?

It seems moving to lighter guns is the only smart move. But hey, since I'm outta the business of runnin' to cover, dodgin' bullets, an' swingin' through the jungle on a dangly vine, I'll have more time to take sharp aim, right? Faced with this situation, having an eclectic collection of weirdos, wizards, Spartans an' Amazons amongst your family and friends can help — and they did!

On a recent blue-sky day, the Hoplite Hoard trucked my busted bod out to the Rat Canyon Range an' commenced covering all horizontal surfaces with featherweight firearms, knives and sundry accessories. Since hospitals take a dim view of patients shooting down their hallways, my experience with recently introduced handguns had suffered. I took the cure, enthusiastically.

Lots of rounds were launched from lotsa tubes that day, but there were two absolutely delightful surprises I wanta share with you — despite the fact they've already been bathed in printer's ink by real GunWriterGuys: Ruger's sweet little LCR and the SIG SAUER P250 Compact 9mm.

Two Triggers Worth Tootlin' About

Get thee to a gun shop! Better still; get thee to a rental range which stocks these puppies. Amazingly enough, all the superlatives you've read about 'em are true, especially about their triggers.

A Tale of Two Triggers: SIG SAUER P250 (L) and Ruger LCR

If you haven't read the mechan'-tech reviews on these guns, do it. They'll explain how the gizmo engages the grabbit et-dang-cetera. But if like me you're more of a grunt than a gunsmith; more caveman than connoisseur, then let's talk, okay?

First, the LCR weighed only 13.4 ounces on my postal scale; less than the cardboard box, lock, brochure and little zippered rug it came with. Loaded with 147-grain rounds, it still weighed less than a pound, at 15.8 ounces. I've shot many small-frame revolvers, and stingin' recoil and nasty muzzle flip has always been the trade-off for light weight and a short barrel. Not so with the LCR.

The unique cam-operated trigger is smooth, consistent through the stroke and feels far lighter than others with comparable pull weights. It's a star on its own, but the greater story lies in how, with the combined effects of that trigger, the rubber grip and angle geometry, and the composite frame, you can rapidly pump five shots into a pie plate at fighting distance with one hand. We shot the LCR plenty; strong hand and weak, mostly with 147-grain Winchester .38 Special + P JHPs until we suddenly realized — wait a minute! This is pleasant! This is one superb dump-in-your-pocket backup, or carry-gun. I'm anxious to see if the optional Crimson Trace Lasergrip preserves the recoil-absorbing qualities of the factory grip. I'll let you know, okay?

The Stealth Service Pistol

After shooting it, that's what I thought: It may be a "compact," but the P250 Compact could easily serve as either a police duty sidearm or military service pistol; just more agile and maneuverable than most. And, 15 rounds plus one up the pipe ain't nothin' to sniff at.

The P250, like the Ruger LCR, delivers some truly stunning design features. Its morphing-mutant modularity is indeed a VeryBigDeal in engineering innovation, but of little interest to me. It is light — one pound six ounces "dry"; one pound 15.2 ounces full-up with 100-grain Cor-Bon Pow`R Ball rounds — but there are other light pistols. For a caveman with big, broad hands and sorta stumpy fingers, the whole package is a beautifully-balanced, positive-pointing piece with a perfect "reach" to the trigger, and the trigger is the main event.

If you've ever handled one, imagine a first-class PPC Match gun; a DA revolver with a long, butter-smooth action. Yup; it's that good, plus the pull weight of the trigger is absolutely constant through its travel, and that travel is geared one-to-one with the arc of the hammer! See "Get thee ..." above.

Well, dang; outta space and I didn't get to talk about knives — but watch for that in a July-August feature, okay? Connor OUT.

THE HOME DEFENSE RIG

About twice a year the Memsaab Helena and I carve time out of our Carnival of Chaos to do a thorough analysis of our safety and security situation. The phones are turned off and we allow no distractions. Yeah; we take it seriously, considering all threats, not just armed intruders. We talk, make notes on weapons, ammo and accessories, and do "walkthroughs" of threat-response tactics — for

The heart of a Home Defense Rig: A Level III SERPA holster and Xiphos weaponlight, by BLACKHAWK!.

around the house, away from home, driving and working. To do any less, we agree, is like buying empty fire extinguishers: meaningless gestures in a game played for lives.

Back when I was a cop, I questioned a badly wounded citizen who was confronted by two armed attackers, one with a knife, the other with an old Iver Johnson .22 revolver. Our citizen-victim was a legal concealed-carrier, and well armed. The way the goblins fumbled the first part of the encounter, he shoulda had every advantage over them. He never even cleared leather. At the hospital I learned why he lost that fight, his gun and nearly his life.

"I really never imagined it would happen to me," he wheezed, and his eyes still held true shock. By that point in my life I wasn't surprised he had gone through the motions of "being prepared" while really being completely unprepared. I had seen too much of it already, even by fellow cops. Simply put, he had the hardware, but not the enabling software.

Helena and I spend more time on possible scenarios and our human responses than we do on equipment. I recommend the practice to you, 'cause I wanna see the Good Guys win. There's not enough space in this magazine to thoroughly discuss safety and security from soup to nuts, so let me sound off on just one thing I feel strongly about, okay?

Envision this scene: You're awakened by a bump in the night; maybe tinkling glass. You jump up in your jammies — or in the buff — grab your Bedside Boomer and head for the hallway. Do you have a tactical light? Your cell phone? Now both your hands are full. How are you at turning doorknobs or switchin' on lights with your toes? Punchin' 9-1-1 with your nose?

Now picture yourself rising again, this time quickly snapping or buckling on a sturdy, snug-fitting belt you've outfitted as sort of a "First Response Tool Chest." Now you have both hands free until you choose to fill one with the right tool for the job. Your roscoe rides in a Level II or Level III active-retention holster; fast, but resistant to goblin-grabs if you wind up in a high-stakes wrestling match. Spare ammo is on your belt, not in a box in the closet.

You have a strobing light and laser mounted on your gun, because carrying fewer separate tools makes sense, though you also have a backup tac-light on your belt — right there by your cell-phone. And you're packin' a less-lethal weapon like a PepperBlaster or JPX Jet Protector, right? You want some options other than 230-grain slugs or empty hands.

Restraints are a good idea too — handcuffs or plastic zip-cuffs. If you do win the first round with an intruder, I can tell you from experience the longer they are un-shot the more convinced they become that you won't shoot, especially after they're disarmed. Sometimes they become dangerously stupid. Believe me; a securely shackled scumbag is easier to manage. If they get active with their legs or elbows, a stiff shot of pepper-snot can restore order and provide entertainment.

For Helena and I, a stout fixed-blade knife rounds out the "necessaries" on a Home Defense Rig. Think of it as a "handgun retention device." One pal of mine adds a whippy collapsible baton, and others carry TASERs or another form of electro-therapy. However you equip your belt, you're better off than you were.

Stylish?

Now, I know what you're thinkin': You're seeing yourself confronting a crook or turning one over to responding officers while wearin' your faded blue flannel jammie-bottoms with the little sailboats on 'em, and a big black gunbelt draped with deadly gear — and you're thinkin' you'd look silly. You wouldn't look silly to me, or to any cop with a room-temp IQ. To us, you'd just look prepared and serious. And who cares what you look like to that predator, especially if he's lookin' up at you through teary eyes, and you're smiling?

Better a Silly-Lookin' Winner than a Dignified Dead Dude.

Another acquaintance of mine sorta snorted derisively when I mentioned my Home Defense Rig. A short time later he experienced one of those "bumps in the night" and investigated, pistol and flashlight in hand. He 'fessed up afterward, and I tried not to laugh. At the top of his staircase, he needed a hand free to unlatch the puppy-gate. He unconsciously tucked his Beretta 92 into the comfy, worn-out elastic waistband of his sleepy-shorts. His shorts rocketed to his ankles; he lost his balance, and wound up head-bonked, dazed, barebutted an' gunless at the bottom of the stairs. The puppy, who had knocked over a potted plant on a stand, came wagglin' over to lick his face.

Now that's silly. And I won't even mention Pete's name ... Connor OUT.

TALE OF A ROAMIN' PONY:
The Colt That Came Home

MAY/JUNE 2010

It was late 1980 or early '81 when a stone-faced man in a dark suit stepped into the shop of up-and-coming gunsmith Terry Tussey. Stoneface surveyed the room with

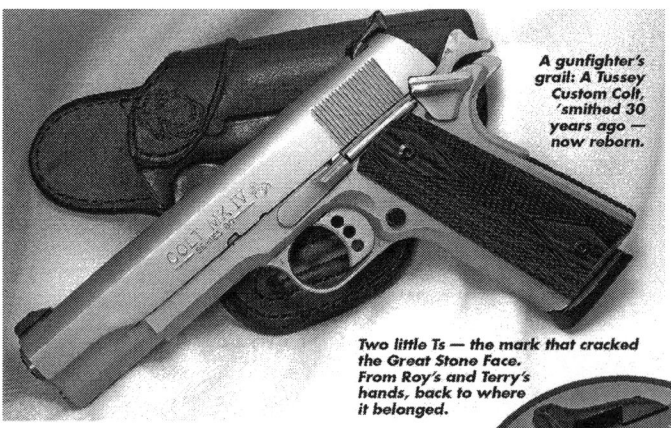

A gunfighter's grail: A Tussey Custom Colt, 'smithed 30 years ago — now reborn.

Two little Ts — the mark that cracked the Great Stone Face. From Roy's and Terry's hands, back to where it belonged.

scorched-earth eyes, and then closed the door. Terry quickly spotted the bulges under Stoneface's arms, and felt a little relief when his coat parted to reveal a gold badge clipped to his belt.

Though decades younger then, Terry already knew serious armed thugs had occasionally hit gunsmiths' shops. After all, that's where the good guns were. And this guy looked nothin' but serious. Sure didn't look much like "Officer Friendly" though. He wasn't.

Stoneface laid a blue box and an envelope on the counter. The box contained a spanky-new Colt Mark IV Series 80 Government Model 1911A1 pistol. The envelope held a sheet listing operations to be performed on it. Most were reliability mods, like lowering and flaring the ejection port; throating the barrel and polishing the ramp; tuning the extractor and smoothing the trigger; combat sights and more, finished off with a frosted matte industrial hard chrome job. Terry spontaneously started to ask a routine question.

"So, the primary purpose of …" and Stoneface cut him off.

"Gunfighting," he said, and tapped the list. "You may shave a little accuracy for absolute reliability, but she's got to shoot into eye sockets at 15 and fists at 50 — with government hardball." He dropped his card on the counter and turned to leave.

"Fists?"

The man silently laid a big fist over the center of his chest. Terry nodded; he understood.

"I've heard you're good," Stoneface said. "Show me."

Terry looked at the card, made a coupla phone calls, muttered "Hmm …" a few times, and then — Oh, boy, did Terry show HIM! When his two descending Ts in an oval were finally stamped on that Colt it was a gunfighter's grail, brutal and beautiful at once; elegant and ominous; a pure bullet-launcher and deadly serious, like the man it was made for.

The Man, The Missions

That stonefaced man was my Uncle John, then commanding officer of one of the nation's largest and most active SWAT units. He had risen through the ranks of SWAT the same way he'd earned combat promotions as a Marine: by single-minded ferocious dedication to the mission, whatever it was, at whatever risk. He was at his best — even his most comfortable — when playing the game "You Bet Your Life" with dangerous men. He didn't do so well with what he called "politics, platitudes and patty-cake."

He may tell his own story someday, but I'll tell you this one to sorta illustrate the man: When unit commanders were ordered to generate yet another piece of PC feel-good fluff — a "C.O.'s Statement on Race and Color" — he gathered his SWAT cops and said, "This is our policy on race and color: We have two races — the 440 and the mile, run quarterly. We have one color: camouflage. Dismissed!" He got thunderous cheers from the troops, and a thorough reaming from the brass. He didn't care. Only the mission counted.

The damages of duty caught up with him a decade later, and he found himself disabled, retired and financially strained. Some guns had to go, and the one he could get the highest return for was that Tussey Custom Colt. It stung him worse than shrapnel and he grieved to let it go, but the stone face never slipped or sagged. He sold it and never looked back.

The Colt wound up in the hands of a young officer who loved Terry Tussey's work, and equally loved guns which could murmur stories in the night; tales of standoffs and shootouts; face-downs with felony fugitives; SWAT missions and stakeouts; drug lab raids and cornered killers; horrors, hostages and heroism. He got both with the Tussey Colt. That young officer was our own Roy-Boy, now the Publishing Potentate, long before he was even His Illuminated Editorial Immenseness. Who'd a thought?

I know Roy shot it a lot, punishing, polishing and praising it. Ultimately it became his Bedside Boomer; his Bump-in-the-Night Gun. Rivers ran, fortunes changed, years passed, paths crossed and recrossed. Terry and Roy became friends, as did Roy and Uncle John. I fit in there somewhere.

Uncle John rarely spoke of that gun, and only when he was delivering his patented parable about letting things go. No matter how much you value something, he said, when letting go is the right thing to do, you walk away and never look back; Shut Up, Get Over It, and Move On.

Rat-Bite Times Two

When Terry learned Roy had that Colt, it sorta bothered him. He built guns for individuals, and he'd built that particular gun for a very particular man. He filed it under Other People's Business and tried to forget it. But like a lone rat in a vast ship's hold, it nibbled at him on a thousand nights, and finally, it bit. He didn't know his rat had a cousin in another ship's hold a thousand miles away, and it bit — hard — on the same night.

When Terry called Roy the next morning, he was prepared to be forceful; his sense of righteousness was simmering. "Roy," he began sternly, "About John's Colt — where is it right now? It's his gun, Roy, and he should have it!"

Roy was stunned. That Colt was on his desk, lying under his hand; removed from his nightstand in the gray dawn. He had already dug out a shipping box for it.

"Ummm …" he muttered, feeling the hair on the back of his neck stiffen and rise. "Uhh … Last night, I, umm … I was gonna send it, umm … today, you know … to John … Holy smokes, Terry! What's goin' on?"

They talked. Terry asked Roy to send the Colt to him, first. Once it was in his skilled hands, Terry lit it up, tore it down to the last pin, and commenced … magic. It was not reworked; it was reborn; not face-lifted so much as forged anew. Our conspirators enlisted an accomplice …

Neither Terry nor Roy could be there when Aunt C handed Uncle John a plain cardboard box and said simply, "Open it" — but I was. He lifted out what looked like a spanky-new Colt Mark IV Series 80 Government Model 1911A1 pistol; new, but far from "stock." Realization began to dawn as Stoneface read the port side of the slide and, and even the Duty Dummy — me — could see clouds breaking over the Man With a Mission's face. He slowly turned the pistol to its starboard side, and his eyes fell on those twin Ts in an immaculate oval — Terry's earliest logo. It was several minutes before he could even rack the slide and gently, reverently pull the trigger.

I can't do the moment justice. Perhaps no one can. It was like seeing an old samurai presented with the lost sword of his ronin years; watching as spirits rise from the steel in wisps of smoke, whispering tales of ancient battles.

After 30 years, the roamin' pony returned. The Tussey Colt came home. Terry Tussey's hands twice made it superior; gave it excellence. It is now in the hands of the man who made it memorable; gave it history.

Why tell this story? First, because it warms and gladdens me, and I can. Second, because some of us, all of us, now and then need reassurance that among good and honorable men, sometimes what goes around comes around, and that can be a good thing. Thanks for reading. Connor OUT.

PREPARE FOR THE ZOMBIE WARS!:
Because crazy is the new "smart".

July/August 2010

Just a buncha regular guys blastin' targets and battin' the breeze.

I'd guess that's what others saw on a crunchy-cold day at the Rat Canyon Range. I dunno; maybe they could sense something different in our gimpy movements, stiff with old wounds.

Chuck, Bob and Steve — you've seen 'em on the street, right?

Under the heavy clothes they couldn't see the tapestries of scars. "What a bunch," I thought; "Broke-down ex-cops, an' shot-up old soldiers — with four outta six of us gettin' it both ways." I guessed between us, we had enough metal, plastic and scar tissue to make a whole 'nother dude. But it was good just to have us all together in one place — and cool that in this group, I qualify to be called "the kid."

During breaks in the range-house warming frozie-fingers around the woodstove, naturally we yakked about Been & Done stuff. I figured we had worked, fought, operated on about every sizeable land mass except Madagascar and Antarctica, and scrapped with everybody from the Soviet Army to Sendero Luminoso; the Pathet Lao to the PLO, plus domestic dirtbags and miscellaneous multi-national mutts.

"We prob'ly killed more men than smallpox," Uncle G observed kinda pensively, creaking on his artificial knees and massaging the hand pierced by a ChiCom burp-gun slug on the Yalu in '51.

"Well, they all needed killin', didn't they?" MacKenzie chirped brightly. Uncle G laughed then, but the group had gone quiet, seeing old sights, old fights inside their eyes …

They were bored, too. The action-shooting bays were under repair, so we'd just been bustin' bullseyes. That's when I broke out some of Joe Quinlan's Zombie Targets and got exactly the reaction I expected.

They Already Knew 'Em …

"Hey!" Van Zyl chortled, "I know these guys! I fought them in Congo!" The others agreed.

"San Diego, below Broadway after midnight, these ghouls come outta the gutters," said Uncle John. "I think they eat winos and runaways."

"Nah," Canfield cracked, "Them're Somali skinnies for sure; right outta Mogadishu; just cleaner. They take a lotta killin'."

Everybody had their own tale and place, from Baltimore to Basra. But Zombie goes beyond ugly ... The guys knew a little about zombies, but after meeting Joe, who was a zombie-movie freak as a kid, I actually did some readin': The Zombie Survival Guide and World War Z, both by Max Brooks, leading authority on the Living Dead. I explained — they have no fear, feel no pain; the only way to slow them down or stop 'em is by bustin' structure; spine, shoulders, hips, knees; and the only way to kill 'em is by destroying the brain. Otherwise, they just keep comin' and they will kill you. Then it hit them.

"Wait," said VZ. "Seriously, we have fought these guys." It's true. We'd fought people stoned outta their skulls on everything from khat to crack, hash to meth; wild-eyed religious fanaticism to Wild Turkey with an LSD chaser. And who's more dangerous than a scumbag so brain-fried on PCP he'd snap the links of handcuffs, fracturing his wrists in the process, and still try to strangle you or stab you with his own protruding splintered bones?

Thugs and suicide bombers soaked in stimulants and painkillers are already epidemic in the Middle East, Asia and Africa. We had all had to shoot some whacko right down to the deck and keep shootin' 'till his clothes caught fire; delivered guaranteed-fatal wounds on loony-goons who were clinically dead but hadn't got the telegram.

"Jeez," Canfield muttered, "We've been fighting zombies for years and ... and it's gettin' worse all the time."

They all looked at those targets a little differently then. Oh, they were still funny in a silly laugh-your-butt-off way, but as the guys thought more about the proto-zombies in their pasts — and the more they mused on What's next? from the rapidly-mutating, intertwining worlds of drugs, pathogens and social psychoses, those targets got "funny" in a dark, slitty-eyed black-chucklin' way ...

Two Good Reasons ...

Fighting drugged-up, body-armored psychotic mutants? That's already happenin'. Zombies? Not much of a jump, huh? Fighting schools like Gunsite have long been teaching "shoot to failure" drills, sorta along the lines of my own philosophy: You don't shoot a man until you think he's dead — You gotta shoot him until HE thinks he's dead. (Or the PC version: "Until the threat is neutralized.")

And there are two other good reasons to train to fight Zombies: First, in this oh-so-sensitive society, shooting virtually any other kinda anthropomorphic-lookin' target will get you accused of bein' racist, sexist, or lethally prejudiced against some color or flavor of cretin or crackpot — and prob'ly get you sued someday. And there is no movement or group, or even a big law firm representing The Undead and filing discrimination-against-zombies lawsuits.

Second, nobody from government will take you as a serious threat to the Glorious New World Order. They already think you're a threat, but now they'll just dismiss you as another nutcase. I'm okay with that. Maskirovka, y'know? In America today, folks, crazy could be the new "smart." Connor OUT.

"FULL OF IT"? TAKE THIS!:
Shameless Plugs For Selected Pistols

Did you guys see that letter to me in the May/June issue (Speak Out, "The Whinery") on page 16? This diplomat starts off with "Connor, you're full of it!" and goes on to accuse me — and the rest of the Handgunner crew, apparently — of bein' suck-up sycophants for gun manufacturers; pimps for the pistol-makers. He named my Jan/Feb 2010 column specifically, where I tootled about the triggers on Ruger's LCR and the SIG P250 Compact. Yeah, that one.

SIG P220 Combat, after bein' sandwiched between rocks and crushed by tractor treads. The rocks broke — the Doomsday gun didn't. 'Nuff said?

Here's how I know (a) he's not a regular reader — not of this column, anyway — and (b) what he's full of. In seven years writin' this diary, I think I've mentioned maybe a half-dozen specific handguns. That must make me the poorest pistolpimp on the boulevard, wouldn't ya think? I bet you can guess why I said what I did about 'em … cause it's true, and it's good! If you tried those triggers, what did you think? Whether either of those guns fit your needs or not, did you get the same kind of impressions I did? Just curious …

Now, to achieve two goals — first, to stick it up The Whiner's snoot, and second, to answer a question readers have asked many times in different forms, essentially this: "The balloon goes up, Connor, and you must reach into your heap o' handguns and grab just one. Which one would it be?" Stand by to get pimped-to-the-max, folks! After all, I'm just a suck-up sycophant.

Ummm … Good Question!

A dozen-plus years ago, the answer woulda been simple: My plain-Jane 4" stainless Ruger GP-100, in .38 Spl/.357 Mag. It's super-strong, Doomsday-durable, and ammo for it was abundant everywhere. It's not my favorite carry-piece or favorite shooter, but a very intelligent "one-gun" choice. I'll never let it go. Since then though, .38/.357 has dwindled in popularity and supply, the survivability of newer pistols has escalated, and …

That "balloon goes up" scenario can take many forms, and venue would be important. Are we talkin' about food riots, the only music is distant sirens, blue suits on the streets in riot gear, and radio messages urging people to "let the 'thorties restore order"? Am I at home base in the High Lonely, stranded in a whistle-stop town on the plains, or stuck in a concrete metro-jungle? Hmmm …

I've got a Kimber Pro TLE/RL II — a present from The Memsaab Helena — which might just be the best-handling, most agile steel-frame 1911 I've ever touched. It's a "Commander-size" piece with a 4" bushingless barrel, Meprolight night sights, checkered rubber grips (done right!) and a dust-cover rail. The action is silky slick, and its precision is palpable. For perhaps purely personal reasons, the balance and "pointability" are perfect for me. Okay; maybe for you, too. It's a great gun for The Big Crapshoot — played for your life.

As a general rule, I don't care for DA/SA actions, but another top contender is my SIG P220 Combat, also in .45 ACP. The P220 already had a legend-level reputation for survivability under harsh conditions, and with the friction-reducing and enhanced corrosion- resistance upgrades built into the 220 Combat for the SOCOM trials, it truly earned it's "To Hell and Back Reliability" tag.

I was present at Firepower TV's proving grounds in 2006 when those madmen heaped two days of horrific abuse on the first five specimens off the production line. Nobody, including the SIG rep, expected any to survive. They all did, firing and functioning superbly. That's when I realized, DA/SA or not, I had to have one — just in case.

But under a rising black balloon, I might just reach over and grab my Smith & Wesson M&P45. Light, extremely accurate, tank-tough and featuring an optional manual safety, which exactly matches the arc of my thumb, it points on-target as naturally for me as a Browning Hi-Power, and that's sayin' something. And, the extra firepower of a half-dozen spare 14-round extended mags to back up standard 10-rounders gives it an edge dealing with mobs of "post-event" marauding morons.

Other Scenes, Other Choices

Or, have the blue-helmeted foreign "guest" troops been invited in to help enforce the U.N. Disarming-The-Rabble Treaty, and my best source of ammo re-supply is, well … them? Then I might grab a recently refreshed Gen-1 Glock 17 and a bagful of mags. I don't care for the Gen-2 or -3s, and haven't tried the Gen-4 yet. But I'll put absolute faith in that old stock Glock.

Am I a movin' covert in the concrete jungle with my name on a "reeducation camp" list and concealment is critical? For that, I'll take my HK P7 PSP, rebuilt by Frank Duren in Nixa, Mo. It's one of the sturdiest, slimmest, flattest, most inherently accurate and concealable pistols ever made.

Wait … is this a "Final Footfall" scenario? End Times, after the impact of that three-mile meteor? The grid is not just down, but gone? Okay, maybe I'm back to that GP-100 again, and takin' my chances on ammo availability.

Whew! Have I shamelessly plugged enough guns? Can't wait for all the baksheesh and freebies from manufacturers to roll in! I'll split 'em with you, Gus. Your half would be … 50 percent of ZIP. Connor OUT

VETERANS DAY NOVEMBER 11, 2010:
Lest We — And THEY — Forget

NOVEMBER/DECEMBER 2010

You've heard of the "Siege of Boston" during our American Revolution, right? At first, it was not a siege but a standoff: We held the hills, but the British held the port and city. They were content to sit out the winter in relative comfort waiting for reinforcements in the spring, and let the ragtag Continental Army freeze, starve and dwindle meantime.

A very young, obese fellow who explained he ran a bookstore approached General Washington; his favorite subject was military history. His sketches suggested improvements to the rebels' fortifications impressed Washington so, he ordered them to be carried out.

Then the lad expressed his concern that without artillery, the redcoats might still overrun their defenses. He reminded the General there were cannons in the abandoned fort at Ticonderoga, in northern New York. It was over 300 miles away and might as well have been a thousand, as winter descended. Washington said he did not believe the guns could be moved in winter, much less transported to Boston. The pale, plump young man volunteered to try.

None of Washington's aides thought the fellow (a 300-pound, clumsy, city-boy they laughingly called "Fat Henry") would ever be seen again.

But Henry did reach Ticonderoga, and 56 days later he delivered 59 cannons

and mortars weighing 60 tons to his general, having dragged them over the Berkshires through repeated blizzards. Faced with Henry's cannons, the redcoats abandoned Boston and sailed for Canada. Henry's accomplishments from that time on were legion and extraordinary. But every November 11, who will lift a cup to the memory of Fat Henry Knox?

Forgotten — Lost Papers

On February 20, 1942, the carrier Lexington was the principal target of Japanese

Our friends at Ranger Up showing Veterans Day wear. If you order, upon checkout enter promo code Handgunner2010 for free Priority Mail shipping. You're welcome, and thank you for remembering that Freedom Isn't Free.

111

bombers during furious air battles around Papua New Guinea and the giant enemy base at Rabaul. Previous attacks on the Lex had failed, but seriously depleted her air assets. When another flight of nine Japanese twin-engine bombers were detected heading straight for the Lexington, Lieutenant Edward "Butch" O'Hare and his wingman "Duff" Dufilho were the only ones who could possibly intercept — and Duff's guns were jammed; useless.

Attacking a Mitsubishi G4M "Betty" bomber could be suicidal. The Betty's defenses included five 7.7mm machineguns and a tail-mounted 20mm cannon. To jump a "vee-of-vees" of Bettys solo, went beyond suicide. Butch bored in, guns blazing. Accounts vary on how many Butch shot down — probably five, with a sixth damaged — but his C.O., also flying an F4F Wildcat, arrived to see three enemy bombers falling in flames at once. The attack failed. Butch became the Navy's first flying ace of World War II, and its first aviator awarded a Medal of Honor.

Before and after that day, Butch O'Hare distinguished himself as a modest, yet fiercely courageous American. He was shot down in November of 1943, while leading a night mission to intercept Japanese torpedo bombers. No trace of Butch or his aircraft was ever found. I do not believe one person in 100,000 who pass through O'Hare International know of Butch and his bravery. But on Veterans Day, will you pause to remember Butch?

Woodrow Wilson Keeble, a full-blood Sioux from Wahpeton, N.D., was being scouted by the Chicago White Sox for his 100-mph fastball when his Guard unit was activated for Korea. Master Sergeant Keeble, already a WWII veteran of the Americal Division, found another use for his pitching arm on October 20, 1951, in the rocky hills of Sangsan-ni. After his unit suffered heavy casualties in three assaults on a Chinese-defended hilltop, he decided to attack it alone.

Hurling grenades and firing his BAR, Keeble knocked out three pillboxes and cleared two trenches, killing 16 enemy infantry as they threw grenades at him and delivered withering fire. Woody took that hill and held it. He was shot five times, and stung with 83 grenade fragments.

Keeble's nomination papers for the Medal of Honor were lost twice in the years afterward. Woody didn't push it; he hadn't fought for decorations, but for his country and his comrades. Thankfully, others persisted; Woody was finally awarded 56 years later, in March 2009. Woody died in 1982. Who will honor Woody on November 11th?

One Small Request

There are so many stories I want to share with you; I had to simply pick three at random. I know you folks will honor our veterans, living and dead, on Veterans Day. But will you help remind others — including many who don't want to be reminded — that freedom isn't free; that countless veterans paid for it?

If you have served — any service, in any role — you paid for it. If not a veteran, if you are a son of liberty, a daughter of independence, a child of freedom, let others know it. I'm proud to stand with you. Connor OUT.

HAPPY NEW YEAR!:
Now Survive It

JANUARY/FEBRUARY 2011

It seems I kicked over an anthill with those "Doomsday Gun" comments in the Sept/Oct Guncrank. It started rollin' with readers, gunwriters, editors and industry folks volleying back and forth about doomsday guns; what designs, features and finishes might be most survivable in end-game scenarios, sans support, supplies and societal stability. Then all that stuff spun up and out, expanding into post-catastrophe then post-apocalyptic survival in general, before circlin' back and down — right on my gourd. "Talk about it," sez His Editoriship …

I'm not styling myself as an expert on survival. I've advised and consulted on "critical preparedness planning," and I have, well … survived. But I'm just a guy who knows some stuff — like these three things:

First, 90 percent of you live in places subject to one or more of these predictable forces: earthquakes, flooding, tornadoes or hurricanes; metro, forest or wildfires, and severe snow, ice or lightning storms. Most

Start point and mid-point: The ASAP Survival Pack supports two people for up to 72 tough hours with food, water, a GPS and a great deal more. The Trident 1911 by Cylinder & Slide, is Fail Zero EXO-coated for lubeless, greaseless performance — this one has 1,000+ rounds through it without cleaning or lubing. There is no end point … For more info: www. americanhandgunner. com/productindex

of you live on grids which may at any time suffer massive system failures. And finally, there is no sizeable city in the US which is more than one week away from empty shelves, widespread riots and looting, and martial law or anarchy. Industrialized society at its best and worst exists only in a precarious balance.

Many feel there is greater potential today than at any other time in our history for the shiny coin to jiggle outta the slot. Such scenarios are kinda like God or jihad — whether you believe in 'em or not makes no difference; they believe in you, and they'll come for you sooner or later.

Second, "Are you prepared?" ain't a question, it's a koan; an interrogative not intended to elicit an immediate answer, but to stimulate thought on the complex, multi-faceted factors involved. If somebody just blurts "Yes," they're not — count on it.

Third, the road to survival prep ain't a road; it's a network of shifting, changing trails, with crossing points at places like "Prolonged Power Outage" and "After the Earthquake" to "The New Stone Age." The network has no terminus; it just keeps going and evolving. Trouble is, most people who even attempt survival prep start from the wrong points.

Start at Marker Zero

I've done both formal and informal advising, and found examples like this: In a big South American city, an affluent family of three had a remote "safe haven" prepped and waiting, and a 4WD vehicle stuffed with supplies in their garage. When riots and gunfire broke out, it was so sudden and fierce in their upscale shops-and-townhouses area — a natural looter-magnet — they literally couldn't get down the sole-access exterior stairs to their street-level garage. It would have cost their lives. The entire side was pocked with bullet holes, violent feral looters roamed free, and a neighbor lay dead on the landing.

They were totally unprepared to just hunker down inside their home for four days. They were weak, nerve-shattered, dehydrated and debilitated when the national police finally restored order. Their $50,000-plus Gelandewagen was defunct anyway, having taken a round through the fuel pump. They started their "preparedness journey" at about mile-marker 80 and were unprepared for marker number one.

A guy boasted to me he had a 70-gallon water heater installed and could use it as an emergency water source. I asked if he knew where the drain tap was, and did he have a wrench handy to fit it? Nope. It turned out to be so jammed in its space he would have had to dismount it to get a drop. I asked another guy, proud of his preps, "You wear contact lenses, right? Got spares? Got spectacles for backup?" He explained he used disposables, was down to his last set, his glasses broke and he hadn't replaced them yet … but he had lots of freeze-dried food an' camping gear! Folks like him are called "supply centers" by survivors.

I knew two middle-aged brothers who had stored food, water and meds, plus many guns and thousands of rounds of ammo. Their door was up-armored and their street-side windows were inch-thick plexi. They lived in a huge old wooden multi-unit building with lofts — a torch ready to be lit. "In case of fire," I asked, "And you have to walk out, what will you take and where might you go?" The AC hummed and rattled, as did they …

From The Inside Out

Preparing to survive almost any exigency should work from the inside out. That means start inside your own body — and those of others you're responsible for —

allowing for basic and crisis-mode needs for 48 hours, inside your own dwelling, without utilities or services, period! If that seems too simple, you're not being thorough enough. Aside from high-energy food, water, meds, communication, sanitation, protection et-al, consider things like, if conditions dictate you emit no light or sound indicating people inside, are you prepared for that?

It's a koan, folks. Start at marker one. And remember my Grandpa Connor's advice: You gotta have what you need, or have what it takes to get what you need. Connor OUT.

AN INTERVIEW WITH MISTER B.:
A 1911 Centennial Adventure

MARCH/APRIL 2011

Don't ask me how it happened — there ain't room here. It took years of clandestine meetings with physicists and fakirs, crystal-gazers and crackpots, mediums, two sidewalk saints and a 16-year-old Cal Tech dropout who built a time-space holographic transmogrifier in his grandma's basement. I'm not even sure if I was transported through a dimension-warp or it all happened in my head, but suddenly I was in a round room surrounded by opaque cloud-like vapors, with the tinglin' taste of chewed aluminum foil in my mouth, waiting to meet a man who, as he calls it, "crossed over" — in 1926!

I was shakin' my head and wondering if I could spit somewhere when a "ding!" like an old-fashioned elevator bell rang. Through the "cloud-wall" stepped John Moses Browning — irritated, grumbling, and flappin' the lower edge of his robe.

"Horsefeathers and fiddlesticks!" he barked, "Soppin' wet! Again! Tell me, sonny," he asked, "Why is it the fans of all my other guns just wanta shake my hand, but the 1911 fanatics gotta be kissin' and drooling all over the hem of my robe? Soppin'! Oh, well,"

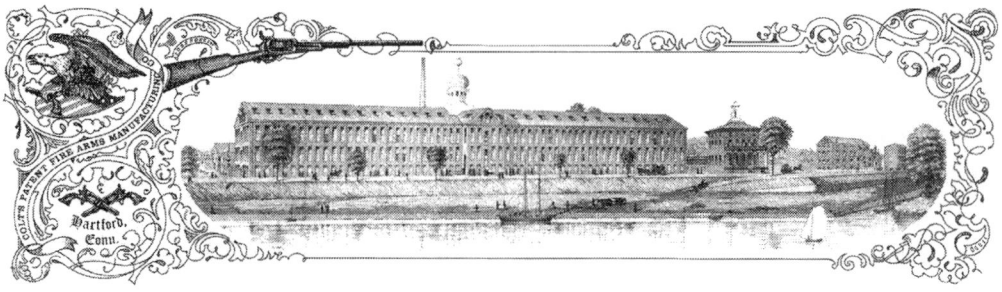

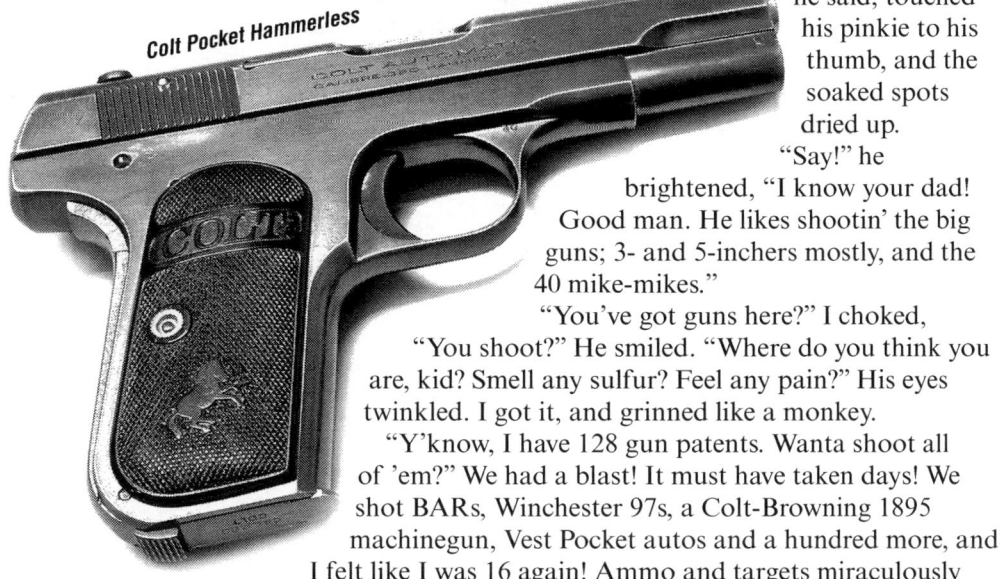
Colt Pocket Hammerless

he said, touched his pinkie to his thumb, and the soaked spots dried up.

"Say!" he brightened, "I know your dad! Good man. He likes shootin' the big guns; 3- and 5-inchers mostly, and the 40 mike-mikes."

"You've got guns here?" I choked, "You shoot?" He smiled. "Where do you think you are, kid? Smell any sulfur? Feel any pain?" His eyes twinkled. I got it, and grinned like a monkey.

"Y'know, I have 128 gun patents. Wanta shoot all of 'em?" We had a blast! It must have taken days! We shot BARs, Winchester 97s, a Colt-Browning 1895 machinegun, Vest Pocket autos and a hundred more, and I felt like I was 16 again! Ammo and targets miraculously appeared, and the reports of the guns were muted, pleasant booms. Then he glanced at his empty palm, sighed, and we were back in that cloud-room.

"We don't have much time, sonny," he said. "That took three minutes, but wasn't it fun? Got some questions for me, do you?" I suffered instant brain-dump; a familiar affliction. All I could do was blurt, "Didja know it's the hundredth anniversary of ..." and he cut me off with a wave.

Mister B Speaks

Yep; sure," he said dismissively. "Of course I like the ol' girl, but for Pete's sake, it's been a century-plus! You folks have done some good things with it, but you're still makin' it with that stupid redundant grip safety? I'm honored and all that, but y'know, I learned a lot over the last few decades, and I came up with a better design. Heard of the P-35? Bravo to my pal Dieudonne Saive for finishing it for me — he designed the staggered magazine, y'know — and I'm not takin' anything away from the nine parabellum; newer loads for it are some real thumpers — but I didn't leave any orders that it couldn't be made in .45 ACP, did I?" He twinkled again. "In my head, I called it the Sweet-P, you know, like a sweetpea. I love that gun."

"Something you folks don't think about is, I had to incorporate a lot of stuff I didn't like on guns because that's what the contracts required, like the grip safety on the 1911. The Frenchies demanded the magazine safety on my Sweet-P, which messed up the trigger pull. I like what they called it though — Le Grand Puissance — sounds cool, huh? Anyway, all it needed was a more positive click to the safety, a tad more mass on the thumb-safety lever, a little more beavertail, and ... like this!" A P-35, exactly as he described appeared in his hand. Rosewood grips were flourished with curling tendrils and blossoms — sweetpeas. Nice.

Carry-Guns

The hundred questions I'd had deserted me. I stumblingly asked which three guns were his top carry-choices. He didn't hesitate.

"My Sweet-P, an '08 Pocket Hammerless, and a BAR, son." He saw my eyebrows go up.

"Why a BAR? Ask the Marines. There are two in dress blues at every gate here; not really necessary, but they insist, and they tell some great stories! Anyway, nothing says 'non timebo mala' — I fear no evil — like a BAR!"

"You're thinking it's tough to carry a BAR, right? Listen; what you folks call open carry we used to call freedom." He turned thoughtful.

"I gave you an interview, so you give me this. Go back with this message and become its champion: It's not enough to reverse those 'duty-to-retreat' laws. It's not enough to defend yourself and assure your safety. You must create a moral duty, enabled by law, to take positive action to attack evil and defeat predators. There must be a duty to act."

"Now," he smiled, "We have just enough time for a quick dark beer. I developed a fondness for it in Belgium. Thirsty?" "Uhhh … Beer? Here?" I stammered. "Sonny," he smiled, his eyes twinkling, "I said this is heaven, didn't I?"

IDIOGLOSSIA FOR GUNNERS':
A Language For Us!

MAY/JUNE 2011

Gotcha, huh? Had to look up "idioglossia"? That's okay; I did too. Here's how it began: I was visiting an old pal at his gun shop when a dude strolled in and Tom's face squinched up like he was suckin' a lemon. They obviously knew each other, but Tom wasn't overjoyed to see the guy. The dude fumbled, trying to make conversation, and Tom was civil, even polite, but not exactly warm an' fuzzy. When he left I barely heard Tom whisper under his breath, "Squib."

I thought he'd said "squid," a sorta uncomplimentary term for "sailor," mostly used by jarheads like me. I found the pejorative particularly strange coming from a retired Navy CPO, so I asked. Tom was a little embarrassed he'd been heard.

"No, not 'squid'," he said, "Squib, with a 'b'! You know, like a squib round; enough power to pop the round outta the case, but not enough to push it out the muzzle."

They had served aboard ship together, on the same damage control team. The guy performed well during drills, but when the real thing happened, he didn't just freeze up; he went into rigid, catatonic hysteria, blocking shipmates from accessing the DC gear compartment and becoming an emergency problem himself.

"So he's a squib," Tom said, "The worst kind of malfunction, where your gun's not only out of action, but now you've got a round stuck in the bore. Nice guy, but a squib."

Afterward I realized two things: First, I hadn't heard anybody use the term "squib" in a long time, and not applied to a person in many more years. It had been in fairly common use when I was a kid. Second, I realized there are lots of firearm and shooting-related terms which used to be part of our American lexicon, but have now fallen into disuse. I think that's sad — and serious.

Our Gutted Glossary

Think about it: Not so long ago, a "doozy" was anything first-rate and classy; the best of its kind. That sprang from the nickname

Americans gave the superlative Duesenberg automobiles of the 1920s and '30s — Duesie. The Duesenbergs are long gone, but "doozy" outlived 'em by decades. The deep and profound relationship of free citizens and their firearms created many more.

A common American farewell used to be, "So long; keep your powder dry." This referred, of course, to protecting your gunpowder from moisture; keeping your weapon primed and ready. Ultimately it came to simply mean being prepared and alert. A dull and useless doofus was a "dud," derived from a dud round, one whose primer got spanked but failed to fire. An unstable person with a hot temper was said to have a "hair trigger," and someone who behaved rashly was "goin' off half-cocked." Being told to "hold your fire" referred not just to refraining from shooting, but to speaking out of turn, interrupting others, or executing any kinds of actions not even remotely connected with shooting.

Today, how many Americans even know what "keep your powder dry" means, much less where it came from? The age of flintlocks may be over, but where did all of our gun-glossary sayings go? There are more citizen-owned guns than ever before, even if the percentage of gun owners may be lower than during our frontier days, so what's causing this extinction? Perhaps examining one formerly well-used phrase can provide an answer.

For over a century, a person who could be counted on to always tell the truth was called a "straight shooter." The expression was common across the social spectrum, including our political plutocracy. In fact, it was a politician's golden moment if a working-class guy would say of him — on camera, of course — something like, "I'm votin' for Farqmuggle, 'cause he's a straight shooter!"

If that happened today, what sort of mindless maelstrom might it prompt? Lefties, libs and lame-os would shrilly shriek it down, and the politico himself rush to a podium to assure the masses that "I am not now, nor have I ever been a ... shooter! " GunSpeak simply ain't PC.

Bring Back the SQUIB!

I think it's time to get gun-speak back into our national glossary, even if it's our own idioglossary. We might remind some people of our armed origins. Or at least, we'll have our own dialect. Either way, we win.

We know what it means to "stovepipe," and it ain't restricted to guns. A guy of whom you'd say, "range loads only," or "no Plus-Ps" may be capable of muddling along, but can't handle confrontation. To say somebody's "Condition One" should be a high compliment, referring to their attitude and alertness as well as their ordnance. One who wanders around in Colonel Cooper's "Condition White" is a clueless cretin. An aging gentleman said to be "worn shiny, 10 percent blue, but the lockwork's crisp!" may be old, but still fully functional — and experienced. What kinda guy rates the phrase, "loose groups"?

Want to help? Send your suggestions to idio4gunners@yahoo.com. I'll gnarfle 'em into order, and try not to malf or have a RUD. Connor OUT.

50 STATES, 50 GUNS:
Let's Get Rollin'!

J<small>ULY</small>/A<small>UGUST</small> 2011

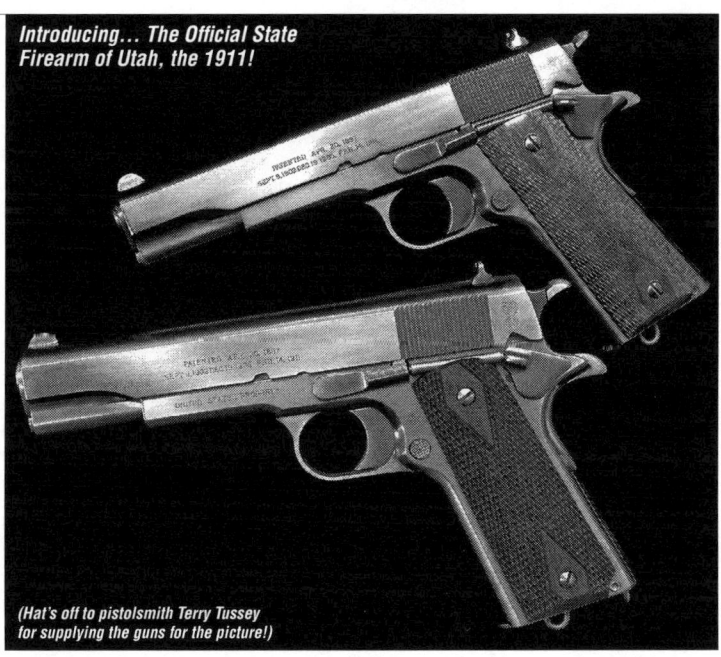

Introducing... The Official State Firearm of Utah, the 1911!

(Hat's off to pistolsmith Terry Tussey for supplying the guns for the picture!)

As I scribble this, Utah bill HB219 sits on Governor Gary Herbert's desk waiting for his signature. Given Hizzoner's past position on firearm issues and the overwhelming support this measure received in the state House and Senate, it seems certain he'll sign it into law within days (They did. Editor). When he does, Utah will become the first and only state with an official State Firearm: John Moses Browning's M1911 pistol. Perhaps you've heard of it? Yup; a State Firearm! How cool is that? Let's say it again and let it sink in: The first and only state with an official State Firearm! This is what I call "a good start."

Years ago there was a significant effort to adopt the flintlock Pennsylvania Long Rifle as that state's official firearm. While it enjoyed popular support state-wide, the idea was apparently strangled in its crib by the usual entrenched political powers of Philadelphia. A handful of similar acts in other states were also shrieked down by hordes of hoplophobic harpies. Maybe this "first" could only have happened in Utah, but now, the time might be right to carry the theme across the country.

Utah is overall and inarguably a gun-friendly state, despite the effects of the Yuppie Invasion of the '80s. The Lib-Leftie influence is mostly limited to the white wine & stinky cheese centers of Salt Lake City and a few smaller trustafarian* strongholds. It's also the birthplace and family home of John Moses Browning, native son of Ogden, and the immensely profitable, jobs-creating corporate home of the global business bearing his name.

This made it awfully tough — and politically dangerous — for Utah's gun-haters to vilify the man or his legacy. While HB219 was moving through the legislature, Utah celebrated John Moses Browning Day on January 24th, with hardly a squeak from the sidelines. Interesting, huh?

Thinkin' Tactical

Since designating a state symbol had nothin' to do with "More guns on the streets!" or expanding concealed-carry privileges, the opposition was deprived of most of their arsenal of irrational scare-tactic rhetoric. As it turned out, all it really gave 'em was an opportunity to look petty, juvenile and silly. On the one hand, they couldn't argue that "It's only a meaningless symbol, like the Dutch Oven being Utah's official cookin' pot, so why pass it?" To do that, they would alienate fans of all 26 state symbols. On the other, they couldn't generate any interest for a claim that "This spells the end of civilization!" The best they could come up with were whimpers and jibes, and the debate also flushed out some "stealth socialists" who had been trying to look "gun-neutral."

One expressed dismay because usually, "These designations come to us from elementary schoolchildren." So adults can't name a state symbol? Arguing that "Guns are only for killing!" didn't fly either, as the grownups asked, "So our police only need guns to oppress and kill innocent people? Our soldiers only need guns as tools of genocide, rape and plunder? Citizens shouldn't have guns for self-defense? Guns aren't lawful tools, freezer-fillers, peace-keepers?" These are debates we can win, folks!

One state senator tried the sniggering-sophisticated approach, asking why not emblazon a gun on the state flag, or arm the bees on the flag? The grownups just looked at him like, "Are you nine years old or what?" I think he had to rack that one up in the "lost credibility" column.

All of this was watched closely by elected representatives in other states, and the question is not IF, but WHEN similar bills start poppin' up. And that's only right. Our founding fathers' most unanimous faith was that self-defense and the right to bear arms for that purpose are God-given; universal human rights which no just government should infringe. And don't think of official state guns as "just a symbol," but as a symbol — a symbol of the fundamental difference between citizens — and subjects.

The most successful waves of state laws of the past decade have been "Castle Doctrine" acts, Right to Self-Defense laws, and concealed-carry legislation. That's a tide to ride, friends.

One Down, 49 to Go

Why shouldn't every state have an official firearm? What should it be? Which state has the best claim on the Peacemaker? The legendary Winchester '94? The Colt Walker Dragoon? The Merwin Hulbert First Model Army Revolver? The iconic Springfield '03? The .36 Navy 1858 Remington New Model? Which gun best fits Alaska, Alabama, Maryland or Missouri?

Here's your chance to help. Go to www.americanhandgunner.com and click on the link on the home page saying "Vote for your state gun!" It'll link to my Guncrank column. There, you can leave a comment. Keep it to 50 words or less, but tell us your state, which gun you vote for and why it fits your state. We'll keep a running tally so you'll be able to see the results. When we have a couple bushels of 'em, we'll get them to the right "State" people. Sorry, but we don't have staff to receive snail-mail, FAXes, smoke signals, semaphore or heliograph. Now let's get rollin'! Connor OUT.

SHRAP & FRAGS
*You Asked For It

SEPTEMBER/OCTOBER 2011

Hot, sweaty, stumbling, dusty. Ticked off over bein' muzzle-swept by morons all day. Pour BIG adult beverage. Spill it. Pour another. Drink it so's it doesn't spill. What's in this folder? Letters from readers, askin' "What's your take on fill-in-the-blank?" Wrong time, wrong mood, though that's improving; see "beverage," above. Okay, you asked for it.

The China Problem: What's the problem? Are we runnin' low on plastic clothes hangers an' cheap folding lawn chairs? Oh; that other "China problem." I hear all this stuff about how buying Chinese products is good because they "increasingly see us as valued trading partners" and it makes 'em more like us (versus "like us more"). And I think, oh, yeah; like, if you invite a 6-foot crocodile into your bathtub and you throw roast chickens, beef briskets and bucks at it until it's 26 feet long with jaws the size of Billy's bass boat. Then of course, he's gonna see you as a "valued trading partner" and won't eat you. Yeah.

UN Headquarters, New York: The world's most dazzling collection of museum-quality football bats — all wrapped in silk suits

Bought a microwave, TV or alarm clock lately? I wouldn't mind the flood of gizmos and widgets so much if they added a line to that "Made in China" tag saying, "Thank you for your money. We buy strategic weapons, T-Bills and American politicians with it." If I ever find a bag of Fritos with that tag on it, somebody else gets muzzle-swept.

We still make the best guns and ammunition in the world though, and lots of 'em, thank God. That may save our bacon when China decides to come after us individually to collect that $1.2-billion per person debt because our government's broke. At that point, some ChiCom general might pause and think, "Geez, they got a lotta guns and know how to use 'em!" Then he turns to a buncha PLA privates and says, "Okay, who wants to go first: you, Yu, or you, Woo? No takers? I gotta put a pistol to your heads?" And a PFC in the first rank thinks, "I got a better chance of him missing me at 6" than one of those Yankee IDPA handgunners missin' me at 50 yards! I've seen 'em on YouTube!" And the invasion fizzles …

Frauds, Fads & Football Bats

The United Nations: People just don't understand the UN. It only exists because the Mafia has strict membership rules. Thugs who couldn't meet the mob's racial and ethnic requirements wanted to have their own club, 5-star resort, and tons of other people's money too. Hence, the United Nations. Say, why doesn't the ACLU sue the Mafia over employment discrimination? Because the mob won't pay to be harassed — we do, and take it meekly. The Mafia busts kneecaps. How long could the UN last without American money? I don't know, but I'd like to find out. The UN is as useful as a huge display of expensive, highly polished football bats.

Everybody Hates Us: Wrong. Lotsa' people love us. Some hate us because basically, they want all the comforts, security and assets of a free, rich, enterprising society without the work, freedom and enterprise required to create it. Like modern American largesse but with seventh-century rules, like keeping your women in coal sacks, being able to order the wife you bought to drown herself in the bathtub, and selling your surplus offspring for cash or khat. Some hate us only because they've been taught to, whether in a Wahabi madrassa, Harvard Law, a mud hut or an Ivy League journalism school; places where people are taught what to think, not how to think.

Some will never forget we've defeated them. Others won't forgive us for liberating them. And a certain percentage of the world's humanoids are just natural-born miserable, gut-eatin' haters, as smart, sane and humane as ticks on a burnin' dog. Simple question about America: How many want in, and how many want out? America and Americans are widely liked, respected and admired. Wonder why you don't hear about that? Re-read all after: "Wrong."

Moron Empire

The Sheep from Goats Conundrum: One reader sees "conservative liberals, whacko conservatives, rich trash, poor heroes," etc., and wonders how to separate the sheep from the goats. Yeah; it's like sortin' a sack fulla' ferrets blindfolded. You can't categorize folks by skin, clothes, income and least of all by what they say. You gotta sort 'em by their core dynamics; what moves 'em. For some, it's Duty, Honor and Country. For others it's Rights, Liberty and Integrity. For the rest, it's Frauds, Fads and Fetishes. Think about it, and it ain't so hard.

Dang! Outta space, and didn't cover Borders or Anchor Babies … but I feel better!

In closing, remember, none of the above problems could exist without the passive or active support of a certain kinda people. The Mongol Empire, history's greatest, once spread from China and India to Moscow and the Hungarian plains. Now there's a much bigger one. Its subjects are everywhere, world-wide. It's the Moron Empire. When they come to recruit you, just tell 'em "Go away, or somebody's gonna get muzzle-swept …" Connor OUT.

ON BEIN' THANKFUL

NOVEMBER/DECEMBER 2011

Recently, I ran into a guy I hadn't seen in five years. He ogled at my new scars (I call 'em epidermal ornamentation) and my jaunty stance of leanin' on my lunar-lander walker-cane. He then mumbled some crap amounting to, "Oh, poor you! Aw, that's awful! How horrible for you!"

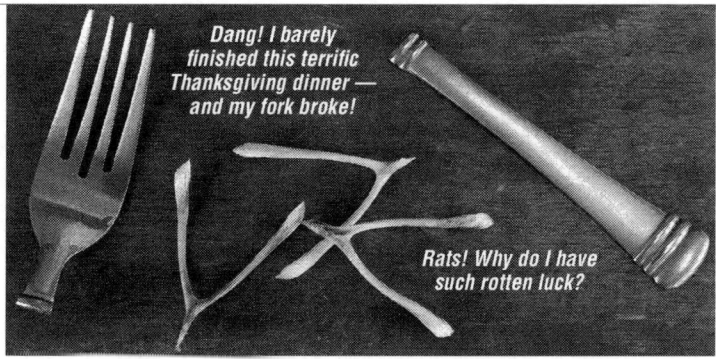

Dang! I barely finished this terrific Thanksgiving dinner — and my fork broke!

Rats! Why do I have such rotten luck?

You know the type. His 5-star dinner is ruined because Chez Henri's is outta' cherry-amaretto-walnut ice cream for dessert. And he's one of those who thinks anybody who's hit a coupla' potholes on the road of life must, be crushed, miserable and moanin' because he dang sure would be. Hey, I didn't say he's a friend; just some guy.

He's also the sort who's nonplussed when a guy like me smiles and says, "Nah; I'm doin' great, and man, am I thankful! I'd count my blessings, but I can't count that high."

Here's a kinda' Connor CAT-scan slice: Sometimes when the Memsaab Helena is putting donkey-liniment on my back and feelin' all those lumps, squiggles an' knots which were not "original issue," I can feel her hands tremble; chokin' up; sometimes I feel the tears pattering. Then she'll squeeze me gently and whisper, "Oh, thank God, John … Just thank God." I know what she's thankful for, and it ain't the scars and broken bits.

And a warm sirocco of gratitude blows over me; faithful friends, a loving wife, great kids; worthwhile work and the feeling that I can still make my own way and contribute to the good; earning the food I eat and the air I breathe. Yeah, I've got tons to be thankful for, and no regrets.

Pass the turkey and a big slice a' THANKS, please …

Less Thankin'

Speaking of which, seems like Thanksgiving is on the decline. Lots of folks take the holiday, but I see less and less of the actual giving-of-thanks. This goes along with the hordes of people living in conditions undreamed of by two-thirds the world, but still feeling short-changed somehow, and deserving a chunk of others' possessions. Maybe too many Americans* have had it so well for so long, they can't be thankful anymore?

Long ago, an old warrior advised me that every time I wake up, before I open my eyes, bring my hands up to head level and then extend my arms out as far as I can reach. "If you don't feel the inside of a coffin or body bag," he said, "You win!"

Not impressed? About 1.5 million people per week lose the life lottery. Feel better now? — Me too, every day. So far, even though human mortality is still holding at 100 percent (death has great success stats), my "Alive at Five, Every Day Plan" is working!

A while back, I had to call for roadside assistance when a tire ran flat. The young man who responded moved very smoothly for having two prosthetic legs below the knees. An Army vet, he lost 'em in an IED blast. He admired my camo, multi-toe cane; I admired his techno-cool Terminator feet, and we both grinned like monkeys.

"I'm so-o-o lucky!" he told me. "They were gonna' have to take my left leg at the hip, but the docs saved it, and these work great! I'm going to get Cheetah flex-feet and be running again!" His eyes shone as he laughed, "Man, I really lucked out!"

Seessee-Bwois

* Americans: More accurately perhaps, "the current residents of a geopolitical entity; the formerly-United States of America."

Throughout my life of lumps, every time I might have felt a twinge of self-pity, I found myself in the company of people a lot worse off than I, who faced their conditions with courage and humor. Those who came the closest to winkin'-out like burnt stars had the best aphorisms to express their attitudes: "Still on the sunshine side of the grass! Woohoo!" and "Ain't nobody pattin' me on the face with a shovel today, dude!"

My old comrade, G.K. Shirpa, has sorta' made it his crusade to point out — gently if possible, forcefully if not — why complaining, dejected, demoralized soldiers have nothin' to mutter about. He's been fighting communists and other vermin since he was a boy in the mid 1940s. He'll see some whole, healthy pup cryin' in his beer, grab him by the stackin' swivel, haul him upright and then poke him in the chest a coupla' times — hard, with a steely finger.

"You know what ees NOT thees?" he demands. "Eez not Russia-soldier bayonet!" He then opens his shirt and searches the maze of scars until he finds the one left by a Soviet blade. "Hyew see dees, whining one? Hyew gotz notting for to cry! You want cry? I geev yew thees!" When Shirpa's done, if his subject ain't properly thankful, at least he won't dare to show it ... I taught him the phrase "sissy boy," which comes out particularly scathing and funny as heck: "Seessee-bwoi!"

Thanksgiving is coming. I know I can count on you folks to remind the whiners and seessee-bwois it ain't about holiday; it's about giving thanks for your breath, your heartbeat, for another shot at feeling the sun on your face. And if some mutt grumbles and throws his sucker in the dirt, feel free to poke him — hard! — And demand: "You know what eez NOT thees?" Connor OUT.

NIGEL'S TAKE:
Chalk & Cheese

JANUARY/FEBRUARY 2012

God bless my ol' buddy Nigel. Now retired from long service with a Guards Regiment and then SAS, each time he calls I learn, laugh, wonder and ponder. He's one of those guys who just knows, 24/7/365, what time it is in Karachi, Kent or Kabul; the phase of the moon and when it will rise in Kinshasa, Krasnoyarsk, or Kansas City; what spots on the globe are not covered by surveillance satellites at that moment, and a thousand other esoteric points. Long ago when his now-white moustache was ginger-brown, he first taught me the difference between a haboob and a shamal, and thankfully, he's still teachin' me stuff.

He was explaining the linkage between the growth of Britain's overarching, individual-oppressing "Nanny State" and the decline of Britons' rights to self-defense, to keep and bear arms, to self-determination; how one could not rise without the fall of the other, and why we — "you Yanks" — are fighting the right battle with the wrong weapons — and using the wrong tactics on the wrong opponents.

"For example," he said, "You tend to place all anti-gun people in one category, failing to differentiate between the irredeemable soldats and the comparatively mild and malleable masses that they sway. They are completely and utterly different, and must be dealt with differently." "How different?" I asked.

"Oh, chalk and cheese, Johnny-me-lad, chalk and cheese!"*

There was a pause. I heard a low Hmm … hmm … yas, quite so, yasss … and I knew Nigel was pokin' something with his pipe and cogitating.

"Johnny-o," he intoned, "They are chalk and cheese, lad!" Over the next hour and a coupla' pints, here's what we worked out.

"Know thy enemy" — and the difference between chalk and cheese ...

Chalk & Cheese Primer

The anti-gun soldats, the chalk, are the hardcore activists, organizers, propagandists and solicitors of the movement. Motivated by either statist political ideology or craven hoplophobia and a fervent desire for a utopian gunless society, they are intense, dedicated and contemptuously dismissive of any opposing view. Omnipresent in political venues, they are rarely the ones who speak. Instead, they recruit, prime, prompt and urge various cheeses to speak.

Chalk is smooth and clean in appearance. It comes in boxes, in tightly regimented formidable little ranks, and though deployed as individuals, their actions are almost identical. They are essentially compressed dust, but they have been through a process, which polishes and hardens their surface. They have pretensions to high education, but in fact, all they can do is scrawl the rote material of their manipulators, often the same thing thousands of times; simple statements for simple minds, empowered by sheer repetition. They also have pretensions to art, but it is really merely ideologically infused graffiti; bumper-sticker visuals.

Their exterior is lily-white, as is, they claim, their motives. They show "diversity" by association with rainbow-hued chalks and soft pastels, which they claim to honor as "fraternal brothers and sisters," but secretly, they hold the colors in contempt; just "silly but useful tools."

Chalk can sound very businesslike — or screeching; a matter of how it is wielded. The message is the same.

> ** In America, we say "as different as apples and oranges." For Brits, it's "chalk and cheese."**

The cheese — the people — is like a big, moist ball of mozzarella. Soft and resilient, the density and texture varies, but good mozzarella has no intrinsic hard lumps. It's easily influenced by minimal changes in temperature and pressure; it can be gouged and pounded and chunks cut out, but with time and firm, gentle shaping, it tends to resume its natural form. If rolled in filth and debris, it can become mottled and ugly, but with thorough rinsing it cleans up nicely. For good or ill, cheese has a short memory.

Under prolonged harsh conditions cheese can harden on the surface, go moldy, sour and unpalatable; but with reasonable care the only way a good cheese becomes bitter and poisonous is through injection by outside influences; it is not in the nature of cheese to be so.

A good cheese is, in brief, naturally wholesome and flexible. It may not be to your taste, and at times may be unappealing. Cheese simply is what it is, not what you might wish it to be.

Protect The Cheese

"First, Johnny-o," quoth Nigel, "Realize the anti-gun campaign is a splinter in a stouter bludgeon. The real war is waged by statists against individual liberties; disarming individuals is but an aspect of it. We Britons would not have lost our arms had we not first lost our individual rights, most notably the right to self-defense. Of what avail are your arms without it?"

"One cannot reason with chalk, Johnny-o," Nigel said, "Nor change its nature. To attempt it is wasted effort. One can only try to keep it in its box, and erase the boards as you can."

"Among pro-gun people, yes, talk about guns. But you will never win over the cheese by talking about guns, but rather, by talking about the cheese's right to be cheese; protecting the cheese's rights."

It's an election year, folks. Know your chalk from your cheese. Box the chalk, and gently, gently, massage and protect the cheese. Connor OUT

TRAINING FROM YOUR SOFA:
The Next Best Thing To Bein' There!

MARCH/APRIL 2012

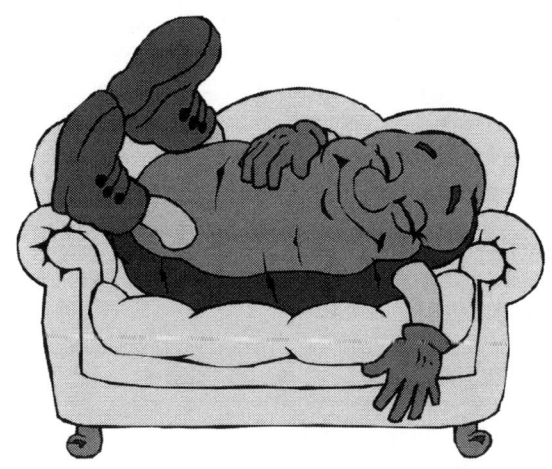

I've never met Clint Smith in person. I've read a lot of his writing, but never shaken his hand. That said, I've spent several hours of informative, personal 1-on-1 time with him, reaping the benefits of his knowledge on subjects from defensive use of the revolver to fighting from and around a vehicle. We haven't had dialogues — it's been Clint talkin' and me listening — but that's okay, because I can listen to myself anytime! It's my dime, so I want to listen to him!

I'm not a gunsmith. Hey, I'm not even a decent gun mechanic! But you name the gun, and I can get a master gunsmith to patiently guide me through the process of stripping it right down to the frame, answering all my questions about how the plunger prods this pin and what the heck this widget whacks.

Paul Howe is an ex-cop and 20-year Army veteran, with ten of those years in Special Operations as a tactical team leader and senior instructor. I like his training style and content, but it's tough to get down to Nacogdoches, Texas for a session at his Combat Shooting and Tactics (CSAT) facility. No worries though, I've got the best of his expertise captured on some little round discs, and more available online. And I know he'll pardon me if I also spend time with Bill Rogers, the master of reactive pistol shooting, and the hard-core training team of Chris Costa and Travis Haley, a pair of real high-speed low-drag guys, if you'll forgive the term.

Veni, Vidi, Video-Vici!

Time away from work and the price of travel — not to mention course fees and ammo costs — may prohibit you from attendance at a premier training establishment, but video's the next best thing to being there. Too, you're not restricted by the tempo of a large group, and you can replay the material any time you like. So, shooters, who's got what?

Go to www.americanhandgunner.com/store, click on the DVDs, and check out Clint and Heidi's latest offerings on home defense, the urban rifle and a whole lot more. Defend Yourself With The Gun At Hand is classic Clint stuff to use what you already have effectively rather than trying to buy your way into effectiveness. And Concealed

Carry For Ladies gives you the best of this husband/wife team on distaff defense. Both are 2-disc sets priced at $49.95 and $29.95 respectively. Their style? They're teaching friends, and that includes us.

AGI, the American Gunsmithing Institute, is best known for their long, thorough courses for working gunsmiths, but you really need to scan their Armorer's Series videos, because they're made for us non-gunsmith types. Most of the courses run 90 minutes to 2 hours and cost $39.95. They cover history and background as well as function, and provide complete disassembly and reassembly instructions. Video really beats books when you can actually see the moving interaction of parts, like the lockwork of a S&W revolver, and just how much pressure a master 'smith applies to a given maneuver.

It could be well worth the cost of picking up an old Makarov and buying the video just for the value of all you'll learn — and the confidence gained — in the process of strippin' it down to the last pin and putting it back together!

Bloodless Battles & Bloody Drills

Most trainers push their students to achieve their best. In The Art of the Dynamic Handgun from Magpul Dynamics, Travis Haley and Chris Costa push 'em to their failure points — repeatedly — and then show them how to adapt and overcome, against all odds. Watching them train, I'm reminded of the old saying about the Roman Legion: "Their drills are bloodless battles and their battles are bloody drills."

The Magpul mantra is "reality, consistency and efficiency," and the emphasis is on deliberate, drilled movements reduced to "running on autopilot" while responding to the sudden intrusion of Murphy's Law instantly and decisively. The 4-disc, 7-hour set covers basics to way beyond, and it's well worth the $49.95 price.

Panteao Productions has put together a unique training outfit. They have recruited a big and growing array of well-known shooters and trainers like Lewis Awerbuck, Jessie Harrison, Mark Redl, Massad Ayoob and Paul Howe, and professionally recorded them at their best.

Anybody can buy the videodisc sets online at $49.99 each — with discounts for multiple purchases — but I think the best deals are Panteao's monthly and yearly memberships. As a subscriber you can stream any and all of their videos online, 24/7/365, as often as you like. That means you'll also have unlimited access to all new productions as they're finished, plus streaming short "Pro Tips" from all the experts. If you've gotta have discs in your mitts, you can then select your favorites and buy 'em at a discount. What a deal, huh?

Get a Blade-Tech training barrel, or some inert rounds. Seize the remote control. Warm up your thumbs, and fall in for training! Connor OUT

SANDBAGGIN' CANDIDATES:
Just A Coupla' Questions And Comments

MAY/JUNE 2012

Okay, candidate, stand in the bucket. Grab the handle. Now lift yourself.

The elections are coming, and I can't get close enough to candidates for federal office to have little chats with 'em. They see me coming and scatter. I think it's the steam whistlin' outta my ears, or the flames shootin' from my eyeballs. Maybe you can sneak up on 'em for me?

Suggested Questions

Do you agree the Second Amendment right to keep and bear arms is an individual right; that it applies to individual free citizens? This is a Yes or No question. Don't spin off sophistry about how you've always supported American sportsmen, how plunkin' ducks and dropping deer is "an American heritage," okay? Yes or no? If yes, we want that in writing, now. If no, we're done here — and so are you.

Are you familiar with the Latin phrase "Panem et Circenses" and the history behind it? If you don't, you're not qualified for public office. It worked for a while in Rome, but didn't end well.

Have you ever met an American military veteran who volunteered to serve, sacrifice and possibly die to preserve Socialism? One who went into battle inspired by the words of Marx, Lenin, Stalin? I haven't.

Do you understand that two dollars is more than one dollar? That's a good start! Now, if we entrust you with one of our dollars, is it okay for you to spend it all on cupcakes for yourself and your pals, and bill us for four more dollars? Think hard, 'cause this is a Pass/Fail question.

Can you name four ways the federal bureaucracy is different from cancer? Three? Two? One? No, saying "Government doesn't intend to kill you" isn't valid; neither does cancer.

Would you support a "Nancy Pelosi Outrageous Arrogance Law"? It would say that any politician who stands next to a 20-pound stack of legislation, grins like a kabuki witch and says, "We have to pass it so you can see what's in it," gets a savage beating and thrown out of office — through the window. The closed window.

Talking Points

The current buzz phrase is "redistribution of wealth," like it's something new. It's not. It's been goin' on since the imposition of income tax in 1913, and furiously since the so-called "War on Poverty" kicked off. And don't call it wealth anymore, because most of us getting redistributed don't have wealth. We just have some earnings left. Say, "we want to redistribute what's left of your earnings," and see how far you get with that. That's called honesty. Try it.

We now have second and third-generation career welfare parasites; those who have never worked; just lived on the public dole. If you won't end it, how 'bout a generation limit on it? Computerized public birth and welfare records can enable that. Like, you get three consecutive generations of freeloaders, then we pull the plug on trough-swilling and tell their offspring, "Sorry, you're gonna' have to get off your butts and work for a living." It would be a start, and it would promote some shared experiences. Shared experiences create consensus. Think about it.

Almost half (47 percent) of US households pay NO income tax at all. Virtually none of those are "the rich." A small percentage is truly impoverished. Many are "career unemployed." There is a psychological and philosophical value in everybody paying something in income taxes, even if it's $10, even if it's paid out of our money, which you gave to them. Paying something gives them a dog in the fight.

Neither mass deportations nor amnesty programs will ever solve the illegal immigration problem until and unless our borders are secured. If you send 'em south, they flow back. If you legalize 'em, more come. If you secure the borders, then you can hash out the problem. We are — or were — a sovereign state. We should act like one.

Warnings: Listen Up!

If you've got the Race Card in your pocket, you can take that sucker out and burn it right now. The overwhelming majority of us — black, white, brown, whatever — don't give a damn what anybody's skin color is, and we're sick of being accused of racism — often, by racists. Stupid, vicious and greedy are colorless, and that's what we're against. You play that race card on us and we might burn it for you — while it's still in your pocket.

Get a bucket with two handles on it. Keep it in your office. Every time you think a new tax or higher taxes will help create prosperity, stand in the bucket, grab the handles and try to lift yourself off the deck. Winston Churchill explained the physics a long time ago. Look it up, and learn something.

Thanks for your help, guys. Politicians are awful slippery critters, and I'd recommend you grab 'em by the ear, but ... I guess I pinched 'em too hard. The screamin' is somethin' awful. Connor OUT.

———◆———

(Editor's Note: Maybe you outta' copy this and keep it in your wallet. Might come in handy if you find yourself close to one of these politician-animals some day. RH)

ASSUME THIS, NOT THAT
If you want to live

JULY/AUGUST 2012

It's always been a quiet street, so we can assume ... what?

The brief: 100-year-old maples form unbroken arches of emerald leaves, shading streets of well-tended craftsman-built homes; a peaceful neighborhood in a very low-crime community. Doors are often unlocked, because who stops by except neighbors and friends? Yes, such places still exist, and good friends of ours, an attractive single mom and her pretty teenage daughter live there. But one recent night a "visitor" to the area, a whacked-out, drugged-up psychopath, crept into a nearby home at random and committed a horrific assault, stabbing one victim until the blade of his cheap knife bent into uselessness. It was an aberration; the neighbors slipped back into somnolence. Not the girls. For them it was a reminder of another place, another time.

They knew this was a statistical anomaly — but they also knew those are the events you prepare for; those rare and dangerous anomalies. Already trained and armed with handguns, they added a 12-gauge pump to their battery and requested a refresher on home defense considerations. Afterward, they picked out some points they had not heard or read before and asked me to write about them. And so ...

Go Ahead & Assume

All your life you've been told not to assume — but there are some assumptions you must make, because the consequence of error is grave. The "qualifier" for assumptions should be, "If you want to live, you assume this, not that." The first is anyone who enters your occupied home at night chooses to, knowing you're inside, and it's not just about opportunistic theft.

Opportunist burglars bent only on theft have no desire to confront residents. They're all about the loot and getting away clean. They typically commit daytime burglaries

after assuring themselves nobody's home. A tiny, miniscule percentage of burglars get a thrill out of creeping undetected through an occupied home while victims sleep, stealing and leaving. If a goblin enters your home at night, the human prey is as much a part of the feast as your possessions. What's your most survivable assumption?

The second is any sound or movement which alerts you, especially if it wakes you, must be investigated, even if it's not repeated. Typically, people wait for sound or movement to be repeated, or, sound-after-movement or movement-after-sound, before they admit the possibility of threat.

Whether they're military sentries or peaceable civilians, people want — and have a psychological need — to dismiss possible threats; to believe singular sounds and movements, not repeated, are phenomena which can be safely ignored. "First-world" people do this routinely, and often enough, they don't suffer for it, but is that a sound assumption? So-called "primitives" and non-industrialized people typically do not assume so. They know something was responsible for activating their spider-sense, and it can only be ignored at great peril.

There's a certain symphony of sounds which you ordinarily sleep through; the routine creaks and groans of structural response to temperature changes, the gurgle of water in the pipes, the subdued hum of routine traffic. Your senses become inured to them, and they don't wake you. But over millennia your survival subconscious has been honed to respond to alien noises, the ones which might signal the presence of danger. They not only wake you, but may give you an instant shot of adrenaline to prepare you for fight-or-flight.

If you're awakened, your socially-conditioned reflex is to turn on a light, the brighter the better, to soothe your conditioned reflexes. Don't. Your vision is adjusted to low light, so use it; protect it. Only use light as a weapon and a search-tool projected in front of you.

More Assumptions

If you see one intruder, do you assume there's only one? If you don't see a weapon in his hands, do you assume he's unarmed? If you see a weapon in his hand, should you assume that's the only one he has? The only safe assumptions you can make are that this person is dangerous; the presence of a weapon only makes them more dangerous, and an unseen weapon can be more dangerous than one you see.

You've got him at gunpoint, and he cajoles, he begs, he pleads, he swears to leave peacefully if you'll just let him go. What can you assume? That his mouth is moving, possibly to alert unseen companions; that he's still the goblin who entered with evil, violent intent. Do you assume he would show you the same mercy he's begging for, if he now got the drop on you?

You've shot him and he's down. Does that mean he's finished? If he's not moving, do you assume he can't move — suddenly and violently? If he's silent, is it because he's silenced, or because he's listening?

Keep the gun on him until police arrive and are present. Recently an older lady in California had to shoot an intruder while she was literally on the phone with a police dispatcher. The goblin wasn't moving. When sirens became audible — still some distance away — the dispatcher told the lady to put down her gun. When can you assume you're safe? Think about it. Connor OUT.

HOME, HOME ON THE RANGE:
Not so much sometimes ...

September/October 2012

The message from His Illuminated Immenseness Roy-Boy was terse as a curse: "Drive 322 miles to [BigUgly] City*. Pick up [XXX] pistol** at FancyPantz Sporting Club & Range***. Shoot, test, group, chrono loads, make copious notes, and ship pistol FedEx next morning, OYT." "OYT" is his shorthand for "Or You're Toast." Thanks, Roy.

I'd never been to the FPSC&R before; not my kinda range. The road in was paved n' striped! Broad paths of machine-made burgundy pea-gravel were flanked by double rows of rocks, the inner row painted white, and the outer row battleship gray — and lacquered! A glass control tower sat atop the main rangehouse, manned by some clean-shaven dude with aviator shades, a headset and microphone, and enormous binoculars. Somewhere close, I thought, there's a ring-knockin' Annapolis grad runnin' this show.

Soft muzak, like a chamber orchestra on Quaaludes playin' the Rolling Stones' "Satisfaction" wafted from hidden speakers. A mellow baritone cut in with "Brass boy to Section C-12!" Instantly this ancient dude who looked like Gabby Hayes wearing Walter Brennan's castoff bib overalls appeared and ran a cordless vacuum "brass sucker" down the spotless shooting line. He had hair like fried steel wool and eyebrows like electrocuted mice. Goggling my battered boots and bristly jaw with his one good eye, he gave me a big 5-toothed grin.

"Connor, ain'tcha? Look like yer pitcher in Handgunner. M'name's Moss." He vanished through a Hobbit-door, leaving a scent of Hoppe's Number 9, fried bologna and swamp-butt. I smiled, and then noticed the shooters had wrinkled their noses in distaste.

Like Another Dimension

I'd never seen so many fresh, vibrantly colored polo shirts outside of a Land's End window display. Two guys wore "Mitt Romney jeans"; tailored, pre-faded, dry cleaned and pressed. The others wore crisp slacks. These guys had hairstyles, not haircuts.

They would have names like J. Chauncey Biddlesworth IV and Hollings H. Hampton, Senior. Nothin' against those boys, mind you, but I couldn't at that instant ever remember having a good time amongst so many un-faded shirts. I dropped my "guest pass," a forged bronze disc with the club seal on it, into the right front pocket of my bush shorts and it fell through the hole — one of the holes — clangin' like a manhole cover on the smooth, epoxied concrete deck. I felt eyes on me and envisioned wrinkled patrician noses. Their electronic muffs musta been turned up. Sorry, Chauncey, je regrette, Hollings.

The shooting counters were smooth as pool tables. Chairs were bright tubular steel with padded seats. There were acoustic baffles overhead, and not a single hole in 'em. Electric target holders glided back and forth over thick, manicured green grass. It was 68 degrees F, blue sky with a polite breeze, and the whole thing put me completely off my game. I couldn't hit squat nor shoot for beans. It was just so … wrong.

Rat Canyon Remembrance

I missed the Rat Canyon Range; the dancing dust devils tearing away targets and flingin' 'em like a hurricane hitting a loaded clothesline; the gaping knotholes knocked out of the warped gray planks of the firing line, perfect for stickin' revolver barrels in to safely park your Roscoe; the overhead so shot fulla holes that when it rained and you were under it, it was raining there too, the only difference being that drizzle was filthy, fulla grit and desiccated bug corpses, so you stood out in the clean rain until the shower passed.

I missed the P.A. system, which was just ol' Rangemaster Robbie's Navy-trained "Chief Bosun's voice," which can rattle your fillings when he lovingly calls out, "Git that muzzle downrange or I'll shoot ya myself, meathead!" or "Stop shootin' an' pull up yer pants, Cooter, I can see yer plumber's crack from here! Yer gonna catch hot brass in it!"

I missed the Rat Canyon range-rats and how they got their range-names****, like "Boot" and "Moon" and "Fiddlesticks"; why there's a sun-bleached sagging left-foot Tony Lama boot hangin' from an overhead beam, what's in it, and why the right one's interred out beyond the 25-yard line.

I felt just awful. Everything was so "right," it was all wrong. Then a suddenly chill wind whipped my Infidel T-shirt. From the southwest, billows of purple-black clouds with bright-flashing bellies hurtled toward us. Moss materialized at my side, a single-action Army stickin' outta one pocket and a 1911 butt outta the other. The parking lot emptied in 60 seconds. Last man out was Aviator-shades, who barked "Lock up, Moss!" and jumped in a gray Mercedes.

"'Fraid of gittin' their fancy cars sandblasted," Moss spat, then smiled. "Wanta do some shootin'? Gonna git fierce quick, but who cares? After, I could fry up some SPAM, heat up some beans, n' be honored t' share a whiskey with ya. Got biscuits too." His bushy eyebrows waggled in the wind, and sand from the un-manicured puckerbrush flats pelted us. We both grinned like monkeys. My assignment got done. Life is good. Connor OUT

---

*Can't name the city. If you live there, my condolences. **Can't name the pistol. You'll read about it soon. ***Can't name the club. They threatened to sue. ****Can't tell ya, no space — maybe next issue.

NO BRASS GONGS, NO GOLD & GLORY
... but he didn't let anybody down.

NOVEMBER/DECEMBER 2012

Each year on Veterans Day we are regaled with tales of heroes — typically, those awarded our nation's highest decorations — and indeed we should and must honor their sacrifices and celebrate their acts of gallantry. But between those draped with honor in public ceremonies and the virtually anonymous souls entombed under government-issued grave markers, there exist legions of those who silently serve unheralded and unknown. This Veteran's Day I'll lift a cold one to Matt Garst, once unknown, now little known, still shouldering his rifle daily and doing his best not to let anybody down.

I first wrote about Matt in the March 2011 issue of GUNS Magazine in my Odd Angry Shot column, a piece called "The Two Americas."* I had found a brief blurb about him in Leatherneck Magazine, and contrasted him with two of our society's trendy, metro-fashionable types, apparently devoid of any real talent or accomplishment except being famous; famous because they're celebrities and celebrities because they're famous. It was easy to get info about those two. Web searches returned over 10 million hits, and each had their own Wikipedia pages. I had never heard of them before — and then wished I never had.

Does That Qualify For Flight Pay?

June 23, 2010, Helmand Province, Afghanistan: 23-year-old Corporal Matt Garst led his squad on patrol, scouting an abandoned compound. Two of his Marines had already walked a narrow trail beside a high wall, but as it turned out, they weren't heavy enough to set off a large IED planted there. Matt's a big muscular guy. At 6', 2" and weighing over 260 pounds including rifle, ammo and gear, he outweighed his men by 30 to 40 pounds. That was enough. The blast launched him and a yard of earth into low orbit.

Matt's troops were on the other side of that 10' wall when the deafening roar thundered. They looked up in horror and saw their corporal's flailing legs kicking out of the dirt column rocketing skyward. He was blown over ten feet vertical and

15' downrange. They ran around the wall fearing the worst. Matt was standing in the smoke still clutching his rifle, cursing as he batted off dirt — and highly ticked off.

"What the #### are you lookin' at?" he barked. "Get back on cordon!" He called in the incident on the radio, refused air evacuation, and led his squad four rocky miles back to their base.

"I wasn't going to let anybody else take my squad back after they'd been there for me," he told a Marine journalist. "That's my job." He grumbled as Corpsmen checked him out, reluctantly took an ordered day of rest, then picked up his rifle and got back into the fight.

There were lots of Ironman jokes, and "Did you qualify for flight pay?" also, "Gimme your armor — you don't need it." He shrugged 'em off, and except for his growing respect and reputation among his fellow grunts, drifted back into American obscurity. His final words on the incident were, "I'm just happy it wasn't any of my guys."

EOD later determined the 3-liter explosive was huge, but had been buried too deep and the earth compacted too hard. Lucky for Matt.

"I hadn't let anybody down."

Another year, another chapter. Matt later rotated stateside, was promoted to sergeant, spun up more Marines, and returned to Afghanistan. Late the night of Dec. 2, 2011, he led his squad and several ANA (Afghan National Army) troops on a gravel road beside a deep, swiftly flowing canal near Kuchiney Darvishan. It was believed Taliban had mined the road, and an Afghan soldier named Zaheed swept it with a metal detector. Suddenly a speeding truck rounded a bend, and Zaheed tried to wave it down, fearing it would hit a mine. The truck struck him, went out of control, and both splashed into the canal.

Sergeant Garst rapped out perimeter security orders to some, shouted, "Follow me!" to others, and leaped in. As the truck sank, Matt saw struggling people through the rear window. He dove deep, reaching into the truck, coming up with two women and an infant. Clutching all three to his chest, he flutter-kicked them to shore against the current, turned, dove back in and pulled out a drowning man. Other Marines got to Zaheed and saved him and several others.

Using his limited Pashto, Matt questioned the men and determined all the truck's occupants were alive and accounted for: two men, three women, two kids and an infant. Zaheed suffered a broken ankle and deep lacerations. Matt deployed more security, figuring the noise might attract Taliban, then bandaged Zaheed and fashioned him a splint from two antennas. Garst arranged transport both for Zaheed to a military medical facility, and home, for the shivering Afghan civilians. Can you guess what he did next? Yup. He formed up his troops and led them back to their patrol base, where he said, "Once we got the family out and on the shore, I felt good — like I hadn't let anybody down." No, you didn't, Matt. Semper Fi, Marine.

MERRY CHRISTMAS AND HAPPY NEW YEAR!

Now give yourself a break ... and a goal

JANUARY/FEBRUARY 2013

I've had to shoot at several public ranges lately, and what I've seen disturbs me. This is a general observation, applying to "defensive shooters," not target shooters, and there are exceptions, okay? But basically, I see this: Guys tryin' like the devil to wring target pistol performance out of defensive handguns; locked into textbook positions, squintin' and squeezin', breathing the classic huff in, half-breath out, but exaggerating it to the point of hypoxia; grippin' their pieces like iron until visible trembling sets in; making miniscule adjustments; finally poppin' that first shot followed inevitably by finger-fluttering of the support hand. You've seen that, right?

It's obvious they're not only over-thinking about the mechanics of what they're doing, but also about how it looks to others. They're thinking about position, grip, presentation, breathing and trigger control as separate segments rather than as an integrated, smoothly-executed process. They squint, shoot and mutter in self-disapproval.

Then if they haven't shot neat cloverleaves of touching holes, they're disappointed with their groups on target. If they're with friends, or just engaged with an adjacent shooter, there's shaking of heads and angrily or sadly grumbling, "I don't know what's wrong; I'm all over the paper" or "Not winning any trophies with this crap."

An awful lot of shooters are really good at mercilessly kickin' their own butts. As often as not, their groups look okay to me, though it seems they've put more agony than ecstasy into 'em. I think, "This guy could do much better if he'd just relax and give himself a BREAK, for Pete's sake!"

"Oh, boohoo" or "Yo! Woo-hoo!"?

Take a Break!

I think a lot of this stuff occurs for three reasons: First, they're trying to replicate the groups shot and published in magazine articles. Forget that. Those are done — and overdone — by people who do it for a living, to establish a handgun's inherent accuracy, that's all. If your Roscoe shoots service-straight, you're good to go. Ask yourself what's more important to you: Shooting teensy-tiny groups under ideal conditions on your best day, or launching effective "war-shots" when you have to?

Second, too many shooters suffer from "observer pressure": trying to look textbook-perfect to others. The only shooter you need to impress is the one shooting at you. On the range, you are The Shooter — onlookers are "range furniture." Forget 'em!

Third, they're having to concentrate so hard on each aspect of shooting — and comin' out herky-jerky and strained — because they're trying to practice under live-fire conditions on the range! Wrong time, wrong place, folks. Live fire on the range is where you express all the practice you've put into dry-fire drills. Dry-fire is where you perfect, smooth and seamlessly integrate position, grip, presentation, breathing, trigger control and tactical reloads, from slowest-smoothest to as fast as you can remain smooth and certain. Live fire is analogous to mid-term exams; dry-fire is the study you put in to be truly prepared for those exams.

Get yourself a Blade-Tech Training Barrel and lotsa inert rounds. Practice routinely for 15-20 minutes per session, tops. Wear the same clothes you wear to work, grocery shopping, stopping at the ATM, takin' your family out to dinner; all of 'em. Take every drill from the draw, because if you fumble that, your other skills may not save you — and you can't do that on most ranges. Step up, back or sideways to positions and draw smoothly, because life won't always let you get set and centered. Dry-fire standing crooked, half-crouched, squatting, on your knees, on yer butt, one-handed holding a sack a' possums, whatever; get smooth and then get jiggy!

Present and fire at 90 degrees, snap back to 145, pop two and swing back to 0 degrees, because "bastards have brothers, and scumbags come in squadrons." From the textbook, write your own book! And all that time, integrate motion, grip, breathing and trigger, so that when you do hit the range, your process is polished and you're ready to have some fun expressing! Call it "ballistic therapy," 'cause it's good for body and soul!

Hit the range when others don't, during rainstorms, high winds, snow and hammering heat. Don't overextend yourself, but get the experience and know how it affects your shooting. Shiver, swelter, shake — and shoot! Shoot in low light until they kick you out. And mix up your on-the-range drills so much you're never frustratedly repeating the same errors under pressure. That's not training; it's torture.

The Goodliest Goal

Here's your goal: Come next Christmas, you can grin next to a silhouette showing a group that'll win no gongs, but they're all in the breadbasket, and say to yourself, "Not so great? I can do it all day long, every day, any night, 24/7/365, in fair weather or foul, in whatever clothes I have on, from muzzle-to-belly to down-the-street; 2-handed or 1-handed with either hand. I can do it on my knees, on my butt, stoopin' or standin', at any angle. My reloads ain't like lightning, but they're sure and certain. My guns run hot an' straight, and I run 'em right. I'm good to go — and ready to rock." Connor OUT

ARTFULLY REVEALING THE BLINDINGLY OBVIOUS

MARCH/APRIL 2013

A month before national elections — with enormous implications for gun owners — and three before SHOT Show 2013 — what's a hack gunwriter to do? The ugliness will be over by the time you read this, but right now, I'd be guessing. So, it's magic tricks! But first, this story:

Long ago and far away in a tiny remote village, an entertainer, a magician of sorts, rolled in with his bullock-drawn cart, accompanied by an enormous oafish-looking assistant. The local kids were delighted and flocked to greet him — me too! After setting his "stage," the ancient wizard gracefully draped

WAIT!

IF YOU HIT A COOKIE WITH A HAMMER —

THE COOKIE CRUMBLES?

a crimson scarf over his docile bullock's massive horns and plopped a little yellow hanky on his assistant's bushy head. The bullock and the assistant froze stock-still. Stalking dramatically about, peeking and peering, the wizard challenged the kiddies to guess what was under those cloths. What could possibly be hidden there?

The older kids had seen the act before, and laughing, shushed the younger ones, telling them "Watch! Watch!" The wizard leaped up, yanked the scarf off the bullock and recoiled in shock: A bullock! Amazing! The bullock snorted and waved its horns. Then he crept up on his assistant, leaped in the air and plucked off the hanky. Shazam! A MAN! The wizard, astonished, fainted dead away as the oaf grinned and did a nimble dust-shuffling dance. The little kids got it and they all shrieked in glee.

His whole act was like that. His "find the pea" trick employed three tiny cups and a baseball-sized "pea," and he made his cart "disappear" behind an open rainbow-hued umbrella. The kiddies howled. What the old guy lacked in prestidigitation he made up in style and slapstick. No "magic;" he just artfully revealed the blindingly obvious. Let me give that a try, okay?

Bullock Under The Scarf

With sincere sympathy for the victims of the Aurora theater massacre, I must ask if anyone else noted this: Dozens of unsuspecting people gathered at midnight to see theatrically-costumed fictional characters portray intense gratuitous violence and imminent slaughter. They were then subjected to intense gratuitous violence and slaughter by a theatrically-costumed self-fictionalized character.

Could anyone have predicted this? Not with any certainty, no. But on the other hand, who would be shocked if, at the midnight debut of a new Friday the 13th movie, a hockey-masked psycho brandishing meathooks leaped from behind the curtains and clawed his way through the crowd? Anybody want to attend an L.A. midnight resurrection showing of The Texas Chainsaw Massacre in a "Gun-Free Zone" theater?

John Lott, author of "More Guns, Less Crime" notes seven theaters within 20 minutes' drive of killer James Holmes's apartment were showing The Dark Knight Rises the night of July 20th. Did Holmes pick the closest theater, the furthest, or the one with the largest audience? Nope. He selected the only one prohibiting guns, including licensed concealed carry. Coincidence? Duhh … Wait! You mean that big sign banning guns didn't stop Holmes? Shocking!

Now consider this: After the massacre, the management of one of those theaters changed its policy and is now a posted "gun-free zone." Some people really can't see the bullock under the scarf.

The Oaf's Hanky

On September 11th, a date with a certain significance in American history, violent anti-American riots "spontaneously" broke out in numerous centers of "peace and tolerance" around the world. In Benghazi, our ambassador and three other Americans were murdered in a virtually unopposed terrorist attack. We were told the Benghazi attack was just another "spontaneous" reaction to a video trailer — which virtually no one had seen — for a nonexistent movie said to be "disrespectful" to a certain "revered personage." Now we know that just prior to the Benghazi attack, American security forces were apparently withdrawn.

Wow, triple-shock! Attacks on a day celebrated by terrorists, marked by numerous past attempts and completed terrorist acts on the same day could not possibly have been foreseen! Duh, could they? And another shocker! The suspected organizer of the Benghazi attack was Sufyan Ben Qumu, an al-Qaida terror attack planner. He had been transferred from Gitmo to Libyan custody on condition he be locked up forever-and-a-day. He was released? Astonishing! Yup; just like Abdel Baset al-Megrahi, the Lockerbie bomber, who was also supposed to be under lock and key forever. And Ben Qumu returned to terrorism? You mean, like so many other released Gitmo Charm School alumni have? Hooda thunkitt? Quick, more scarves and hankies!

I know this is gonna sound crazy, but first, I think smart people might want to avoid places which have been proven to be magnets for mass murderers, especially when events there may be additionally attractive to whacko sociopaths. Second, I suspect if certain people and groups have murdered thousands of your peers, promise to kill as many more as possible — including you — and swear eternal war against you, well, gee … they might mean it. Third, I'm afraid this will sound completely nuts, but — I think if you remove security from a tempting target, then bad guys — if there's such a thing as bad guys — they might, umm … make mischief. They might even do it on anniversaries of days they've killed lots of you. Even if we say we wanta play nice.

I'd like to take my own bullock-cart magic act on the road, but my village only has one idiot, so I have to stay here. Connor OUT.

MIA FOR SHOT SHOW 2013
AND The Annual Hoplo Hunt

MAY/JUNE 2013

It's comin'! Still three weeks away as I write this, but it looks like I'll miss SHOT Show again. Sometimes it sucks to be "indispensable." Yeah, it guarantees I have work — my "day job" — but it also means I'll be stumpin' around a freezing, windy firing line while hordes of dealers, manufacturers and gunwriters soak in a sea of new! and innovative! firearms and accessories, some of which will actually be "new" and "innovative." Well, poop ... I was sniveling about it to Uncle John, and he just laughed and punched me.

"Which parts are you gonna miss?" he chuckled. "The famous, ferocious SHOT Show flu? The 9-dollar mystery-meat burgers at The Ptomaine Tavern? Being run over by marketing reps draggin' those bucket-carts of press releases? Getting trampled by mobs jostling to see The Fabulous New Gun! that turns out to be the same ol' gun in hot pink or zombie-green?" I knew he was just tryin' to cheer me up, but ....

"Well, I'll miss seeing a lot of good people," I said, "And ya gotta admit, the Hoplo Hunt was always fun."

Annual Hoplophobe Hunt

The Hoplo Hunt is a little-known SHOT Show activity. See, every year a handful of dedicated antigun hoplophobic journalists from the lamestream media finagle SHOT Show press passes. Their mission is to "rip the rotten, racist, radical mask off the murderous gun industry" and write Pulitzer Prize-winning exposés. They routinely fail.

A small group of us would stalk 'em just for fun. We never confronted, harassed, or debated them — because we didn't have to. Eventually, you'd find most of 'em frozen in catatonic states between enormous displays of firearms, having suffered "data overload" seizures and, to put it delicately, enuresis ignavus: involuntary wetting due to acute pusillanimity. The others often get, well ... healed.

Healing The Hoplos

144

Female infiltrators tend to be young, bright, brittle types with hidden digital video cameras and the vague impression that women who like guns are haggard, hoary harridans with more tattoos than teeth, totin' double-barrel shotguns. Miss Winifred Wimple's hoplophobia rarely lasts through Media Day at the Range, an event held the day before SHOT Show, where members of the media get to shoot the latest guns and burn tons of free ammo. There, she gets gob-smacked with reality.

Her first shocking observation is that those gun women are, umm… feminine, and attractive — ladies who can talk Dolce & Gabbana and Smith & Wesson too! And they have something she had only seen women possess in movies: confidence and self-assurance. Surrounded by armed Amazons, she wilted until they learned she'd never even held a handgun.

Never? Oh, honey! We're gonna have SO much fun! Miss Wimple disappears, emerging 5 days later as Winnie, with a grin, a Glock, a cherished "Shooter Ready!" T-shirt, and epiphanous insight into her new self.

The male hoplos are generally urbane, sophisticated-lookin' (that usually means emaciated and pale, resulting from too much tofu and not enough sunshine) dweebs who think a 12-pocket vest is good "gun show camouflage." That could be, but he's wearing that vest over a starched button-down, a mauve bow tie, and Italian skinny-sole loafers.

His problem is, he comes lookin' for "gun crazies," but he runs into people like the Brownells, the Hornady family, the Hoffmans of Black Hills Ammo, and others who just stick out their mitts and welcome him with open, sincere smiles and handshakes, like he's never experienced at any leftie-lib gathering.

Many gun-folks avoid hoplophobes instinctively, sensing that "sumpin just ain't right with that fella," but he's just as likely to get shanghaied by a buncha Texas gun dealers who throw log-sized arms around his narrow shoulders and haul him off to a steak-an'-taters dinner, whispering among themselves, "Heck, he cain't he'p bein' the way he is — He's prob'ly Yur-peen, y'know, from one of them itty-bitty countries in Yurrp where all they git ta eat is snails an' cabbage."

By evening's end, he's buying rounds of boilermakers for the boys, is admiring his newest-bestest-buddy Big Red's beautifully engraved 1911, and has learned how to yell Yee-Haa!!! with the big dogs. By close-of-show, he's ditched the bow tie and geek getup for comfy flannel and jeans, won Big Red's 1911 in a hand of Texas Hold 'Em, has an invitation to a feral hog hunt at Red's place outside Nacogdoches, and that smile? He knows his new pals Shorty, Slim and Lufkin Luke will be there too, to help him get snapped in with the .45-70 Marlin Guide Gun he ordered.

Dingell T. Berry had never shot a firearm before — and found he liked it! — And could actually shoot pretty well after some coaching by the boys at the Clark County Range. He'd never had men argue over whose home he would first be a guest in, and settle it with a coin toss. Never had a nickname before either, nor been bear-hugged by what felt like real bears when they bade him farewell at McCarran International.

"Ding," Red told him, "You's always a good man inside, pardner. You just needed ta git peeled outta that plasticwrap and sorta un-hogtied, y'know? Now, adios don't mean goodbye, 'cause we're gonna see you come spring, okay? So adios, my friend."

Yes, some hoplos can be healed. Try it on your own turf, because we need all the friends we can get! Connor OUT.

GETTIN' INTERESTING, AIN'T IT?

JULY/AUGUST 2013

There's an ancient Chinese curse that goes, "May you live in interesting times." It sounds like an odd blessing, but in those days life was pretty mundane except for episodes of horrendous famine, pestilence and war. Well, we've got some interesting times, don't we?

The slaughter of schoolchildren in Connecticut was for all of us a grievous tragedy; another instance of a "gun-free zone" becoming a killing-ground, safe only for the madman. For some though, it was a political opportunity to energize a failing campaign. Sandy Hook provided would-be tyrants and blue-sky believers the catalyzing event they had waited for. Government and media massaged the message so that for millions of well intended if uninformed people, implements — semiautomatic rifles and so-called "high-capacity" magazines — were responsible, not a depraved shooter. That fit the political agenda. Never mind the almost universal factors of "gun-free zones," powerful psychotropic drugs affecting mass shooters and blazing warning signs that these are dangerous people! Why such intense focus on rifles, despite their miniscule use in violent crimes?

I think an acquaintance, a former Soviet Army soldier — now a US citizen — explained it best: "The nation is like a huge sponge which routinely refreshes itself with blood, sweat and treasure. All governments squeeze out what they dare. The citizens' rifles are like needles hidden in that sponge. You can only be squeezed so much; never squeezed dry. This is why first they want the rifles. Then, all other guns. Then, everything." He added something more foreboding.

"It seems in every century," he sighed, "there must be a Soviet Union. Is it America's turn?"

As I write this in February, the federal government is engaged in unabashed assault on our derided Constitution. New York, California, Colorado and other states compete to see which can create more "instant felons" and ban more guns. Other states are moving legislation to defy anticipated federal laws, which violate the Second Amendment.

Hundreds of sheriffs have pledged not to enforce such laws. DOJ is in a curious position. They demand states not enforce federal immigration laws, refuse to address cities and states contravening federal drug laws, but insist any federal gun laws be stringently enforced. Lady Justice, with her scales, is supposed to be blindfolded, not bipolar.

Firearm, magazine and ammo companies prepare to leave their home states. Others will not sell to agencies or even individual officers of "oppressive states." Millions of citizens have pledged resistance and non-compliance. People are buying guns every 1.5 seconds. Some historians whisper the country is more divided, socially and politically, than it was on the eve of the Civil War. It ain't a pretty picture.

Cutting Through The Fog

If the fog is thick enough, not only can't you see your enemies, you can't even see where to draw your line in the sand. That's fine with our foes. Debate, division, disputation and confusion favor them. Their advice is "Don't get excited (until it's too late)." We're drawn into endless debate over magazine capacity, background checks, nonexistent loopholes and meaningless cosmetics, the question becoming how much we will give up; what losses we'll tolerate. There are, I believe, few certainties, among them: registration means ultimate confiscation, period, and nothing surrendered will ever be enough.

So you're feeling outnumbered? You're in good company! So were those who founded this nation. Take heart, friends; the Constitution was written precisely to protect the rights of a minority from the tyranny of a majority. That's why our much-maligned founding fathers constructed not a true "democracy," but a constitutional republic. They knew the paroxysms, chaos and failures of the Greek models, and wisely selected the best features to form an imperfect — but exemplary — form of government. And if no one else will defend the Constitution, the people must. It's ours.

When it comes to Second Amendment arguments, we need to get beyond the endless bickering about left and right, liberals and conservatives, Republicans and Democrats, and especially personalizations of the issue, like Obama versus whoever. It makes no difference whether you're disarmed and your rights trampled by Marxists or Martians, rightists or Rastafarians. Our Constitution's framers were not only smart but also wise. They recognized any person or element seeking to enslave the free citizens of the new Republic must first disarm them of effective weaponry. The Second Amendment was written to safeguard against tyranny — not against any particular polity or person. Someone who favors a "progressive socialist" government should be just as vehemently opposed to infringement of their right to bear arms as one who might favor government by military junta.

The Line in the Sand

The core issue — for all humans who wish to live free of domination by totalitarian force — is retention of the ability to resist oppression; to fight tyranny in any form. Would you rather be disarmed by a right-wing ruler than a leftist?

There is nothing more iconically American than resisting overreaching government. With great reservations we consent to be governed, not ruled, by our Constitution, not by imperial edict.

I don't ask anyone to adopt my stance; only to cut the fog, define your position, and know where your line is. My line in the sand is here. My answer is NO to all of the above, communicated to every official from my county sheriff to the president. I don't care if I stand with three, 300, 30 million ... or alone. But I wouldn't mind some good company. Connor OUT.

THE CHESHIRE MAN

September/October 2013

We'll call my friend Bill and his oldest dog Bruno, okay? It happened in a small, nice suburban development in the mid-South, buffered by 20 miles of fields and woods from the nearest urban center. Bill can't recall a single crime in the neighborhood in years, as though all troubles — gangs, drugs and grief — stop at the interstate.

At about 2:00 a.m., old Bruno's aging bladder signaled him to awaken Bill and answer nature's call. Bill got up and let him out, expecting, as usual, to wait 5 minutes, then let him back in. Routine. Bill almost nodded off again, but Bruno's bark — his "General Quarters!" bark, not his "Let me in, Dad" garrumph — put Bill on instant alert. He stepped into saggy-baggy old sweatpants and floppy slippers and shuffled for the front door.

Bruno was just inside his invisible electric fence, giving canine hell to a dark figure a few feet away, slightly bent over, murmuring soothingly to Bruno. Bill flipped the light on. It was a young man; tall, mid-20s maybe, long wild hair, wearing sneakers, jeans and a short-sleeve T-shirt. There was frost on the grass and windshields, temp about 30 degrees. Looking for a car or bike, Bill saw only a skateboard out in the street. He called sharply for Bruno, who reluctantly withdrew a few feet. Bill's spider-senses tingled.

"I can tell by the tone of your voice you're upset," the man said more loudly than necessary, but low. "I'd like to come up and talk to you." He began slowly advancing. Now Bill's bells rang. He was standing half in the door, holding a pistol behind his back. "We're not talking," Bill said. "You need to leave."

"What's that behind your back?" the guy chuckled — and advanced. Bill blurted the first thing that came to him: "A big-ass flashlight!" Now the dude laughed, low — and took another step.

Tipping Point

Will that flashlight ... kill a deer?" He smiled broadly. Bill was suddenly and acutely aware of his shrinking options and poor situation. Should he abandon Bruno and slam the door? Shoot? His sweatpants were almost falling off. His slippers would flip off with any sudden movement. The man showed no fear, not even concern, and a weird, carefree, even amused attitude. As Bill later said, "He radiated casual violence."

Bill took his best verbal shot: "Yes it will!" he bellowed. "Go! Move along!" Still

You've got the hardware — what about the software?

smiling like a Cheshire cat, the guy gazed at Bill for a long moment, then coolly turned, walked out to the street, stepped on his skateboard and wheeled away. Bill noticed that unlike every skateboard he'd ever heard, this one was silent. A few minutes later he realized it had to have been set up for that: "Rigged for silent running."

Bill freely — and wisely — admitted the incident had shaken him, and he was miserably unprepared for it. He had faced danger before, but he realized it had fallen into two categories: In most, he knew the dangers he faced and had some time — a little or a lot — to psychologically prepare himself for them. Then a couple of times lethal danger had sprung upon him so suddenly he reacted instantly, aggressively and instinctively. This was different, and he was unprepared. All those other situations were unequivocal. This one wobbled from second to second.

Bill's a shooter; a good one, with solid guns and a level head. Bill was prepared, with the right hardware, attitude and game plans, to "repel boarders" in a home invasion or deal with an ATM stickup or sudden violence in his business. We talked about it at length, and I wish I had room here to repeat that. I'm sure your heads are already sparkin' with conjecture and conclusions about Bill's encounter. Was there an unseen accomplice nearby? Is that why the dude spoke louder than necessary? A T-shirt in 30-degree weather? Was that because he was drugged up — or just got out of a warm van? That careless attitude: was he armed and experienced, crazy and fearless — what? And at flashpoint, does any of that matter?

Preachin' To The Choir

Yeah, I know. But remember, Bill is a choir member too. And sometimes the songbook is missin' a few pages, so excuse me re-stating what I've said before: Never step out — not even halfway out — without a gun, a light, a knife and an attitude. Always be prepared — clothing, footwear and in your head — to run, fight and climb fences. It's not that difficult or even inconvenient once you adopt the survivor's philosophy and totally dismiss any concern about being thought paranoid. The world is a dangerous place. Run "worst-case scenarios" constantly — and have scripted lines to fit a variety of spontaneous, unpredictable scenarios. Give some thought to having "the right lines," but far more thought to the right actions.

My S.O.P. is to never open a door or turn a corner unprepared to deal with Zombies, Nazis, PCP freaks, giant rabid wolverines, Martians, mad mullahs and laser-guided psychotic polar bears. You don't have to go full-boogie Connor though. Just remember: Bill's Cheshire-grinnin' goblin is out there, somewhere — right now — runnin' silent. Connor OUT.

THE TOOTSIE ROLL TALE:
A Veterans Day Story

November/December 2013

For too many Americans, November 11th signals "that 3-day weekend before Thanksgiving." Others know it's Veterans Day and feel it deeply. But for many people, Veterans Day is a vague and fuzzy concept, lacking a compelling memory; a story, a visual aid; something tactile to focus on. Those are the ones you want to hand a piece of candy to. A couple of weeks before Veterans Day buy a bag of those tiny Tootsie Rolls, the ones called Midgees. Put some in your pocket and begin handing them out, along with this story:

After World War II, the Korean peninsula was divided into the communist North and the democratic South. While South Korea was recovering and rebuilding, North Korea was arming to the teeth, receiving countless tons of weapons, munitions and war supplies — and encouragement to use them — from Mao's China and Stalin's Soviet Union. In June of 1950, North Korea invaded the lightly-defended South with infantry, tanks and artillery, nearly rolling up the entire country. South Korea had no tanks, anti-tank weapons or artillery. Then a coalition of UN member nations, led by the US, intervened.

After weeks of bitter fighting, North Korean forces were pushed 'way back over the border at the 38th Parallel. For a brief and shining moment, it appeared the invasion had been defeated — and the North's Russian and Chinese sponsors had taken a slap in the face. Mao's response shouldn't have come as a surprise, but it did. He sent a million-man army against the allies.

The Frozen Chosin

By November 26, 10,000 men of the First Marine Division, along with elements of two Army regimental combat teams, a detachment of British Royal Marine commandos and some South Korean policemen were completely surrounded by over ten divisions of Chinese troops in rugged mountains near the Chosin Reservoir. Chairman Mao himself had ordered the Marines annihilated, and Chinese General Song Shi-Lun gave it his best shot, throwing human waves of his 120,000 soldiers against the heavily outnumbered allied forces. A massive cold front blew in from Siberia, and with it, the coldest winter in recorded Korean history. For the encircled allies at the Chosin Reservoir, daytime temperatures averaged five degrees below zero, while nights plunged to minus 35 and lower.

Jeep batteries froze and split. C-rations ran dangerously low and the cans were frozen solid. Fuel could not be spared to thaw them. If truck engines stopped, their fuel lines froze. Automatic weapons wouldn't cycle. Morphine syrettes had to be thawed in a medical corpsman's mouth before they could be injected. Precious bottles of blood plasma were frozen and useless. Resupply could only come by air, and that was spotty and erratic because of the foul weather.

High Command virtually wrote them off, believing their situation was hopeless. Washington braced for imminent news of slaughter and defeat. Retreat was hardly an option; not through that wall of Chinese troops. If the Marines defended, they would be wiped out. So they formed a 12-mile long column — and attacked.

There were 78 miles of narrow, crumbling, steeply-angled road — and 100,000 Chinese soldiers — between the Marines and the sea at Hungnam. Both sides fought savagely for every inch of it. The march out became one monstrous, moving battle.

The Chinese used the ravines between ridges, protected from rifle fire, to marshal their forces between attacks. The Marines' 60-millimeter mortars, capable of delivering high, arcing fire over the ridgelines, breaking up those human waves, became perhaps the most valuable weapon the Marines had. But their supply of mortar rounds was quickly depleted. Emergency requests for resupply were sent by radio, using code words for specific items. The code for 60mm mortar ammo was "Tootsie Rolls" — but the radio operator receiving that urgent request didn't have the Marines' code sheets. All he knew was that the request came from command authority, it was extremely urgent — and there were tons of Tootsie Rolls at supply bases in Japan.

Tootsie Rolls had been issued with other rations to US troops since World War I, earning preferred status because they held up so well to heat, cold and rough handling compared to other candies.

Tootsies From The Sky

Tearing through the clouds and fog, parachutes bearing pallet-loads of Tootsie Rolls descended on the Marines. After initial shocked reactions, the freezing, starving troops rejoiced. Frozen Tootsies were thawed in armpits, popped in mouths, and their sugar provided instant energy. For many, Tootsie Rolls were their only nourishment for days. The troops also learned they could use warmed Tootsie Rolls to plug bullet holes in fuel drums, gas tanks, cans and radiators, where they would freeze solid again, sealing the leaks.

Over two weeks of unspeakable misery, movement and murderous fighting, the 15,000-man column suffered 3,000 killed in action, 6,000 wounded and thousands of severe frostbite cases. But they reached the sea, demolishing several Chinese divisions in the process. Hundreds credited their very survival to Tootsie Rolls. Surviving Marines called themselves "The Chosin Few," and among themselves, another name: The Tootsie Roll Marines. Join me in sharing their story — and some Tootsie Rolls. Connor OUT.

151

YEAR OF THE GAMMA RAT

JANUARY/FEBRUARY 2014

Hey! A show of hands here, okay? Think back 5 or 10, maybe even 20 or 30 years; what you were like and what you were doin'? Now, how many of you ever seriously envisioned living this long? How many of you are more kinda surprised that you're even here, standing on the doorstep of Twenty-Fourteen?

Lots of you, huh? I thought so. Geez, we oughtta form a club and have T-shirts that read, like, "HERE I STAND — Only by the grace of God and the poor marksmanship of my enemies." (And, of course, their stupidity, lack of discipline, failing courage and hesitation in the pinch, well that helped too.) Take a bow, folks — you've earned it.

In the Jan/Feb 2013 issue, I laid out a yearlong plan for sharpening your skills as an all-terrain, all-weather shooter. If you didn't get it, go to the website and click on "Digital Editions"; it's on page 30. That was, you might say, about knowing what you do and how you do it. To help bring in 2014, I'd like to share a couple comments about knowing who and what you are.

Inner Warriors, Inner Waiters

There's a lot of crap being said and published about "The Inner Warrior," and what makes a warrior. Most of it, I think, is overblown, hyped-up, romanticized claptrap, implying if a person doesn't grin like a goblin and salivate at the prospect of bloody slaughter, they are somehow inferior to those who would just as soon not, thank you very much. The image painted, mostly by chair-borne commandos and recreational Rambos, is of some chiseled sci-fi superman, draped with ordnance, radiating rage and shooting blue lightning bolts out of his … umm … eyes; one who "lives for the fight." I don't think that's an "inner warrior;" more of an "incipient psychopath."

The first time I heard Uncle John say, "There's an inner warrior — and an inner waiter," I thought he was makin' a joke about stand-up guys versus wimps. I shoulda known better. That wasn't it. Here's his take, paraphrased and plagiarized:

The man with an inner warrior is indeed excited by fighting; stimulated by combat. He's good at it; he has the right stuff for struggle. He tends to run to the sound of guns, and he's centered in conflict. He's valuable in that regard. But he needs tempering and restraint, or he becomes a danger to himself and others, and he overreaches, courting disaster. Above all, he must have the moral compass to choose what he fights for wisely and ethically and never, ever let his ardor for the fight twist him so he fights for the fighting and becomes a war-whore.

The person with an inner waiter is one who serves, and takes great satisfaction from it; a nurturer and protector; one who runs to cries for help and to the sounds of pain. They are uncomfortable with confrontation and avoid it; they may flee from threats and only if cornered or defending the defenseless will they fight, but when they do the latter it is with ferocity, and they will acquit themselves honorably. They're inner waiters, not inner wimps. They have the heart; they need only to realize there are times they must fight, and have the tools and training for that moment.

The best people have both an inner warrior and an inner waiter, and the very best of them have the two in balance. As the Japanese say, "Bunbu ichi; pen and sword, in accord." I think of the men who stood with Washington in the snows of Valley Forge; the farmers and tradesmen, loving fathers and faithful sons, tillers of earth and milkers of cows; mostly men who would choose peace over battle anytime — but did not flinch at facing privation and violence. Balance.

Who and what are you?

The Gamma Rats

You know about Alpha Rats and Beta Rats, right? Scientists love to study 'em. Their behavioral patterns are so easily documented and quantified — and so similar to human behaviors. Here's my take on RatWorld: The Alphas are the powerful, often vicious bosses of the rat mazes. The drive for domination is their prime dynamic. The Betas are their more numerous, submissive, craven and fearful subjects. The Alphas rule by hoarding the best foods and establishing their own harems. Lesser Alphas terrorize the Betas, fight each other and when the moment is ripe, overthrow the ruling Alphas. Almost overlooked are the relatively rare and few Gamma Rats.

The Gammas stand apart, staking out and defending their space, finding their own mate, showing no interest in dominating the Betas. Essentially, they avoid all but necessary, cautious interaction with Alphas and Betas. How do you know if you're a Gamma?

You don't understand why anyone would lust after power and domination over others, or why so many fall into blind subservience. You don't seek the shelter of the mob; you'd rather make your own way. You're neither psycho nor sycophant. The human Gamma's attitude is, "Give me liberty — I'll handle the rest." You want peace and privacy, and you're willing to fight for it. Let's make this "the year of the Gamma Rat." Connor OUT.

THE STATE OF ONION

MARCH/APRIL 2014

Be careful flippin' on your TV, folks. Coming soon is the annual State of the Union speech, followed rapidly by dozens of gasbags givin' State of the State, State of the City, State of the Snollygoster and state-of-whatever speeches. That much hot air blastin' outta your TV could desiccate your eyeballs an' singe your nasal hairs.

I call my address The State of the Onion, because when you peel it, tears come to your eyes. Below are some random excerpts from my eight-hour speech, delivered a capella and sans teleprompter to a rapt audience consisting of — Sancho Panza, my dog.

My Fellow, Uhh...

I would begin this with, "My fellow Americans" but there are some problems with that. First, we have more illegal aliens — a lowball estimate is 11.7 million — than the whole populations of over a hundred nation-states belonging to the U.N. Just thinkle on that for a moment. We could tell Denmark and Norway or New Zealand and Bulgaria, "Hey! We've got more illegals than you've got people put together!"

Second, after two generations of indoctrination passing for education, almost half of our younger denizens consider themselves "global citizens" — "citizens of the world" — rather than Americans. Because, you know, America is "bad," and bein' all one-worldie is, like, gooder, y'know? So perhaps I should kick off with "My fellow residents, accidental or otherwise, of the lands lying within the geopolitical boundaries of the administrative entity known officially as The United States of America." That's more accurate, but it sucks, and that's also a solid clue as to The State of the Onion...

History Repeatin' — Again

For a long time, the citizens of Rome had a good thing goin'. They voted enthusiastically for their leaders, cherished citizenship, and the concepts of civic duty and public service were honored. Then came that whole "decline and fall" thing, accelerated by the policy of Panem et Circenses — Bread and Circuses. As the people grew more affluent, privileged and

lazier, some wily Roman senators figured out all they had to do was provide free food and ever more enthralling free spectacles in the "circuses" — the arenas and coliseums — and they could rape the republic and exercise complete power over the empire.

Mobs of morons loved it. They didn't have to work! They didn't have to think! There were plenty of vassals out there in the "roll-over states" working to refill the government coffers with the fruits of their sweat and sacrifice. All the Roman citizenry had to do was sign up for the dole, the annona — welfare — and they were fed, housed and got free admission to see gladiator fights, staged and choreographed battles with real blood, wounds and deaths, mass rapes followed by slitting-of-throats and the ever-popular throwing of Christians to the lions.

Citizenship could be purchased, and civic obligations were nil. Military service was neither compulsory nor widely respected. Romans were too good for manual labor; that was for immigrants and the unsophisticated. Behavior previously considered shocking was condoned and even celebrated. The senators told them, "No worries; we'll take care of things. Enjoy yourselves!" It didn't end well for the citizens. They learned too late that there's always free cheese — in a mousetrap. Hmm ... seeing any parallels here?

Forty-seven million people are on welfare — "SNAP Cards" and such — and a fraction of those actually need it. We're even paying for a program to convince people who initially refused welfare to sign up for it; a "getting past NO" thing. In 35 states, welfare pays better than minimum wage, and in 15 states it pays better than a $15-per hour job.

Gladiators and spectacles? We have "cage fighters," "ultimate fighters," Hollyweird and video games offer spectacles gorier and more horrific than actual combat, "murder for the masses" featuring killing without conscience, senseless slaughter without risk, consequences — or reasons.

At a time when Americans really need a TV series on the Sons of Liberty, our pre-Revolutionary War band of patriots, instead we get the Sons of Anarchy, a top-rated cable show glamorizing the exploits of a gang of murderous dope-dealin' bikers.

Citizenship for sale? There are "instant citizen" birthing centers on both coasts. They offer five-star accommodations, delivery rooms and doctors. Affluent foreigners bring their nine-months-along relatives to the US on visas, birth is induced and bingo! An instant citizen, who must of course, be attended by three to 33 relatives — in America.

We're graduating university students who can't read and write at the 7th-grade level of 40 years ago. In a survey of 166,000 people aged 16 to 65 in 33 developed countries, Americans scored below the international average in reading, math and problem-solving, gettin' stomped by 16 other countries. It was noted though, Americans ranked very high in possession of college degrees. The message: lotsa parchment, not much learning.

In a seemingly legit nationwide poll, 70 percent said this country's headed in the wrong direction. I'll buy that. I think it's steamin' in the wrong direction at flank speed.

But There's Hope

People are waking up; the long-silent are rising and speaking out. We have countless immigrants who've come for the right reasons, and they're more resolutely American than many of their native-born neighbors. There's hope from another direction too — we'll talk about that next time.

For more of my address, you'll have to check with Sancho. He might have made notes. Border Collies can do that, ya know ... Connor OUT.

UNLIKELY ALLIES?

MAY/JUNE 2014

Warm day, blue skies, and that meant a crowded range. The small bays were all taken and we had to use the long line; any-centerfire, targets from 15 to 100 yards; mixed clots of sunshine shooters. As more shooters arrived, we couldn't help noticing they avoided the half-dozen "illustrated kids" one position away from us.

You've seen 'em: 20's to maybe early 30's, lavishly tattooed, some multicolor punked-up hair, a smattering of facial hardware, dressed kinda like Ukrainian circus performers dragged through an Army-Navy surplus store. Neo-Retro-Metro-Post-Apocalyptic Industrial? Okay; I exaggerate a little, but you know what I mean, right? And along with the leathers and tats, also wearing a little attitude, like "We see you lookin' at us like freaks. What's your problem?" I ignored 'em. Obey range rules, don't muzzle-sweep me and we're all good. But Uncle John was watchin' 'em.

Four guys, two girls, taking turns with a worn-shiny AK, a couple of Euro-pistols and an old Smith Model 10; pawn-shop poppers, and having problems with one pistol. When the buzzer sounded to clear and bench guns for target changes Uncle John said, "Stay. Wait 'til I wave you over. VZ, take off your jacket." They tensed and looked up suspiciously as he approached. He stopped, raised one hand palm-out, and deadpanned "Klaatu barada nikto — I come in peace." That unbalanced 'em for a moment — and me too. Then their lead dog popped a big smile.

"Yeah, from the movie, right? The Day the Earth Stood Still?" The instant he smiled, Uncle John stuck out his mitt for a handshake, and the kid reflexively took it. Good psych move. You could hear the ice crackin' and the whole group warmed right up. In five seconds he had 'em, explaining "You don't have a pistol problem, you got a magazine problem," holding them side-by-side. "See the lips? Run this one, toss and replace this one; it's junk." In 30 seconds, they had a new uncle. He waved us over.

Another psych move: We're not very warm-and-fuzzy lookin', and at seven feet-plus, VZ flat scares the kapok outta people. But he does have a colorful collection of tattooed dragons; classic Asian dragons on the right arm, European dragons on the left. Ten seconds and he's explaining, "Zo, ven I point mine nose Norrss, left arm iz Vest, right arm iz East, for za dragons, you know?" And they're eatin' it up, especially the chick with the purple stripe in her hair, goin' all googley-eyed. Another instant uncle.

The Illustrated Kids

We had a great time! They were smart and eager to learn, but their only "training" had come from — choke, gag — TV, movies and the internet. We went over safety, basic marksmanship, cleaning and maintenance, ammo tips, lots of fun shooting and just getting to know them. Now, not everyone who looks like them is like them, but if you see illustrated kids at a range, chances are good they resemble this bunch.

Uncle John calls 'em Millennial Orphans, springing from fractured homes and forming their own "families." Some came from big money, and walked away. Virtually all have some college, and many graduated. They were force-fed the educational establishment's progressive propaganda-pap until they puked — too smart to become good little automatons. For many, the big awakening came about 2009.

"Our teachers and professors had hammered us with America is evil, defy authority, capitalism kills and crap like that," Lead Dog said. "Then all of a sudden it was don't question authority; obey the government; embrace the collective. Don't think, just obey. That's when we started teaching ourselves."

They discovered new heroes, the real revolutionaries — our founding fathers — and fell deeply in love with some neglected, derided old documents: the Declaration of Independence; the Constitution; the Bill of Rights. And they saw how far we've drifted from them.

"They told us capitalism was wrong because lots of power could be held by a relatively small group," Purple-Stripe explained. "But it's clear they want to replace it with a system where another even smaller group has absolute power, with the brute force of the state to enforce it. Not happening; I'll die first. That's why it's important for them to disarm us. And that's why we have these guns. The founding fathers warned us." She shook her curls. "Strange, isn't it, I had to leave college to get an education?"

They prize self-reliance; they're vehemently opposed to Nanny-State social programs, mass government surveillance and cyber-snooping. They generally support the police, but not a police state. They work, often at menial, low-paying jobs, but they've discovered the inherent dignity of a job well done, and they support each other loyally. They're suspicious and distrustful of older generations, whom they see as having given up their revolutionary heritage without firing a shot. They're not planning to fire that first shot, but like Captain John Parker at Lexington, they feel, "If they want a war, let it begin here."

I found myself thinking of Nathan Hale, Maggie Corbin and Henry Knox, only in their 20's in 1776, and wondering if they had dressed or acted a little "different" in the eyes of their elders.

Stick out your hand. Try that "I come in peace" thing. We need to know, help and influence each other.

Later, I asked Uncle John how he knew so much about these kinda kids. "Pretty typical of the millennial orphans I've met," he said. "Huh? You've met a lot of 'em?" He smiled.

"You don't get out much, do you?" Not enough, I guess. Connor OUT.

THE BOOT DROPPED:
A Rat Canyon Range Tale

JULY/AUGUST 2014

The curt phone message scrawled on a sticky-note read "Boot dropped — call Chief R." I was stunned. Boot dropped? I thought; geez, he was maybe mid-50's and healthy as a horse! I shook my head and called Robbie, the retired chief boatswain and rangemaster at my old home shootin' facility, the Rat Canyon Range.

"Boot dropped?" I sez, "Dang, Chief, what was it — stroke, heart attack? What the heck happened?" Robbie paused, confused, then laughed.

"Aw, not Boot, ya meathead!" he blurted, "He's fine. The boot — MY boot! It dropped, like fell! And you're on the list, so …"

Harken back to yesteryear, folks. In the September/October 2012* issue I told you guys about the weather-worn left-foot Tony Lama boot hung from an overhead beam, the mate to it interred out beyond the 25-yard line, and some of the guys' range-names, including "Boot," "Moon" and "Fiddlesticks." Since the boot has fallen, it's time for that tale.

The Boot & "Boot"

Long after retirement, Robbie still wore his old Navy khakis every day at the range, his only salute to fashion being his love of tall, fancy cowboy boots, the gaudier the better. He was driving a D8 'dozer, mining an overload of slugs outta the berm of the handgun pit. He had deeply undercut the berm when a rare, apocalyptic thunderstorm struck, dumping record rainfall and causing flash floods. Bein' no stranger to wet conditions, the former blue-water sailor kept working — right up until the whole hillside collapsed into a soupy clay pudding — right over the 'dozer blade and halfway up the tracks. It wouldn't budge; just churned in that snot-like moosh.

Robbie hopped off the side, and bloop! — went right up to his hips in red-brown glue. A coupla guys sheltering in the range shack threw him a stout line, hooked it to a truck up on the gravel, and managed to pop him out — sans his starboard-side thunderbird-tooled $500-a-pair Tony Lama cowboy boot … He didn't smile for a month.

Robbie hung the port-side boot from an overhead beam with a twist of wire through the pull-on loops and offered a $100 reward for recovery of the mate. Two teenagers tried, and had to be rescued; pulled right outta their sneakers. When the clay-snot dried a little, Crazy Ivan cruised over with his monster D10 and yanked Robbie's 'dozer free. A week later the Chief 'dozed all that slug-sprinkled sludge flat over the whole range.

A month after that, the native clay was like concrete, with a dusty top layer pimpled with slugs. Robbie asked everybody to pick up a few slugs per trip when coming back from the target lines. With nowhere else to put 'em, they began reaching up and dropping them into that boot, which Robbie routinely emptied until loose slugs grew scarce. The boot hung there fulla lead, straining at the loops — waiting …

Before Boot became Boot, this Hungarian-Romanian immigrant, a heckuva good guy, was bein' called "Hey you" and "buddy," because his first and last names contained about 27 letters each, mostly consonants. It sounded kinda like "orangie-zsherbett kielbassy-fitz-kibble." His English wasn't too hot, but that was okay; ours was barely warm. When he got excited or frustrated, forget it; he'd choose one word in sorta-English and just repeat it loudly. We'd go along with it until he calmed down.

"Hey you" was a pal to all, a fine shooter and a master woodworker. He could make anything from a violin to an amazingly intricate folding chair from exotic woods we couldn't pronounce either, like the one he brought to a summer hardball match. He shot, unfolded his masterpiece chair, sat his six-foot-five body down and relaxed to watch — right under that lead-filled boot.

Boot Gets Knighted

We had a problem with wasps at Rat Canyon. We sprayed 'em and sometimes burned 'em out, but they loved the place. There he was, fannin' himself with his cap and focused on the firing line when a wasp flew up his shorts and stung him on the thigh just below his tenders …

"Buddy" launched outta that chair like a Pershing missile, ramming his head into that boot at Warp Nine. He went down on his butt almost as fast, but when he popped up like a Jack-in-the-box we knew his chimes were seriously rung. His eyes were spinnin' like pinwheels, his fists were up like John L. Sullivan in a title fight and he quartered jerkily, spastically around, trying to find and focus on whoever had attacked him with a sledge hammer.

We circled him warily, out of fisticuffs range, everybody jabbering until I yelled "Shuddup! He don't understand! Point to the boot an' yell boot!" They did. As he slowed down, weaving, he finally got it.

"Boot?" he inquired drunkenly. "Boooooott? Boot!" At that instant the rusty wire snapped, the boot dropped, and poor ol' Boot passed out cold.

Otter had been takin' video of the match and got Boot's dizzy-dance. We showed it to Boot at the hospital. "Ah, BOOT!" he cried. Robbie tapped him on the shoulders with a hospital spoon like he was knighting him and declared, "Henceforth, your range name is Boot." He didn't know "henceforth" from a Hottentot, but he understood.

"Eye yam Boot," he grinned. "Boot. Iz good."

Robbie hung the slug-filled boot back up with the same rusty wire — and the betting began: How many days until it drops? How many slugs are in it? Two bets, two prizes — but what? Moon suggested splitting the money in the Fiddlesticks Fund, and Fiddlesticks agreed — a tale for another time. Connor OUT.

SUPPORT ARMED BEARS
AND the Right to Bear Arms

SEPTEMBER/OCTOBER 2014

Drumroll, please … Ta-DAH! Folks, I want you to meet the new unifying symbol of armed free peoples (and other critters) everywhere; a symbol almost impervious to sniping from the Left. "The Left" is pretty encompassing, so let me narrow the definition: The sniveling, sanctimonious, rainbow-chasing, crystal-gazing, unicorn-riding, ideological infants who think universal peace would break out like a rash if only all guns were outlawed. You know who I mean, right? Well, Panda is almost invulnerable to their attacks, for these reasons:

Panda is black. Panda is white. Panda is Asian. Panda's a vegetarian, for Pete's sake. One hundred percent of Panda's intake and output is natural, organic and biodegradable. Panda's "carbon footprint" is zip, and his "greenhouse gas" emissions are near zero. In fact, they're about 1 percent of the greenhouse emissions of a college sophomore after dining at Taco Bell.

Is Panda also Hispanic? Latino? Check out the gunbelt: traditional tooled leather bearing classic silver conchos with turquoise inlays. And, Panda's name is Joselito — or maybe Joselita — we can't tell, because Panda is soft-spoken and has a speech impediment — which also makes Panda a "special needs" case! Panda may also be a bit gender-confused. Even panda experts can't tell a panda's gender by sight. They have to do a "parting-the-fur" inspection. Heck, pandas can't tell the gender of other pandas by sight only. True fact, folks.

Pandas are an endangered species and the victims of disappearing habitat. When found in the wild they're thrown behind bars in panda-breeding concentration camps, then cruelly harassed 24/7/365 by clicking camera shutters and goofy humans going "OOooohhh! AAAHHHhhh!!! Aren't they so CUTE?" in every known language — humans who don't realize the juiciest bamboo shoots can never be as sweet as … freedom!

Multi-ethnic, vegetarian, "green," organic, one-with-nature, gender-confused, "special needs," under constant surveillance, subject to species discrimination, politically imprisoned and threatened with extinction — is there any other creature on earth more deserving of the right to bear arms, and more justified in self-defense? Is there any other creature more truly politically correct, more invulnerable to the craven criticisms of the lefties? I think not, my friends. Support the right of armed bears to bear arms! Stand with Panda!*

With Their Own Clubs

With Panda, my friends, we take the offensive, using the symbology which our enemies so often twist against us. They capitalize on our desire to get along with them, then insist we submit to their demands. They claim to be all about "celebrating diversity" and recognizing "individual-ness," right? Let's give it back to 'em! There are two movements we need to launch. The first is "race/ethnicity." They say they honor diversity? Beat 'em over the head with it!

Are you white, black, Native American, Asian? Demand that on all governmental forms, our diversity is recognized! White crackers should demand a "Saltine-American" check-box! Rednecks and rosy-cheeks could be "Rufus" (red) or "Ruddy Americans." Darker-complected whites, very light blacks, and many Hispanics might share the term Café au lait-Americans. C'mon; are all Blacks alike? Just saying "black" is like saying "wood." Is there a difference between ebony and sugar pine? How insulting! Saying "Asian" is like saying "soup." All soups are the same? Ridiculous! Is there any difference between Jicarilla Apaches and Algonquian Ojibways? Just ask 'em! Hispanics and Latinos comprise dozens of distinct groups. Send blizzards of letters and hordes of e-mails, bury them in phone calls; drive the agents of political correctness crazy with their own ideology!

Ballistic Therapy

Research has shown that shooting firearms can release the same enzymes in the brain as passionate kisses. We all know shooting calms, soothes and invigorates us, right? It's a proven physiological palliative for stress, anxiety, depression and frustration. This is a genuine medical concern, folks, and ballistic therapy needs the official recognition it obviously merits. How many thousands — or hundreds of thousands — of physicians, psychologists, even psychiatrists could and would testify to shooting's non-narcotic effectiveness? And how many millions of shooting enthusiasts?

We need volunteers; spokesmen and women; letter-writers and phone-callers; e-mailers and Twitter-tweeters, all demanding our "drug of choice," our most efficacious therapy be recognized, supported, and YES, even subsidized! Like, "Okay, Sandra; if I have to pay for your birth control pills, you can help pay for my ammo!"

So you think you've detected a hint of humor in this? It's true. But I'm also dead-bang serious. We are an endangered species. Both blue-sky dreamers and hardcore socialists want to disarm us; the former group because they have marshmallow fluff between their ears, and the latter, to clear the decks for unopposed governmental tyranny. The fight is for all the marbles — and that's when you most need laughing warriors! Connor OUT

Go to www.americanhandgunner.com and click on the Web Blast link near the top to get your very own downloadable poster of Connor's Panda!

*Want a Panda T-shirt, maybe a bumper sticker? Of course you do! Go to www. dannco.com, look for the "Connor's Cut" tab and check 'em out. It's a Connor's Cut project, so it benefits veterans' charities — and makes zero bucks for me. Cool, huh?

I MUSTA BEEN HAVIN' FUN, HUH?

'Cause a decade somehow blew right past me ...

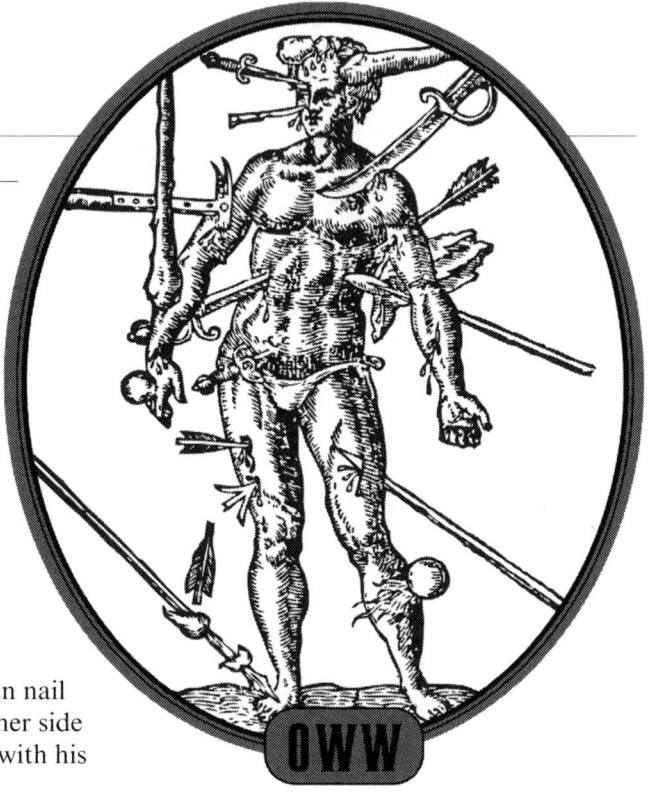

NOVEMBER/DECEMBER 2014

I think I've told you before — the Memsaab Helena went to college on an athletic scholarship. The ranches of the High Rockies grew some fit, tough girls. Her specialties were the classic Greek events: javelin, discus, hammer, shot put, long jump. She might have made the Olympic team if not for an unfortunate suspension. She and her coach were on the sidelines watching another university's decathlon star competing. She shook the javelin in her hand and asked, "Want me to take him out? I can nail him easy from here." On the other side of her coach was a reporter — with his recorder runnin'.

Anyway, there was this trick she used to do at competitions; a real crowd-pleaser. A trainer's table about 30" high would be carried onto the field, and she would crouch beside it. Now imagine this 6' redheaded Amazon exploding upward from a flat-footed crouch to land on top of the table cocked and locked, then hurling that javelin some amazing distance. Crowds went wild — and so did I.

Time passed and she stayed in fighting shape, frequently bustin' out her javelins and discuses. At family gatherings, folks would demand "the table trick" and by golly she delivered, usually on a stout picnic table. What a girl ...

Reluctantly, she yielded again last week at a big family-and-crew barbecue. It had been years, but she did it! — and still looks like a champion.

Done With That

Others watched the arc of the javelin. I saw her get off the table — carefully; not her usual jump. Her smile seemed weak and her knees rubbery as she excused herself and wobbled around the side of the house. I followed. She was bent over, one hand braced against the bulkhead, not-quite-dry heaving. Ever the oaf, I laid my hand on her back and asked, "Sprain something?"

"I think," she whispered, "I sprained … organs. Is that possible?" I offered my shirt. She dabbed her lips and straightened slowly. Oaf redux, I asked, trying for a laugh, "'Member that time you jumped off and the picnic table collapsed, like you'd killed it?" She said Yes, managed a grin, and snapped her fingers.

"We were celebrating your first Guncrank Diaries column! When was that?" Before I could think, she continued, "I hope somebody got video, 'cause I'm done with that. Throwing, okay; table-trick, no more!" Then family called …

The next day I got a letter from a guy who's been readin' Guncrank from Day One. He wrote, "It's been over a decade, you know. Your kids were teenagers." There was more, but I was stunned dumb. A decade? I checked. Yup; mid-2003, and the 10-year mark had whistled right past me. He asked for an update.

You Asked For It

Our son, introduced to you as "the Refrigerator Raider," raids his own 'fridge now. After graduating from state college he went on to a big university we called "FancyPantz U," where he reported he was "surrounded by sissies and socialists." But he done good anyway. After beatin' the campus cops at a USPSA match, they invited him to join their team, use their range and stash his guns in their lockup. A year later they quietly gave him his own key.

He works hard, gets paid well, shoots regularly in IDPA, Bull's-eye and 3-Gun, and instead of tuckin' $20's into pole-dancers' thongs, he upgrades his reloading equipment, which resembles Lake City Arsenal.

Amazingly, Little Red graduated college too. Her professors found her "bright, determined and rather intimidating" — a quote from one of 'em. Ha! That's our girl! The company she works for discovered her true talent. They deal in "critical life-support products." If the goods aren't delivered on time, people can die. When the CEO smells sloth or incompetence, he fires Little Red at it like a bullet. She's known as "that hot-shot trouble-shooter outta home office;" liked by the hard-working, feared by the slackers.

If you see a fiery red SUV streakin' down the highway piloted by a fiery red girl, pull over and brace for turbulence. She visits often; says home base is "The one place I can still be nine years old, right, Daddy?" Damn. She still owns me.

Old hardcore Handgunner readers remember my Uncle G, Commander Gilmore. He wrote The Ten-Ring for years, and handed off the space to me when Roy wasn't lookin'. He has more artificial joints than a Transformer, still writes Back Blast in Shooting Industry Magazine, and can still crush beer cans in his hands — full, sealed ones. Don't let him give you a "noogie;" it'll be permanent.

Uncle John's scars are now like Egyptian hieroglyphics. He didn't go to Marine "Boot Camp." It was "Barefoot Camp" then, before boots were invented. He reminisces about when he was Yoda's drill instructor at the Jedi Knight Academy. Four doctors who told him he'd be dead in a year are long deceased, and he swears he didn't do it.

Three cross-country moves, two multi-state moves, two in-state moves. Way too many hospitals. If I had as many surgical instruments stickin' outta me as I've had stickin' in me over the past 10 years I'd look like a sci-fi sea anemone. My dog, Sancho Panza, has mysteriously gone gray in the muzzle — and so have I. Life is good. Connor OUT.

STEEL PLATES & A FULL MOON:
Another Rat Canyon Range Tale

Okay, settle down. After 'splainin' how Boot got his range-name in the July/ August '14 issue* and promising to tell you how Moon and Fiddlesticks acquired theirs, you've clamored to hear 'em. So, here goes.

Moon was dealt a crummy hand of poker and flipped it into an ace-high straight. He was born with extreme curvature of the spine; his torso radically elongated and arced in a deep crescent. His limbs were foreshortened, less so in the arms, but there was hardly space for knees between his hip joints and his feet. His mom was distraught, but his father wigged out and promptly abandoned them, screamin' about "the wages of sin."

Dad was a loony latecomer to some splinter cult religion who went from readin' a pamphlet to being a raving robed zealot almost overnight. Daddy's only contribution — other than biological — was giving Moon a complicated faux-biblical first name taken from some made-up wandering wizard in the cult's myths. The guy was supposed to have summoned magic prune juice from a stump or somethin'.

All of Moon's internal parts, from pumps to pipes and cognitive software worked just fine. His mom said as soon as toddler Moon figured out he wasn't equipped like his playmates, he decided to make his body the strongest, most agile machine possible.

He did it, earning varsity letters in football and baseball his senior year of high school, and almost taking one in gymnastics. He could hold an "iron cross" position on the rings until spectators got dozy, but some events were heavily loaded against a guy whose body looked like a giant warped hot dog with golf tees for legs. He was voted Prom King too, because he's a great guy, never disparaging others because they didn't have his "advantages." His mom finally remarried that year — to Moon's gymnastics coach and history teacher, who thought Moon was just the finest son ever. Step-dad was an avid shooter, and a plank owner of the Rat Canyon Range.

Challenges & Triumphs

Moon builds custom homes and commercial buildings, and I've seen him go up four stories of scaffolding like a gecko on crack — with no ladders. He's a fine builder, and a master at runnin' racks of plates with his Smith & Wesson .45 ACP wheelguns.

When people see him machinegun-blastin' steel with his revolvers, they ask why he doesn't go to the big matches, where he would undoubtedly win trophies. He'll pull out a photo of his wife and four sons, all "normal-shaped," — whatever that is — and grin "Got all the trophies I want. I do this for fun." Yeah; that kinda guy.

Moon has challenges, sure. He likes T-shirts and polos, but he would need like a size Medium but Xtra-Xtra Tall to cover his long torso. Those don't exist. His wife will buy two shirts, then piece 'em together to get enough length. He has virtually no hips, and appears to be butt-less. Remember those stupid "shants" that were popular a few years ago? Neither shorts nor pants, they ended at calf-length — for everybody but Moon, and they were actually a bit long for him. They saved Shirley a lot of hemming though. He bought a big supply of 'em.

Then there's that hipless-buttless thing: If his shants aren't snugged up tight against the friction of his shirt, they tend to kinda, well, slide off … And, he still had that stupid first name you couldn't even make a decent nickname out of.

Moonrise In November

It was a crisp November Saturday, and we had some just-for-fun events set up after the match; a combo bowling-pins-and-exploding-pumpkins thing, Halloween-masked monster-poppin', stuff like that. We had three 6-plate racks of falling steel targets, and Moon was gonna try to beat his own range record whackin' 'em; 18 shots, with two reloads en route. Moon offered to donate $100 to the Fiddlesticks Fund if he set a new record, or $50 plus $10 each for any missed shots if he didn't. We knocked that down to $50, $25 and $5. He and Shirley protested but finally agreed.

Otter had happily gone Hollywood with his video setup. He had wireless clip-on mics rigged to the PA, and would narrate and record from a little platform just behind the shooter. When Moon was called, he snatched up his youngest son from behind and spun him around for a kiss. He didn't know the child was clutching a full cup of cocoa … Somebody loaned Moon a T-shirt which didn't even reach his belly-button. The show went on.

Moon's like a "Zen shooter." He leans forward, takes a breath and the world ceases to exist. As he hammers, his lean increases and he exhales kind of a primal hiss between his teeth. That day he was blazin'! As he whacked the last two plates, those shants lost their tenuous grip and dropped to the deck, takin' his skivvies with 'em. There was a hushed silence. Then, hey, he does have a butt!

Zen-master Moon straightened, clearing his roscoe, completely oblivious until Otter stepped up, flipped open the preview window, and showed him a replay. He turned beet red, snatched up his shants — and then exploded in laughter. The PA boomed:

"Shirley! Boys! Come see this — it's EPIC!"

Now you know how he got his range-name** — and why we love him. He got his new record too. Connor OUT

**Always wanted to say this: "My name is Moon, and I approved this message." — Moon

BIRTHDAYS, BACKUPS & CALENDAR DOODLES

MARCH/APRIL 2015

Sunrise. The house was quiet. Me an' the Memsaab were sippin' first cupsa coffee, the only sounds bein' her pencil tapping on the calendar and Sancho Panza snoring by the kitchen door. Then …

"Aw, nuts! I missed Louise's birthday! It was last month!" She snortled and tossed her hair in frustration. She's got a cute snortle, by the way.

I asked, "Thelma is still your number-one girl, isn't she? Do ya think Louise needs the Full Monty?" Helena wrinkled her nose.

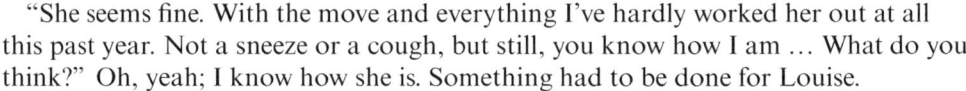

This is what your carry roscoe looks like when you pull it out? Fix it now before you, um … need it.

"She seems fine. With the move and everything I've hardly worked her out at all this past year. Not a sneeze or a cough, but still, you know how I am … What do you think?" Oh, yeah; I know how she is. Something had to be done for Louise.

"How 'bout," I suggested, "we strip her down, scrub her clean, give her a careful checkup an' take her out to dance? We'll eyeball her good, and if she misses a step, we'll get her a date with Kenny." Helena had that furrowed brow, not-quite-tickled but grudgingly pacified look goin'.

"Okay," she sighed, "That should be all right. I just don't want to let things slide just because she's, you know …"

"Your number-two girl," I said. "I know, honey."

The OCKC

Thelma is Helena's primary carry pistol. Louise is Thelma's "understudy;" the exact same make, model and series. She shoots both, but Thelma is shot about 20 rounds to one over Louise. If "Thelma & Louise" doesn't ring a bell, Google-search the 1991 movie. Kenny is our go-to gunsmith, and "the Full Monty" is a complete firearms micro-inspection, disassembly down to the bones, a solvent-tank bath and cleaning and refreshment of lubes and protectants. The OCKC is Helena — the Obsessive-Compulsive Keeper of the Calendar. And she's really obsessive about "her girls." She tracks my primaries too.

You don't have to be as crazy — I mean "focused" — about it as she is, but I highly recommend putting "birthdays" on your calendar, not for all your guns perhaps, but definitely for primary and backup guns. There are two kinds of handguns you should pay special attention to. First, those you shoot a lot, and/or carry on your person routinely. Second, those you rarely carry or shoot — like maybe your bedside boomer or a household hideout.

Shot-a-lot guns build up gremlin poop in places you never see during routine maintenance. One of our crew recently developed unexplained extractor problems. Hidden behind the extractor he found a compressed slug of carbon that looked like a fat fossilized mouse turd. Carry guns are constantly subjected to condensation, corrosive sweat salts and infiltration by lint, dust, threads, grit — you name it, especially if carried in IWB holsters or in direct skin contact. Evil lurks in trigger assemblies, under grip panels, behind bushings, in firing pin holes — everywhere.

Guns that get dumped in pockets, purses, go-bags and car consoles are magic magnets for malfunction-inducers. An acquaintance made an impromptu stop at a range to put a few rounds through his pocket piece. He got one round off, then the trigger seized. His 'smith extracted what looked like busted white gravel. Apparently, it was a fractured age-hardened breath mint. It could have become the equivalent of a cyanide capsule.

Guns that snooze more than they're shot need checkin' too, because lubes can go gummy or turn to varnish and greases can migrate or congeal to concrete. And the worst of it always seems to happen where you can't easily see it.

Commence Doodling!

Two dynamics are at work here: First, most of the time you won't know these problems are building until your weapon fails. Second, mercifully less often, those failures may occur at the worst possible time. Bust out your calendar and commence doodling! Here are a few other doodle-worthy suggestions.

Talk to your 'smith about the most commonly-needed replacement parts for your primary Roscoes — springs, firing pins or strikers, extractors, ejectors or screws. Order spares yourself. If they're needed in a pinch, you'll have 'em ready and he won't have to order them — or deal with "out of stock" delays. Meantime, you've got your understudy, right? You don't have one? Doodle that, dude. Ditto for your backups, buddy. As a wise gunfighter once said, "the best spare part is a spare piece."

Assign a date to survey and inspect your magazines or speedloaders. Need more? Need better? A full set to devote to training only? Are your mag springs as springy as spanky-new? How 'bout inert rounds for your dry-fire drills? Make notes, Nathan. If you carry daily, but your spectacles and daily-wear sunglasses don't provide ballistic protection, ain't it time to remedy that? Okay; maybe not right now, but scratch it on the calendar and plan it, Pete. How old is the ammo in your primaries? Really? And it ain't growin' barnacles?

An annual inspection and re-thinking of your home security belongs on every calendar. Determine what needs to be done or upgraded and create before-ya-drop-dead deadlines. For firearm protection and placement 'round the house, find the right balance of security and speed of access.

I'm writing this on October 4th, Damon Runyon's birthday. I mark it because of something he once said. A street guy and a gritty realist, he had a crap-shooter's worldview. He said "All of life is six to five against." It's true. So stack the deck and load the dice. Connor OUT.

THE GUY WHO WAS THERE

MAY/JUNE 2015

Sounds crazy, but sometimes Roy and I just talk like regular folks. We were both cops in the LongAgo-FarAway, and sometimes we share cop moments; funny ones, stupid times, "rolling code" and such. One came up that's long haunted me and the moment went dark. "Get it out," he said. "Exorcise it. Write it." So...

Uprooted by The Miskito Rebellion, a buncha sad, culture-shocked native refugees were dumped into a run-down World War II-built federal housing project. Repeatedly closed, reopened and abandoned, the most recent residents had been Cuban dopers "freed" by Castro during the Mariel Boatlift. Officially vacated with the utilities turned off, the mangiest rats in that pack just hid out, stayed and continued their drug businesses. They found fresh customers among the new arrivals.

Apparently, back on the Miskito Coast, some of the natives had chewed a mildly hallucinogenic herb as a stimulant/relaxant, probably about as potent as two Miller Lites. But the Cubans were pushing "Sherms" — brown Sherman cigarettes dipped in PCP. The natives' systems and psyches weren't prepared for that kinda madness. It made for some grisly, horrific crimes.

The Call

I was working patrol, graveyard watch. The call was "Unknown disturbance, possible stabbing." The only telephone was in the housing office. I got a best-guess location and floored it. A horseshoe-shaped building, dark, one light coming from an open door. A dozen clamoring refugees, some with knife cuts and slashes, pelted me with fractured Spanish and Misumalpan. "He kills all!" My cover unit was minutes away.

eased in. Blood spatters on the walls and floor of the front room. I inched through an inner door. To my left was a space between the wall and a humming refrigerator. It was filled with a waist-high heap of bloody laundry — I thought.

One dim naked bulb lit the kitchen to my right and a rusty back screen door. The shadows were dark, fresh blood slashes bright crimson, everywhere; walls, fridge, cabinets, floor, not dropped, but flung, sprayed. I thought, all this needs is horror-movie music. The bloody laundry moved and a head poked up. I admit it. I jumped. Wild black hair, deep facial cuts, scared sad eyes.

imploring, broken voice whimpering, one dripping hand extended to me. Holstered my sidearm, knelt and pulled away bloody clothing — and there was another head capped with black hair and a smaller pair of coal-black eyes. A girl, about five years old, bad cuts on her arms and hands — and two little feet? More digging. Yes. Another little girl, maybe two, three years old, her shoulder cut to the bone. Mother had burrowed into the laundry, hiding herself and the girls in that heap of rags as they bled and waited.

Momma sprayed me with word-salad and pantomime, and I got that "He gets the big knife to cut us in pieces." Then her eyes popped wide as the screen door opened behind me. Spun on my knees. He was holding a machete in his raised right hand. I pulled my Smith & Wesson Model 19, leveled it and shouted for him to freeze, drop the knife, suelta el cuchillo!

Nothing. No reaction. I realized he wasn't seeing me. Staring at her? I couldn't tell. Still yelling I scrambled upright, into his line of sight. Nothing. His arm seemed to vibrate — but he still didn't see or hear me.

Less than eight feet away. Head shots are a stupid gamble — but how much woodchopping could he do with two, four, six rounds in his body? I put the orange insert of my front sight on his nose. It would be too melodramatic to say I began to squeeze the trigger, because really, all I knew was the trigger was moving and the hammer arcing back. There was no anger, no murderous rage in his eyes, just deep ocean floor, blankness, nothing. Replayed countless times over all these years since, I could only think "If a cancer cell had eyes, they'd look like that."

The End — That's All

A flashlight beam played across the screen door. It swung out. My cover officer burst in, the rookie behind him blundering into his back, unbalancing him, but he swung the 4-cell flashlight hard, whacking Murder-Man on the side of the head with a thonk! He dropped like a sack. The machete hit the edge of the sink, did a high flip in the air and clattered on the deck. In another blurry second my cover cuffed Murder-Man, and the rookie, horrified, blanched dead white screamed "Oh Jesus, oh Jesus, oh sweet Jesus!" looking past me.

Momma had tried to rise. Long strips of flesh hung from one arm and a flap of cheek dangled. The bloody children tumbled out and another, a tiny infant, fell to the floor squalling now but seemingly unharmed, perhaps shielded by his mother's shredded arm.

Roaring in my ears; hardly heard the sirens coming, tires squealing, cops and EMT's filling that space, squeezing me outside, standing dumbly staring up at the night sky, gun still in my hand. A lieutenant asked "Did you shoot?" Uh, I don't know. I knew only one thing for sure: Murder-Man would have cut them all into pieces. Pieces. Every one.

It wasn't about skill or courage or justice or any of that crap. I was just The guy who was there. Late, but there. And now I look up into another inky-black night sky and think, Thank God. That's all. Connor OUT.

STUFF YOU DON'T READ:
The Back-Beat Story on Connor-Style T&E's

July/August 2015

Some tools of the Test & Eval trade.

The shop was quiet. I sat with electronic range muffs on and my eyes closed, holding a pistol to the left side of my head. I was slowly squeezin' the trigger when the door squeaked open and RJ blurted, "Sir? What the heck are you doin'?!" He's our youngest DARM (Deputy Assistant Range Monkey). His eyes were buggin' and he looked like he was gulpin' golf balls. I put the gun down and laughed. "What did it look like, kid?"

"Like you were gonna blow your brains out, but, uh … you didn't want the noise to hurt your ears?" He blushed furiously. "Wow, that's messed up — and weird, sir." I laughed 'til I 'bout peed myself.

Told him I was listening to a trigger. See, my hearing is damaged from gunfire and ordnance, more on the right than the left. So, I turn the right muff off to suppress ambient sounds, and turn the volume to maximum on the left muff. Amplified, you can sometimes clearly hear what your finger can only sorta detect. If you listen close to a glitch or rough spot, you can hear things like, is it a steady frictional sound, a tik! or a grritt? Is it repetitive or erratic? Duzzit change location?

You can see how that leads to three questions: Is this glitch in the design, is it only in this pistol or is it a serious manufacturing problem? Then, is it correctable? A "frictional" can fade with use. A consistent tik might be just a trigger-connected safety working. A grritt is always bad news. Maybe fixable, but bad news.

I do the same thing with slide cycling and revolver rotation; feeling and listening for problems, inconsistencies or sometimes just characteristics of the design. If during rotation a revolver cylinder drags consistently at a given point, or the trigger pull stiffens, would that ring your bell? How 'bout inconsistently? I wanta know before I shoot the weapon for T&E, and then compare findings after putting a coupla hundred rounds through it. Often, any frictional "white noise" from both triggers and actions vanishes with proper break-in, and actions smooth right out. Often, not always.

Kickin' Tires, Checkin' Oil

I bust out the magnifier and hit the pinpoint light to inspect firing pin and striker noses, and extractors, checking both the face and the claw. If there were any dings or wear after only, say, 400-500 rounds, wouldn't you wanta know about that? Does the extractor wiggle like a loose tooth or does it have good tension? If a trigger has a little play front-to-back, no big deal, but if it has wobble side-to-side, whattaya think? Worrisome? I'm not a gunsmith — not even a good gun mechanic — but I can figure out where potential wear, chatter and bash-points are, and I wanta see 'em up close and personal before and after shootin'.

I test safeties — and then try to spoof 'em. The first time you put a manual safety on, then pull the trigger and find the gun woulda gone bang! if there'd been a round in it, well … Your attitude on consumer testing changes. If a manufacturer says a pistol will not fire if it's even slightly out of battery, who checks that? I think it's my job. Am I wrong? Have you ever tried repeatedly to see if short-stroking a trigger will make it seize up? Tried casually "bumping off" a safety feature, or bumping a hammer off full cock, or tripping a tensioned striker system with a blow in the right place? I do it.

Using inert rounds, I'll put a gun in carry-condition, stick it in a coat pocket with keys and coins, then gnarfle the coat like a mad monkey to see how much persuasion it takes to fire it. You'd wanta know, right? If I tell you that firearm X requires a complete, proper, deliberate pull, you can bet I've tested it.

On the range, I always shoot firearms canted to 3, 6 and 9 o'clock to see if that'll jam 'em, then shoot 'em as close to straight up and straight down as I can get away with. Most can handle it, a few can't. I figure, better I learn this in the dirtbox than have you learn it in a fight — right? Often I shoot autopistols up close to a vertical support on the right, to see if brass bouncin' back at the action might cause a malf.

I pay attention to extraction and ejection, and where brass is thrown. I'm looking for consistency. Different loads will throw differently, but if the distance and angle is erratic with any or all loads, that indicates a problem. If it's one type of ammo, I run chrono tests on it. If it shows a wide "extreme spread" in velocities, there's your answer. If it's not the ammo, then it's the gun — maybe not an immediate problem, but of the "bite you in the butt later" variety.

Expended brass is checked for all the usual suspects: inconsistent primer indents, split case mouths, gouging and tearing of extractor grooves, all that. Then comes all the post-poppin' exams.

Why Don't You Read This?

If it ain't remarkable, I don't remark on it. There ain't enough word-space for everything. Like now. RJ asked if all professional gunwriters do this stuff. That stumped me.

"I dunno," I said. "I ain't one, and never asked one." Connor OUT.

DRAGONS UND MOPES

SEPTEMBER/OCTOBER 2015

I talked about Van Zyl in the May/June 2014 issue. A reader scoffed; called VZ a figment, a fraud. Roy gently rebuked him in the September-October '14 Speak Out, but it still rankles me. A figment? So, a bit about him:

Born Congo, schooled Brussels, bored stiff in Belgian service: "Ridiculous." While on duty, entire family asphyxiated by a fire that never touched 'em. Adieu Belgique; joined French Foreign Legion, met best friend Edward, a short, wiry, entrepreneurial Brit. After the Legion, formed a business: training, consulting, fighting from Pointe-Noire to the Philippines, then into import/export. When Edward settled in the PI, VZ wandered, then gravitated to us.

A giant physical prodigy, a shade over seven feet tall, thick-muscled and fast, none of the clumsiness often found in XXX-L men. Dragon tattoos encircle massive arms. He intimidates people; "menacing," they call him. Great guy, but only two expressions: displeasure and calm. Never saw him smile until the day our over-mountain neighbors visited with their little twin girls. Beautiful, peach-cheeked toddler angels with heavy, tousled golden curls. The parents were "discomposed" seeing VZ, but from the instant, literally, he saw the twins and they saw him, the trio were bestest, loving pals. He knelt:

"I am VZ, and you are … Mopsy Vun, und Mopsy Two, okay?" "BEEZY!" they cried, like they'd known him forever, and climbed him like alpinists up a bluff, nestling in his arms. They accepted their new names as easy as breathing. Pretended he couldn't tell them apart, which tickled them enormously, leading to much teasing and "fooling him." They became "Beezy and the Mopsies," even to some people in town. He made his dragons dance for them; never did that for us. And there was that smile. Mrs.

Mopsy began visiting often, because first, the Mopsies loved and demanded their Beezy, and second, it gave the mother-of-twins a rest! A CAT-scan slice:

Wolf & Tiger On Watch

Mom and Dad Mopsy in our kitchen sippin' iced tea. Mrs. Mopsy suddenly twitched, "Where are the girls?" Helena laid a shush-finger to her lips and beckoned "Come see." In the shade of the big black oak, the Mopsies lay tumbled like plushy-toys in our hammock, deep in sleep. Sancho Panza sat alert atop a ruined kiln, ears up, scanning 360 for threats. VZ sat on a stump, one huge tattooed arm extended, gently, so gently rocking the hammock — and smiling at the Mopsies.

"Would you rather they were guarded by a wolf and a tiger?" Helena whispered. "Oh, I think they are," replied Missus Mopsy.

The thought occasionally winkled that VZ slipped too naturally into playing tea party, reading the Mopsies' moods, washing little faces, steadying drinkies so as not to spill, making up games. Couldn't figure it; dismissed it. Then Edward arrived to visit VZ. The Mopsies were playing with Beezy. Edward was visibly shocked, then broke into a wide chimpanzee-grin. That evening I overheard scraps of a chat between them: "Ja," VZ said, "Chust like dem, but wiss blondie-curlss, not dark." Edward patted a big shoulder, said "Sent from God, p'raps. You've mourned too long, my friend."

I soft-cornered Edward alone and asked, "His family. That fire. Little girls," and he stopped me cold. "Zipped lips, tick-a-lock," he muttered, making the gestures. "I'm sworn, mate. But happy for 'im. He deserves this." I'm an idiot. But finally, I understood. My heart broke for him. And I ticked that lock, until now.

Mark Of The Mopsies

Busted bits, tumbled-down kilns and clay-pits show that long ago somebody made crockery here. One pit contains putty-colored clay. Another, seemingly unused for much, holds reddish clay. Beezy und der Mopsies loved playing there. The Mopsy Mob were noon-to-dinner guests one day. I was duty messenger, dispatched to announce chowtime. VZ and the twins sat on a cut in the putty-clay pit, surrounded by light-colored shapes like mini-loaves of bread and several red-clay fish, pretty realistic except for the big X's for their eyes. I called out "Supper in ten." VZ waved me closer.

"Za Mopsies told me story of loaffs und fishies, purr-fect! Zo, dey make wonderful loaffs and fishies, yes?" The Mopsies beamed up at his praise — I mean, sun-beamed at him. They'd been patting out a big red oval. "I finish platter," he told them. "Mopsies go to momma, wash up for dinner, okay?"

They rose and in turn, each held his face between her hands, kissed him on the lips, said "I love you, Beezy," giggled like GiggleGiggleGiggle and tootled to the house. I told VZ not to touch his face; I had to show him something. He nodded, his eyes glistening a little.

Got a mirror from the house and held it in front of him. Two perfect sets of tiny brick-red handprints, slightly overlapping each other, decorated his cheeks. He stared at his reflection. I'd thought he would laugh. But again, I'm an idiot. The intimidating giant, the "menace" shuddered and shook, rivers of tears streaming down, cutting through the Mopsy-paws, falling from his face. He turned away from me. "I finish platter," he choked, "Und you shuddup aboud dis! — forever, yes?" I agreed.

Time passed. I nagged him. He released me from my oath. Told him some folks think he's a myth.

"Gut!" he said, "I am myth. C'est bon!" And he smiled. Does that a lot now. Connor OUT.

MUH INFLOONSHEZ?
—Yeah, I Gotz Sum—

November/December 2015

Only a few people in publishing know me on sight, and it's okay by me. Unfortunately, one is a pretentious drunk who cornered me at a fancy veterans' charity wingding. Spilling his cocktail on my shoes, he slurred like, "Sho, hooo wush yur litterararial, uhh… (took him four tries to say "literary") infloonshez, huh? Hoo?" I was thinkin' I could knock him out and claim he fainted. But Helena suddenly appeared, grabbed his "dry arm," spun him around and pointed him at the bar. She was wearin' the bloody-murder crimson gown with the plunging front; the one which guaranteed no man would remember anything above her shoulders or below her waist — their loss, believe me.

"For me," she commanded, "Jameson's, straight up. GO!" He balked. She swatted him on the butt and said "Skedaddle!" He silly-grinned, shakily, stupidly — and skedaddled. We split for the exit. Not our circus, not our monkeys. But the drunk got me thinkin': Do I gotz "literary influences"? Yup; I do.

Me No Likee Anglish

As a half-wild boy in the islands I was functionally illiterate in several languages. I happily strung scraps of French, Dutch, Malay, Chinese and sorta-English together with a thread of Melanesian pidgin, now formalized and known as "Tok Pisin." I loved it. Mipela likee distok velly-velly. Then Dad returned from a long cruise. He was not amused. My headgear got forcibly "adjusted" and he buried me in books. I would learn to read, write and speak proper English. It was a "March or Die" proposition. But English was boring — and tough! I needed help and inspiration. I got Joe.

If you haven't read Joseph Conrad's masterworks; Lord Jim; Heart of Darkness; Typhoon; An Outcast of the Islands; Nostromo and more, maybe you should. I was hooked instantly because he wrote of sights, sounds, smells and tastes I knew! The flat cerulean glass of the Java Sea turning to a billion flashing silver coins as baitfish fled pursuing Bonito; curling Polynesian combers crashing on the outer reefs and trade winds singing through the prop roots and fans of pandanus palms; the musty smell of drying copra; the perfume of a cargo of vanilla at the dock, and the tang of fresh-caught lagoon crab — this guy knew my world and painted it beautifully with words. I devoured his books. Then Dad dropped the bomb on me.

Ol' Joe Conrad was born Jozef Teodor Konrad Korzeniowski in Poland in 1857. He knew only a few words of English as a teenager; couldn't speak or write it for beans until his twenties — and all his books were written in English! Ever tried to read Polish? I figured if he could whisk Polish to perfection in English then maybe I could drag my lingual mélange to mediocrity in it. Me kowtow you bikpela man. Whoops. I mean, "I salute you, sir." He stoked my English fire.

Rud, Mikey, Winnie et al

Ask anybody: "Who was the most prolific writer in the English language?" Nine outta ten will name Willie Shakespeare. The tenth will reply "Duh." Willie wrote a bunch, but Rudyard Kipling beat him by miles of type. Yeah, I read Shakespeare and I did learn something from him: All of life is either tragedy, comedy or just boring. But from my buddy Rud, I learned you can write anything; "serious literature," children's books, poems, ballads, sagas, fantasies, human dramas, history — and social critique. Some may like it, some won't, and it doesn't matter, as long as you connect with someone. But the main thing is, whenever it fits, write for people like you're talking with them, and write in the language as they speak it.

Kipling could and did write perfect prose, but much of his work was written as Tommy Atkins and Stella Sedgewick spoke it in barracks and barrooms, woolen mills and sheep farms. High literary society was scandalized — and the people loved it. "One of us, this chap is," they'd say, "Money or no, he's a pukka bloke." If you need examples, just check out his "Barrack-Room Ballads" — and enjoy!

The first three things I ever stood and recited in English were the opening poem to Kipling's Jungle Book, the classic Gunga Din, and perhaps the best thing ever written in any language on being a good man: his poem "If." I guess the drunk would say Kipling was one of my main "infloonshez."

From Mikey — Miguel de Cervantes, author of Don Quixote, the first modern novel — I learned heroes don't have to be perfect: the Man of La Mancha was two beers short of a six-pack, but a brave and noble warrior. And in friends like Sancho Panza, simple loyalty always trumps sophistication. Yeah, I know something about tilting at windmills too.

From young Winston Churchill, the thrill-seeking lancer of the 4th Hussars, I learned you must not only see the "big picture" but the smallest details. If you read nothing else of his works, read The River War, and here's a challenge: "Track the biscuit!" Then you'll understand.

There were more, sure, and a common thread ran through it all. None sat at home and wrote of things they hadn't lived; hadn't personally experienced. The message to me was Go! Do! See, risk, learn — then write. Thanks to them I knew what my life would be. And to my greatest influence: Thanks, Dad. Me likee Anglish now. Velly-velly. Connor OUT.

THE CHRISTMAS CONUNDRUM:
Shopping for Salt-Crusted Sarcastic Savages

JANUARY/FEBRUARY 2016

The crude cackling continued out back as I stepped into the kitchen. Helena was washing dishes. I snuggled up behind her and whispered "I don't think Uncle John and Uncle G will be with us much longer. They may not even make it to Christmas." She stiffened and asked "Why is that?"

"Cuz I'm gonna kill 'em!" That got me a whack with a sudsy spatula. A fresh barrage of belly-laughs came through the screen door. "Heard that, meathead!" they guffawed; "Got our hearing aids turned up, dummy!" Then a voice said more softly; more like a rusty chainsaw, "Why didn't we drown that mutt when he was a puppy?" And the reply, "Maybe he just needs a good Atomic Wedgie, huh?" Those two ... Helena asked "Same-old-same-old Christmas conundrum, hmm?"

I had been trying to get 'em to give me some hints on what they might like for Christmas. These two are the most infuriating family you could ever love; the crustiest, most caustic kin you could ever cherish. They raised me — no easy task — after my dad died, and when Helena and the kids came along they folded 'em into the wolfpack, standing overwatch like Viking berserkers while I was off playing Action Hero; gentle as sheepdogs with them, but deadly as demented dragons to anyone threatening their litter. Christmas brings out their best and worst.

Neither one are what you'd call "well-funded" or even semi-secure. They live cheap, not broke but not flush. But every Christmas they deluge us all with thoughtfully-chosen and often, in my opinion, too-expensive gifts. I've tried to talk to 'em about it and I get "Shuddup. We do what we want. It's our money. And, shuddup!" It helps that they laugh then, but still ...

It's worse when I ask what they want. Their eyes go slitty, their lips draw tight and they act like they're reaching for daggers in their cloaks. I get "What did we teach you about saving money, ya moron? We don' need nuffin! Save us the drumsticks an' two slices of pie. Bring us coffee Christmas morning. Now drop it, dummy." This year was worse, 'cause they were having fun with me.

The STO Gift Guide

The old buzzards fished me in, pretending they were gonna be cooperative. Uncle John took the lead:

"Okay. I want a set of Klapper-Grips for my 1911," he said. "I like the ones with the textured desert camo finish." I bit; I asked what they were and where I could find 'em. "Each grip panel has an acoustic sensor, a 20-lumen LED light and a buzzer-vibrator in it like on your cell phone. I'm always leavin' my Roscoe layin' somewhere and forgetting where I put it. Old-Timer's Disease, y'know. With the Klapper-Grips, I just clap my hands an' the pistol lights up, buzzes an' vibrates." Keeping an absolutely straight face — the only one he's got — he continued.

"You can find 'em at The STO Store, online." I hadda ask what STO stood for. "Senior Tactical Operator," he deadpanned. "That's what me an' Uncle G are, y'know — Senior Tactical Operators." I caught just a whiff of rat in the air, but couldn't even open my mouth before Uncle G busted in.

"While yer online there, meathead," he says, "What I really want for my bedside boomer is one 'a them new STO SnoreFire 9000 weaponlights. Just like a regular weaponlight, except it's 'shot-activated'. You fire a shot and it turns on for ten seconds. Great idea, huh?" My brain was still operating in the "semi-normal world" mode, so I asked incredulously why he would want a light that only turns on after you've fired a shot? Shouldn't you identify your target first?

"Nah," he waved his hand dismiss-ively. "I live alone; no pets since Bogey crossed the river. Somebody's dumb enough to enter my house, in the dark, and wake me up? WAKE ME UP? I only wanta see what I shot, an' see if it needs more shootin'. Then I wanta get back ta sleep." They drive me nuts — and the drive gets shorter all the time.

Red-Headed Genius

"You poor baby," Helena soothed. "I got 'em covered. Thick, soft oversized Merino wool socks, with no elastic. Elastic restricts their circulation. For each, a set of four large illuminating magnifiers to scatter around the house. Plus, they both get a 48" telescoping tool-grabber so they don't have to bend over to pick up stuff they've dropped. And these," she said, fetching a padded box from the closet and pulling out two crystal liquor decanters.

"Uncle John's bread-and-butter whiskey is George Dickel #12, right? And what does he call it? And you know how Uncle G is about his scotch. What does he always say when you're teasing him and reaching for it?" She turned the decanters, exposing deep cut engraving. One read "Doctor Dickel's Magical Elixir #12." The other read simply but elegantly, "MY Scotch — Not Yours — MY SCOTCH!" Perfect.

"And for you," she laughed, "I got — a clue, 'cause you really need one!" She pulled me to her fiercely, muttered throatily, "C'mere, ya big gorilla!" and puckered up for a kiss.

If you've got old, mean, loving, ornery angels on your list; folks you could never repay for all they've done for you, show 'em at Christmas. Get creative. And kiss a redhead. That's always good. Connor OUT.

PICKIN' PERFECT PACKIN' PISTOLS:
Tougher than pickin' pecks of pickled peppers

MARCH/APRIL 2016

Elsewhere in this issue you'll find a blurb on the daily-carry preferences of Handgunner's professional gunwriters — and mine too! You may find my choices a little different, maybe surprising, but I assure you those choices weren't made lightly. I confess, for many years my daily-carry guns depended more on habituation, ego, self-image and other stupid influences than on any well thought-out criteria. Being much older, a tiny tad wiser and far more busted-up, I've actually tried to be smart lately — semi-smart, anyway — about my packin' pistol picks.

Conditions have changed and so have I. I'm out of the Traveling Action Hero business. In the aftermath of my Spinal Surgery Saga, I can no longer carry enough ordnance to fight the Battle of the Bulge comfortably on my belt all day. My speed, mobility and flexibility are, to put it mildly, "challenged." My most likely shooting scenarios have transitioned from "Looking for trouble and finding it" to "Avoiding trouble, but ready and willing to overwhelm it."

If somebody — or a buncha somebodies — force a violent reaction, I won't be executing any Ranger Ricky tactical snap-rolls, escape-or-evade-while-delivering-fire maneuvers or sprinting for cover. If I have to fight in the open, it'll be like a tank with both tracks blown off: the turret still swivels, but I'll likely live or die right where the fight starts and ends. My fighting abilities are less like a stalking tiger and more like an old snapping turtle. If limited to short, hard blows and a deadly bite, I want that bite to be decisive. Is this ringin' any bells for some of you out there?

Choices And Criteria

Hence, I decided my primary carry piece should be a .45 ACP — but only if it met other criteria. It should be light, flat, smooth and simple; fast into play and agile for snap-shooting. It should point naturally, instinctively, and I shouldn't even have to see the sights to consistently score deadly hits at 1 to 10 meters — and very importantly, single-handed with either hand. For targets at greater distance, sights should be very rapidly acquired and up to the challenge. Ability to shoot picture-perfect rapid doubles I judged less important than controlled, repeated singles cadenced about one per second. Ideally, it should be a point-and-squeeze weapon, safe but speedy with minimal controls. Another question was, if grappling with some goblin, how easy or

Four constants: Gun, light, knife and attitude.

difficult would it be for someone to wrest it away from my one-hand hold?

I owned three roughly suitable pistols. I also had the TP45 on loan from Kahr, to shoot head-to-head against its lower priced near-twin, the CT45. Wrote that up in the Jan/Feb issue. I was poised to return both because, well, you just can't keep 'em all, no matter how good. But then I commenced comparative testing.

I shot 'em all, standing, sitting, kneeling and turned-turtle; from in-contact range to 25; all angles and around obstacles; pulling and presenting from under shirt, jacket and parka. I simulated drawing and firing seated in a vehicle, leaning on my cane, holding horizontal and vertical objects, pushing and striking with the off hand; whatever came to mind. Note: Many of these drills were with unloaded pistols — but still informative. Note #2: It was also a great and valid excuse for a lot of shooting!

I wasn't surprised the TP45 did well — it had performed superbly during T&E — but I was surprised it beat the others resoundingly on "either-hand" shooting and close, fast engagements. I kept it.

Selecting a backup to carry in my OTD — Out The Door — bag, I wanted sheer firepower and high capacity; best met with a double-stack 9mm. The weapon must be drawn easily from its flap-covered holster-compartment. If my OTD isn't hanging from a shoulder it's usually suspended from the headrest of my passenger seat, in front if I'm rolling alone and in back if I have a companion. I may need the gun fast. Angles and reach dictate use of a relatively short, snag-free, very easily grasped and drawn weapon. Candidates underwent the same kind of drills I had run for my on-body carry piece.

My SIG P250 Compact won that competition in a walk. So, my backup with two spare mags yields 46 extra rounds of "And that goes for your whole gang too!" An added bonus was both it and the TP45 are double-action-only designs with strikingly similar trigger pulls, and their minimal controls — mag release and slide lock — are virtually identical. Under duress, matching operating systems can be a big plus.

Not Sayin', & Just Sayin'

I could recommend both weapons to you, but I won't. Selecting your daily carry Roscoe and backup-bag gun should reflect intensely personal preferences. I do recommend basing your choices on the same kind of demanding drills I employed — and will review from time to time. And this:

Please, never step out your door, no matter where you live — not to the backyard, the barn, the mailbox or your Maserati — without a gun, a light, a knife and an attitude. Never drive without considering dangers greater than the usual morons, drunks, dopers and texters. Returning home, remember, evil may await. The new national sport seems to be The Anger Games. You may not want to play, but you might have no choice. And I want you to WIN. Connor OUT.

IN PRAISE OF "PURE PLEASURE GUNS":
It's less about goals — and more about souls

It sure is nice to have an Ammo Factory in the family. In our outfit, that's my cousin MacKenzie, Uncle John's son. His reloading room looks like the inner sanctum of a major ammo manufacturer, and he has a passion for turning out better-than-factory fodder. I dropped by one afternoon with a bucket of brass for him to work his magic on. He was stacking hefty paper boxes into a .50-cal can marked "POOTS." Yeah; I had to ask.

Shot hot 'n dirty, the Tussey .38 once defended Uncle John's life. Now it soothes his soul.

"Oh," he laughed. "These are light-loaded, soft-shooting .38 Specials for Dad's Tussey .38; his Pure Pleasure, he calls it ..." We GunBums do most of our shooting together — it's a family-and-friends thing — but everybody knows Uncle John sometimes slides out stealthily for solo range sessions. He doesn't talk about them; just comes back happy. On that Great Stone Face others might not see "happy," but we do. His rage-radiation level drops to zero. In the chain-reaction chaos of my recent life I'd almost forgotten about those solo sessions. What is a Tussey .38? Glad you asked.

Harken back to the May/June 2010 issue, folks, and a Guncrank entitled "Tale of a Roamin' Pony — The Colt That Came Home." It's available online in "Digital Versions." It was the story of a Colt 1911 built by master gunsmith Terry Tussey for Uncle John about 1981, when he was commanding officer of his agency's SWAT unit; how a decade later it went astray, then 20 years later, was retrieved, refreshed and reborn in secret by Terry, and how that Colt came home. The Tussey .38 tacks a tail on that tale.

The .38 "Extra-Special"

Shortly after Terry crafted the Colt, Uncle John brought in another box. This one contained a special order from S&W: a round-butt 6-shot K-Frame .38 Special with a 3" heavy barrel. He wanted the entire top machined flat then fitted with a full-length rib with integral target sights. The hammer was to be bobbed and the action slicked; the trigger smoothed and rounded on the edges, plus other enhancements. Finally, all but the rib was industrial hard-chromed and graced with a set of smooth, contoured wood grips. The result was a superb shooting, hefty but eminently packable backup for the Tussey Colt, or, stand-alone wear around the station in a custom hip holster.

For whatever reason, Terry didn't tell Uncle John he didn't work on revolvers back then; he's almost exclusively a pistolsmith, and a great one. (He does selected revolver action jobs and other touches now.) He just did it — and Uncle John loved the result.

But the S&W, like the Tussey Colt, was sold when Uncle John was disability-retired on "half pay and full bills." You've got to understand when Terry works on a gun, he does it for that shooter. And the distinctive Smith was crafted for one man. In 2010, while Terry was refurbishing the Colt 1911, he launched a broad search to locate the original 3" .38 Special. He couldn't find it. If you run across such a 3" Smith bearing Terry's circa-1981 twin T's engraved in an oval on the frame, you have an almost unique revolver. I say almost, because when he couldn't find the original, he re-created it, and as he'd done with the Colt, simply surprised the stuffin' — and some liquid leakage from the eyes — out of Uncle John with it. Why? Because, he said, it was the right thing to do. Tells you something about Terry Tussey, doesn't it?

Uncle John has carry-guns, backups and home defense guns. While the Tussey .38 could ably fill such roles, now he shoots it only for the deep, soul-satisfying pleasure of it.

Not A Routine — A Ritual

I nagged him into a demo. As Uncle John explained it, a Pure Pleasure Gun needn't be a slick tack-driver or even ultra-reliable. It can be a poor and arcane design, perhaps destined from birth for an early trip to the junkyard. The cartridge can be obsolete, the ergonomics awful, but for whatever reason, it appeals to you. The important thing is you delight in it, and can shoot it without expectations of excellence or anything. It may be a cranky, gritty P38; a pitted, unwieldy Enfield No. 2 Mk 1; a Brazilian contract Smith & Wesson 1917 .45 ACP that's two percent blue and 98 percent dings and gouges. Your "pure pleasure gun" may be your only gun, and this is okay too.

You don't try for tight groups or fast splits; you don't think defense scenarios or competition stages. You just "zone-out and zen-in" on the feel, the smell, the push of recoil and lose your goals, your cares, your imagery and ego. Uncle John caught me checking my groups — the Tussey .38 can shoot clover-groups — and waggled a thick finger at me: a warning. That's not what you're here for.

It took me a while, but I got it. The overwhelming majority of my shooting is "business" or intensive personal training. Both take real concentration. Sure, I get a certain level of enjoyment out of it, particularly when all goes well and the elements come together. But with pure pleasure shooting, it's not about the machine; it's about the mindset. It feels good.

Just think about it — but not too hard. Connor OUT.

MOOHOOHAHAHA! IT LIVES!
Spooky Stuff Indeed

JULY/AUGUST 2016

Yeah, that's a long gun in the photo, and this is HANDgunner. But when Roy-Boy, our Publishing Potentate slips, you jump on it. He'd been on the road, and I suspect, gargling "special" cough syrup when I told him about FrankenGun. He went woozy, burped contentedly and slurred, "So, uhh … Write it up!" Ha! I'd told him about it simply because I don't get tickled easily, but Frankie tickles me into spontaneous incontinence. Besides, it reminded me of a FrankenGun 1911 I have — so it applies. Here's the story:

My go-to gunsmith "K" doesn't want his name mentioned because he's already swamped with work. We're 1,600 miles apart now, but phones and FedEx facilitate conspiracies. During one tele-whining session we bemoaned our teetering piles of orphaned AR parts. Try to sell 'em? Nah. We'd get some doofus in a tin-foil hat offering us two bucks and a possum in a poke sack. Then K bumped into Rob Sutton of X-Caliber Barrels. They chatted. Rob observed, "So you haven't tried one of our barrels yet?"

Later, Rob delivered an 18" beauty with a .223 Wylde chamber and 1:8" twist; hefty but not heavy due to deeply cut spiral fluting fore and aft of the mid-length gas port. Jet black nitride covered the 416R stainless, but to K it sparkled like diamonds. He fired up his nuclear-powered FlugleTronic Laser-Peeper (whatever; that stuff is all Space-Cowboy techno-gullah to me), 'scoped the bore and chamber and declared it immaculate. Short of bucks but long on stupid and caffeine, we commenced dredging our junk bins and oily cardboard boxes.

"We Gotz Partz, Inc."

The process was like magnetizing that barrel and draggin' it through a junkyard: You get a little gold and a lot of garbage. I'd been evaluating three excellent HyperTouch triggers from HIPERFIRE, and needed a test-bed for a 24C, their competition model. K unearthed an Armalite gas block. I found a lonely, ignored FailZero bolt. From that point the makers, origins and quality became unknown factors. Most parts were unmarked and the majority were used and abused.

K retrieved a dirt-cheap receiver set, and fortunately, it miked out "straight." So did a nickel-boron finished carrier from a company that was born, wheezed, and perished as an infant. The free-float handguard was a $30 clearance sale pickup. The only receiver tube I had was rifle-length, so we needed an A2-size buttstock to match. That deformed-lookin' thing in the photo was a prototype of a design with a trap door compartment for a 20-round mag; odd but comfy.

The only other identifiable parts were a Spike's Tactical melonited gas tube and a long-discontinued Brownells compensator resembling an elongated septic tank. Everything else, including pins, springs, buffer, latches, dust cover and miscellaneous widgets were UFO's. Finally, the Frankenstein monster was complete. But was it … ALIVE? Moohoohahaha! (Envision lightning flashing, thunder crashing over mad Dr. K's laboratory.)

But just because something's assembled doesn't mean it runs — and doesn't cough, stutter, choke or maybe blow up. He met the other three Shootin' Coots at his range for a fun-shoot. First, he explained, he had to test this monstrosity, and would they notify his wife if things went wrong? They laughed at it. Then he shot it. Then they shot it. K called me that night, happier'n a shoat in a slop trough. "You won't believe this," he said. The Shootin' Coots all demanded FrankenGuns.

Some Kinda Heavy JuJu

A week later I received FrankenGun and their stack of targets. Half-inch groups. Three-quarter inch groups. Some one inch groups. I was pleased, but had a bellyful of qualms; big wiggly ones. K and the Coots are all seasoned competitive riflemen. I'm not a precision shooter. I'll snap-shoot torso targets with the big dogs, but I'm not your guy for threading needles. K and the Coots had used a 1-4x tactical 'scope. To stack the deck, I mounted a Rapid Reticle 2.5-10x40mm RR-900 Tactical.

Time to face the music. I packed up the same four flavors of ammo used by the Coots and brought along my cousin Mac, to ride the spotting scope, witness my shame, daub my tears of frustration and laugh at me.

No Lead Sled, no sandbags; at 100 yards, just laid the handguard into the U of a Boyt screw-stand and settled in. Fired three shots. Mac wriggled on the spotting scope and murmured Geez … Now the center target. Another Geez. Now the right. Then Geez! Let ME shoot that thing! Yeah. We rotated for an hour.

The tactical ammo, with slugs from 55-gr. to 77, delivered 3-shot groups averaging 0.75" and a fantastic 5-shot group of 0.687"! Our sole box of target ammo, 20 rounds of 69-gr. Federal Gold Medal Match produced five 3-shot groups running 0.5" to 0.625" and a 5-shot cluster of 0.625" — with four shots overlapping.

Function was absolutely flawless. Folks with rows of gold cups may not be impressed, but us spastic combat monkeys? Stunned dumb. To celebrate, we shifted to "Steel Valley" and effortlessly, mercilessly pummeled plates from 100 to 500 yards until sunset. There were two tickled shoats in the slop trough that night.

Up until we shot it, we agreed that later, with more time and money, we'd dismantle this Franken-mess and build something decent with that cool barrel and nice trigger. Our new agreement is, we ain't touchin' a thing; not a single thing. There's heavy juju goin' on here — and cavemen don't mess with magic. Connor OUT

Watch for a detailed account of FrankenGun in one of our upcoming annuals. Connor doesn't deserve it, but Frankie does. — Roy

MY HEROES:
You've got your role models — I've got mine

SEPTEMBER/OCTOBER 2016

Look up there to the left. Yup; it's a plain, cheap rubber doorstop. I've kept 'em handy for years, placing one where I would routinely see it — on my desk, a shelf, windowsill, whatever. It reminds me of who and what I am.

When they're new, shiny and unmarred, what do they do? They stop doors. Made for tough, unrelenting duty, in use under pressure they appear at repose and are casually overlooked. Of course they'll do more than stop doors. I've cut strips, chunks and cores out of 'em many times, to make washers, patches, and plugs; strips to reinforce more expensive but weaker materials — and then returned them to their original role. When deterioration and wounds have lessened their capabilities, all it takes is more force to wedge them into place. They still serve, silently.

I've driven them under a rogue washing machine which would otherwise dance a spastic rhumba over an uneven concrete deck until it popped its hoses. Four cheap inert doorstops, maybe one tenth of one percent of the weight and mass of that shaking, whirling, out-of-control machine stopped it dead. They take a continual beating, true, but the furor is quieted; the friction relieved.

A doorstop can and will become old, dinged, scraped, gouged and battered, as time and travail take their inevitable toll. Scarred, ugly and aged, what do they do? They stop doors.

My Digital Role Model

Back in 2000, I bought one of the first ProChrono Digital chronographs from Competition Electronics. Cheap at about $125, higher-class chronographs cost three or four times that much. But it had a prodigious memory, with

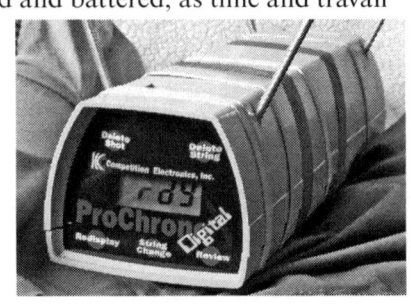

total recall of shot strings, velocities and myriad details. If somethin' fishy occurred, like two slugs recording the exact same velocity, it let you know with a bold "DUPE." If something went wrong or she wasn't sure, she owned up to it instantly with an embarrassed err for "error." But over countless thousands of rounds fired through her screens by myself and many others over 16 years, when I flipped her ON, she happily chirped rdy – her cute way of saying "Ready, boss; let's do this!"

But oh, the beatings it has taken; the damages it was never designed to suffer! It has been busted completely open, scattering parts thither and yon, three times. First, a pal whacked it as he turned, swinging a rifle case. The ProChrono hit the deck, cracked in two and parts flew. The case is a two-piece plastic clamshell, not meant to ever be opened. I presumed she was KIA. The next two times microbursts of wind came outta nowhere, plucked it and the tripod up and swung 'em to the deck like a hammer.

Each time I puzzled over which parts went where and what their jobs were. I kinda-sorta figured out stuff like this is the lookie-up slug-peeper and this has gotta be the Cybertronic Thinkleator-Rememberie-Widget. It's not that difficult if you have aptitude. I don't — but I'm persistent.

Repairs were made with broken toothpicks, shaved matchsticks, acrylic glue and plumber's putty. Note: Do not glue the case back together. Just wrap it in target tape and rubber bands, because you may have to open your patient back up again until you get it right. When all the little ruptured ducks were back into their rows and I hit the ON switch, she'd sing out "rdy," and go right back to work.

Check the inset photo, bottom right: February 2016, one of the lads failed to compensate for optic height-over-bore. That's the scar left by a 77-grain Sierra MatchKing at about 2,600 feet per second. She lives. She performs.

Quite Like Us

Sometimes a tough, simple, ugly ChunkaJunk can and will take on the heaviest, most violent chores and just soldier on. Sometimes a fragile, complex and sophisticated device can withstand more than anyone could ever reasonably expect it to, but given some care and persistent support, it will respond with a cheery face and absolute accuracy. Whether they are born to it and bred for it, or the cruelties of chance have visited horrors upon them, they remain true to task and purpose; true to the best of themselves — and to us.

How many of you ugly chunks have been the doorstop? How many times have you been that wedge, willingly taking the pressure and friction to keep others from mutual and personal destruction? How many of you fair and fragile specimens have suffered the flurried blows of fate and overcome them? I see something of myself in that damaged doorstop, a certain tall redhead in that taped-up chronograph, and many of you in both. Think about it. With respect, Connor OUT.

A KISS GOODBYE

NOVEMBER/DECEMBER 2016

Call him Dan. It's one syllable of his real name. He was an American veteran. He died in 2009, but I didn't learn that until mid-May 2016. I promised him I wouldn't write this until after his death, and I wouldn't name him. It's time. I hope he got to try his experiment — and I hope he got an answer.

Dan was a paratrooper, 101st Airborne. He described himself as a "heli-borne rifle-humper," serving two tours in Vietnam. Dan fought, survived and even thrived in combat in the Central Highlands. The 101st was the last Army division to leave Vietnam, and he was one of the last of them.

"America may have run outta fight," he said, "But I didn't. We won, and the politicians gave it away." Back at Fort Campbell, Dan didn't fit into the shrinking and demoralized Army. He mustered out as a sergeant and went abroad looking for fights. He found several, first as a contract soldier, then working for American OGA's — "Other Governmental Agencies." He stayed busy.

When people asked where he was from, he answered "A cliché." As an infant a few days old he was left on the stoop of a tiny orphanage in farmlands southwest of Springfield, Ill., sleeping in a wooden crate atop some diapers. A car's taillights were seen receding into the night, "Prob'ly headed for Route 66," he was told. The crate bore markings from a dairy products company in Chicago, and those were the only clues he ever had to his origin. Never adopted, he was the last kid out the door when he turned 18. The orphanage closed. He joined the Army.

One Tough Soldier

Tough? He was the kind of soldier other tough soldiers pointed to and said, "That's one tough sonuvvagun. Good man." Physically, he appeared built from rocks and steel cable. Mentally, he was agile and adaptive. Emotionally, he was blessed with the ability to form a closed, calm bubble of concentration, undisturbed yet tactically aware while focusing on complex tasks in the midst of furious fire. I've seen it. I wanted to applaud, but I was, you know — busy. Dan could seem virtually pitiless and devoid of emotion, but one thing was well known: When a fight was over and young men were grievously wounded or dying, especially if calling for their mothers, he tended to them like a mother himself, holding their hands, stroking their heads, murmuring to them as they passed. They touched him, deeply. The contrast freaked some people out. Though we spent very little time operating together, we connected. He opened up.

I saw him reading a well-worn, wrinkled letter beginning "My dearest son," and ending with something like, "Always, your loving mother." I asked, "But you're an orphan, right? Never knew your mother?" He smiled; said he'd fought alongside a guy who regularly received such letters from his mother. The guy would read 'em, then burn them. Dan asked if he could have one, and the guy agreed. Never having received such a letter himself, he treasured it.

Dan said he had thought and even read about the love of a mother for a son; the mystical, almost inexplicable connection between some of them. And he had never assumed his mother didn't love him. Maybe she didn't, but ...

"What if she really, really loved me, but had to give me up? If she's still alive, does she think about me, loves me, wishes she could make things right? If she's gone, did she die wishing that?" Who's to say, he said, when those boys call out for their mothers, that their moms don't hear them? Maybe they do — and maybe they even talk back to their sons. He asked, "Ever consider that? Sometimes, when those boys are fading out, it's like they hear their mothers and suddenly they relax, sometimes even smile — and then they pass. Who's to say it doesn't happen? Tell you what, Connor," he said. "If I go down hard and I can do it, I'm gonna call out for her. She might just be waiting."

That Last Kiss

Seriously wounded once, in a hospital, his cot was farthest in a room full of wounded-and-recovering men. It was up against a flimsy fabric curtain on a cord, separating them from a space holding several terminal cases. He called it the Waiting-To-Die Room. Other staff shunned it, only entering to briskly, brusquely check pulses and sometimes flip a sheet over a face. But one nurse on night shift went from cot to cot, sitting with each, whispering, holding their hands, sensing when they'd breathe their last — and then kissing them.

"Back to duty, Middle East," he said. "In an empty hallway checking a status board. There was a cartoon strip pinned up. This kid was depressed about going to school or something. A little girl kissed him and he brightened up, went out the door. The little girl smiles and says We all need someone to kiss us goodbye. Damn it, Connor, I cried like a baby." He stood, turned away, wiped his eyes. "Will she hear me? That's what I want to know." He walked away.

I thought of my own mother, long passed, and how many times she'd said she loved me. Yeah. We all need someone to kiss us goodbye. Connor OUT.

THE WORLD'S GREATEST GIFT-WRAPPER
That's Me – but you can do okay, too. Maybe.

JANUARY/FEBRUARY 2017

Yeah, I know this is the Jan/ Feb 2017 issue, but you're gettin' it now, right? And you'll find my "2016 Gift Guide" in it. That should help you fill in those blanks on your gift list. But there's still something else haunting you about Christmas, isn't there? A dark, nasty secret over which you've wept into your soppin' pillow on so many December nights since you were a clumsy, gawky child: You suck at gift-wrapping. And you don't just suck at it; you suck muddy canal water with a five-horse Briggs & Stratton motor through a 2" intake at it. We know it. You know it. Your family and friends have been shamed

Gift wrapping essentials: Bricks, tape gun, paper, T-shirt scraps.

by it all these years, telling timid little lies to soothe your tattered ego, like, "Oh, this package is so ... interesting," while they quietly murmured amongst themselves, "What is wrong with him? He can tie his own shoes, but ..." and sadly shook their heads.

Remember the time you put a 6"x8" gift box in the center of four yards of wrapping paper, and when you were finished, it looked like there was a big desert tortoise trapped under wadded paper on one side and a 3"x6" bald spot on the opposite side, with the cardboard showing through? Yes, we all saw it. It was posted online and went viral. Millions laughed at you. But buck up, little buckaroo. There is hope, and its name is Connor.

Stand By For Brilliance

Tough to imagine, I know, but I sucked at gift-wrapping worse than you. I sucked at it like suckin' curdled buttermilk through a battleship bilge pump at it. Everything I tried to gift-wrap came out looking like either a shopping cart smashed by a semi and draped with hot wet gift-wrap, or, like somebody tried to wrap a live, angry badger by spraying him with glue and then throwing scraps of colored paper at him. No kidding. Then — as often happens with me — I had a flash of brilliance; an epiphany which shook the heavens.

I heard the voice of Obi-Wan Kenobi saying "Use the force, Luke!" No, wait. That was something else. It was the voice of James Earl Jones rumbling "Dude ... Embrace the SUCK! EMBRACE IT!" I did. I embraced it, reveled in it, steeped like a teabag in it, went giddy-mad with it and developed ConnorWrappery into an art form. Well, whattaya gonna do when James Earl Jones speaks to you from an old combat boot? Brush it off as just more PTSD? No! Now, when people glance at a Himalayan-sized stack of presents across a wide room they can point unerringly at mine and happily declare, "That one's from Connor! Get that other stuff outta the way an' lemme get a photo!"

Tips & Techniques

Use some traditional Christmas wrap, but liberally fill in gaps with used, wrinkled My Pretty Pony and The Hulk birthday paper. Ragged swatches cut from old T-shirts, aluminum foil, and scraps of cereal boxes work too. Never attempt neatly folded seams and ends! Smash 'em down and tape 'em into submission! Forget carefully applying teensy strips of clear cellophane tape: Load your industrial tape-gun with 2" wide shipping tape and wield it like a Viking berserker's sword! Make 'em work to unwrap your gifts!

For a festive appearance, augment shipping tape with duct tape, electrical tape and Band-Aids. Pro Tip: Anoint Band-Aids with smears of ketchup or red food color and a coupla drops of dirty motor oil daubed from your dipstick. Rub it in. Band-Aids that look used lend an endearing personal touch.

Never use conventional gift-box ribbon. A 1,000-foot roll of bright yellow and black plastic CRIME SCENE — DO NOT CROSS tape costs under 20 bucks on Amazon. com. It's stretchy, makes cool big flouncy bows, and of course it's fabulously tres chic! Big musty rolls of old kite string are cheap at garage sales too. It breaks easily, so take a dozen turns or more in each direction and tie it off with granny knots. Save your busted shoestrings too.

I like giving gift certificates from outfits like Cabela's, The Kansas City Steak Company and BePrepared.com. Put 'em in little gifty-envelopes, tape them to a brick, or between two bricks, and commence wrapping! The hollow cavities in standard concrete cinder blocks can hold cool stocking-stuffers like Gun-Tips and Bore-Tips by Super-Brush, folding knives and other goodies. Bricks and cinder blocks give an exciting "mystery heft" to your gifts.

Throughout the year, be alert to unique gift containers like old, dented Hello Kitty and Buck Rogers kids' lunchboxes with sprung hinges; discarded mailboxes, damaged bird houses and more!

One example: If you're giving a range buddy a roll of Paul Clean .22- to .50-cal. patches (see the "2016 Gift Guide" in this issue), try winding the Rollpatch around the inside of a bald, worn-out go-cart tire, then wrap that. Deflated ancient basketballs can hold lots of gifts too.

See? Even if you don't have your own flashes of brilliance or inspiration from the disembodied voice of James Earl Jones, you too can be a gift-wrapping superstar! Connor OUT.

BEFORE THEY GET BURIED
Prepare to pounce, penny-pinchers!

MARCH/APRIL 2017

Springfield Armory's 1911 Range Officer 9mm is definitely a bargain to watch for.

As I write this in late September 2016, the marketing monster of SHOT Show — January 17–20, 2017 — is already fixin' to flatten you with hype and horsefeathers about all the NEW! and REVOLUTIONARY! handguns to debut in Las Vegas. And who knows? There might even be some new-ish and interesting stuff to sniff amongst the examples of paint-on performance and "fetish firearms," like single-shot .380's you can wear as cufflinks or 12-pound four-shot .444 Marlin revolvers. But there's another dynamic to SHOT Show you should be aware of. I've benefitted from it for years and now I'm cutting you in on it.

A certain slice of our handgunning community just has to have whatever guns the marketing mavens proclaim as the newest and hottest — like, right now! — and they'll often pay "way over list prices to get 'em first. You know who I'm talking about, right? I call 'em The Gimme Gang. They crow and strut and show off their new pets to whomever they can corner, and put maybe one box of rounds through them. Then they lose interest, and the piece gets banished to the back of the gun safe while they chase another "newest, hottest" handgun.

Is this a bad thing? Nah; not necessarily, because the following year, those become the guns The Gimme Gang are dumpin' for chump change in order to help fund a new buncha handguns. That's when skinflints — I mean, "budget-minded shooters" — like you and me can pounce! Deals will be out there. Just keep your ears open and your nose in the wind.

Pounce-Worthy Prey

They're one or two years old now, but this hardly makes 'em obsolete, does it? Here's a selection of handguns I've tested and evaluated, and been pleasantly surprised by.

I'm not a big fan of the .40 S&W cartridge, though I shoot a lot of 'em. These two pistols tickled me, and if you're a 40-fanatic, you might like them too. They're both slim, flat, compact and eminently suited for concealed carry. I tested and wrote up Kahr's CT 40 in the May 2015 issue of GUNS Magazine. It's one of their "Value Series" pistols, priced at only $449. This is $200 less than its premium-line brother, the TP 40. Most of the money-saving differences are purely aesthetic and none are critical to function or reliability. The major money-saver is substitution of a conventionally rifled barrel for the TP 40's polygon-grooved tube.

After factory-recommended break-in, the CT 40 ran perfectly. Its rock-solid reliability was no surprise, but its accuracy was, and at only 21.8 ounces with a very slender girth, its behavior under recoil, even with hot tactical loads, was exemplary.

The Performance Center Ported M&P Shield pistols I reviewed for the July/August 2016 issue of Handgunner weren't new designs, but really valuable upgrades over the original Shields — and great bargains, particularly the .40 S&W variant. For only $70 more than the "standard" Shield you get HI-VIZ "LitePipe" sights, the porting treatment, which I would describe as "3rd-Gen intelligent porting," and, thanks to a Performance Center trigger sear and striker plunger, significantly better trigger pull, break and re-set. Shooting them alongside un-ported, unenhanced models, the combined effect was truly notable, especially in controlled rapid fire. I rate it as a "best buy."

Now For The Nine's

Testing Springfield Armory's 1911 Range Officer 9mm was pure pleasure from start to finish. Dead-bang accurate and smooth-cycling, the powder-puff recoil you get from shooting 9mm target loads from a hefty, full-size 1911 can easily rope you into long, high round-count range sessions, and at about half the cost of sending .45 ACP's downrange. You'll find my review of it in the May/June 2015 Handgunner.

Its goody-list is long, including a match-grade hand-fitted barrel, bushing and slide, and bold, fully adjustable target sights. Whether you're an instructor needing a piece for demonstration and training, a competitive shooter, or you just like repeatedly punching the center out of bullseye targets for "ballistic therapy," the RO 9 can fill your bill nicely.

If some chump dumps a gently-used SIG SAUER P320 9mm at a loss, grab it! In my opinion, the P320 has the best off-the-shelf trigger of any production striker-fired pistol. If you insist, you can get one with a tabbed or hinged trigger, but I tested the standard smooth trigger, and it was, in a word, sweet. I covered all the P320's morphing mutant capabilities in my review in the January 2015 issue of GUNS, and you can read the Digital Version free online. But aside from its size, shape and caliber-shifting potential, if all you did was select one caliber, size and grip combination and stuck with it, you'd have a stunningly strong, simple, superbly accurate pistol which outclasses many others at twice the price. I admired the P320's engineering as much as its performance, which was excellent.

Now look in the mirror and practice saying this: "Well, I dunno. This pistol's kinda yesterday's news, ya know? But I guess I could take it off your hands for the right price" — and try not to smirk, okay? Connor OUT.

THE SUN CAME UP
Same as usual, but somehow ... different

MAY/JUNE 2017

L ate October 2016: I found myself facing two distinctly disparate yet strikingly similar events. Both featured cackling witches, prancing goblins, masks concealing true identities; fake superheroes and mindless zombies; promises of cheap treats and playing of cruel tricks, followed by messy mornings-after.

One was Halloween. I got through that just fine, and enjoyed it. I was an eager, enthusiastic, even a valued participant. The other event was the national general elections of November 8th. The witches were uglier, the goblins more ghoulish; the tricks were nastier and there were no "treats" at all. I did not feel like a valued participant. On the drive

home from voting I passed a small cemetery and wondered how many of the dear departed had already voted by absentee ballot.

At home base we declared an "Election-Madness-Free Zone" early on the 8th. No TV, no internet — and put our phones on mute. Whatever was gonna happen would happen, and might have very little to do with actual living, legal citizens of the United States of America casting their votes, and maybe more to do with pre-stuffed ballot boxes, not-so-mysterious "glitches" in voting machines and inexplicable electronic counts.

We had been told loudly and stridently by "experts" who would and must win, and win in a presumed landslide. We chose to light the grill, scorch some beef, then spend a quiet chilly evening sippin' drinks, gazing into a fire and not entertaining "what-if?" questions. I took the phones off mute about 0230. A waxing half-moon rose under an arc of glimmering stars. The skies were not on fire. I thought, well, that's good, and turned in.

The Morning After

I'd intended to sleep in a bit. Not happenin'. My son was shouting on the phone. "Dad! Turn on the TV! Go on the 'net! They're cryin' like babies! You gotta see this!

It's fantastic!" I had to cut him off and ask what had happened. Then I looked for myself. Wow. It was true. I had missed "the end of the world!" during the night, but the videos were viral. Across the "mainstream media" spectrum, there they were: the nation's sophisticated, elite, urbane, self-proclaimed intellectuals; predatory politicians, alleged "journalists" (actually just unregistered lobbyists), and social commentators, most weeping rivers of tears and spewing gobbets of snot, choking in disbelief. Melted makeup pooled in puddles on talk-show tables. Some simply stared, goggle-eyed, lookin' like they'd just been whacked in their foreheads with a knacker's mallet. Others, shaking their fashionably coiffed heads, clenched their soft little fists in trembling, childish frustration and rage, and stuttered "No! N-N-No! How could this be?"

Simple, ya buffoons: While you were high on hair spray and dizzy from puttin' a hard left spin on events and calling it "news," we were simmering. Yeah; us, the folks who fix your fancy cars, who make sure your lights come on and your toilets flush. We, who truck your food, entrain your high-end appliances, install your climate-controlled wine cellars. [News Flash: We don't resent your material success — We resent your attitude toward us.] We, of the small towns and stable little cities; of the vast unincorporated areas in the "fly-over" states; the people who, when you weren't ignoring and overlooking us, you continually — and falsely — accused of racism, sexism, misogyny and yes, sheer stupidity if we didn't vote as we were told we should. You've blamed us for every tragedy and travesty in human experience from slavery to shin splints, and you didn't think we'd eventually get sick of you?

I think I might speak for millions when I say this election wasn't about Left versus Right; it was about Looney-Tunes Left versus NOT-Looney-Left. And it wasn't really about "our" candidate versus yours. I think a toad in a tutu coulda run for president against your sacred cow and carried 30 states. It was more about these two things: Your ideology and your arrogance; your anti-Americanism and your superciliousness. Against the massive power, influence and money of government, Hollywood and the media, all we had was our votes — and we used them. You're lucky it wasn't rope. You can only sneer and jeer at workin' folks so long before we strip off our work gloves, put down our wrenches, turn off our drill presses and poke you in the snoot.

Meantime In America
Violent crime continues to drop everywhere Americans are lawfully armed, and self-defense is a recognized natural right. Conversely, murderous violence continues to rise in the urban strongholds of "commonsense gun control" and the Nanny State. None of the Hollywood hotshots who swore to leave the country if their Anointed One lost the election have been seen draggin' their Gucci bags over the border. Sniveling, whining overgrown toddlers are still weeping in their university campus "safe spaces," coddled by witless professors-of-whatever. The nation, I think, needs several million pair of one-size-fits-all Grownup Pants — but with built-in diapers. You "experts" lost, to which I simply say, "Well, boo-hoo. Grow up."

What happens now? I dunno. Long, long ago in a galaxy far away, taking fire in a helo jinkin' like a bat on crack, a door gunner smiled and yelled at me, "Bes' strop yerseff in tight, sargint! She's gon' git reeeaall BOMPY a'fore she smooves out!" He fired a burst, turned back and grinned, "Iffen she DO smoove out!"

I'm hopin' she do smoove out. Connor OUT.

MEMORIES
Poppin' up like posies — or punji sticks, whatever …

JULY/AUGUST 2017

Most people take casual strolls down Memory Lane. Me, I tend to trip and plunge off the north bluff of Memory Mountain, smashing into every boulder, tree stump and frozen dead Yeti on the way down.

You know how it goes. You get a fleeting glimpse of a face; hear a voice, a scrap of song or some distinctive sound, like helo rotors pullin' hard; catch a certain scent on the breeze. Instantly, your cranial cogs are kicked into gear, and ...

I was pullin' wadded newspaper out of a package, saw a photo an' Bang! – that's Ank! — exactly as he looked in the '80's. An old photo? He'd be in his late 60's now. But it was him, absolutely, in every detail. I read the blurb. No, it wasn't Ank. It's an American actor named Adrien Brody. I Googled him, just to make sure it wasn't somehow Ank in disguise. Nope. Seems he's famous, though I hadn't seen any of his movies. I woulda been freepeen gout if I had. It isn't just a resemblance, either. Add broader shoulders, more muscle, a French accent and we're talkin' doppelganger for Ank.

The Real Ank

The real Ank, a French-Moroccan, served in the French paratroops and then became a "contracted representative of French and other Western interests;" the sort who humps a ruck and rifle; a good soldier. His given name was Henri, pronounced Ahn-ree, but after learning the diminutive for the Anglicized "Henry" was "Hank," he insisted on using it, because, he said, "Eez Americain neek-name, oui? And I will be un Americain someday!"

The problem was, like many French-speakers, he couldn't pronounce the H-sound for beans. No matter how hard he tried, "Hank" always came out "'Ank." So, we called him 'Ank. After much de rigueur teasing by our multinational crew, he gave a Gallic shrug and accepted it. Why, he was asked, did he want so badly to be an American? He would look shocked.

"You kee-deeng me? More free! Very big, purple mountain majesty, wave of grain, cool! 'Ot dogs at baze-ball game! Yankees, Indians of Cleve-land! Cruising in Chevy

Camaro! More pretty chick-ladies, all kinds! Cheeseburger, chili! Taco! America! Ronal' Reagan, President, keeks ass! Land of free, home of brave! Bon temps!"

Another problem: 'Ank learned sorta-English phrases only by what they sounded like to him, with poorly-connected meanings. There was an incident ("Bones in the Bearded Barley;" no space to tell it here) in which one of our guys had a little nervous breakdown. 'Ank reported on his condition.

"Ehhh, 'e's freepeen gout, but 'e will be okay." Huh? "You know; freepeen gout, like," — 'Ank bugged his eyes, stuck his tongue out and wagged it, spun an index finger around one ear — "Creh-zee, okay? Lost marbles; gone boogla-boogla-boogla!" Took one minute to laugh our butts off, another to figure out he meant "freaking out" or perhaps "flipping out." That was not how he'd heard it. Again with the Gallic shrug. Ahh, 'Ank ...

Mo & The Kek

When the Soviets invaded Afghanistan, a hereditary tribal chief sent his youngest son to live with relatives who ran a bakery in New Jersey. He wanted at least one son to survive. When his father and brothers were killed, Mo returned to the rockpile to lead his clan's fighters. He told them to call him "Boss Man." They didn't know English, but presumed it was a title of respect. They trusted him implicitly.

"But you," he said, "We are equal. You call me Mo, hokay? Name is Mohammed, but," he waved his hand, "Half dese guys named Mohammed. Look!" He raised his voice slightly, called "Mohammed!" A dozen heads swiveled attentively. "See? Much confused. Wotchu gonna do, hey?" He waved them off, like "Never mind," and they went back to cleaning rifles and sharpening knives.

Squatting over an ops plan, maps and drawings spread out on a flat rock. Many questions: Can your guys get from here to here, without being seen? In how long? Is the river too fast, too deep to cross here? Mo frowned, squinted, asked hushed questions of his XO, who looked like a backwoods Abraham Lincoln with an AK. At each juncture, Mo would nod, grunt and mutter, "Shoor. Pitt-suh kek," and each time, those men closest nodded to each other with half-smiles and repeated, "Pitt-suh kek."

Finally Mo stood, spread his arms over the maps and plans, fired some unintelligible word-salad in Dari and loudly declared "Pitt-suh kek!" Smiles bloomed like opium poppies; the men grinned, their heads bobbed, waves of words, "something-BossMan-something-Pitt-suh KEK!" rolled from man to man downhill. Huh? What the heck is pitt-suh kek?

"Oh," Mo explained. "Means easy; no problem. I teached them. Good plan, good fight, but not, you know, suicide thing. Is American saying, pitt-suh kek. Like, you bake a kek inna bakery; frostie outside, candle on top for birthday? Don' you know KEK? If something is pitt-suh kek, means easy."

"Piece of cake," Mo. Gotcha, buddy.

Ah, man. So much more: Watta-boo; Chip TUbeeg and the OO-Lung; the Russian's sincere but mangled and misapplied farewell wishes "Break your leg!" — and no room to tell 'em. Untold, they'll rattle around in my head for days ...

For most people, strolls down Memory Lane are typically brief. Me, I'm still gasping at the bottom of the bluff, with a sack fulla lumpy memories. And a frozen dead Yeti. Connor OUT.

TRAINING, BULGOGI & CARDBOARD
... with a side of salsa, please.

SEPTEMBER/OCTOBER 2017

At my range, there are certain advantages to being big, scarred, ugly and weird. The image is heightened by raggedy post-apocalyptic clothing, and fancy fashion accessories like my dented straw sun helmet and a lunar-lander walker-cane wrapped in Camo Form digi-cammie tape. I would also carry a katana with its sheath stuck through a sash, if it didn't keep getting bollixed up with my cane and trippin' me. My compromise on that is a World War I German trench knife jammed under my belt. I'm all about the bling, y'know.

The effect is also enhanced by being known as "that psycho Connor character." For one thing, bored, wandering, busybody Range Safety Officers tend either to pointedly leave you alone, or approach you very gingerly — especially if they've heard about the RSO who disturbed my shooting for no good reason. The look on his face was so cute when I lurched up close and roared, Trouble not the tiger in his lair nor the lion at his meat, manling! I 'bout tinkled myself snickering after he fled.

Later, the club prez reproved me gently, but I had a good excuse for my sand-blasting decibel level: "We both had ear plugs in. You know how that is." He just laughed and shook his head.

I'd get a lot more self-training done at the range if folks weren't always comin' up — behind me! — which sorta freaks me out — to ask about the training classes they presume I'm giving. I'm not. Wrong guy for the job.

Wrong Guy

Yeah, I've done lotsa teaching over lotsa years. But, for about 45 percent of it, my students' qualifications were often limited to herding goats, harvesting millet and getting stomped by invading armies. Another 45 percent was spent training police SWAT units and pre-tuned military personnel. With Group A, the emphasis was on "sneak, peek, shoot & scoot." With Group B it was weighted toward blinding speed and overwhelming violence. Both groups were rapt, intent learners and each, in their

Range essentials: Multi-sized cardboard targets, shot timer, Kraut trench knife, Tibetan monk's beads and Corning TB6-Y Tactical Banana.

ways, taught me as much as I taught them.

The remaining 10 percent was made up of training a wide and varied mix of American civilian shooters. From them I learned first, many were better shots than most metro cops. Second, the weapon-handling skills of lots of these "amateurs" were right up on par with some high-level military people — and they didn't even know how good they were. But muddling in their midst were mugs who flat scared the kapok outta me, frequently prompting me to scream "If ya muzzle-sweep me one more time, ya moron, I swear I'll pop a pill right through yer gourd!" While the miscreants pouted and sulked, I went off and checked my shorts for passed peach-pits.

Such frankness, I was advised, was "impolitic." Thus endeth my career in "open-to-public" training. Generally speaking, I'm not cut out for "general" activities.

Once they learn I'm not offering classes, folks wanta know what kinda drills I run for myself — suspecting I possess some secret sauce for success. Nope; most of it is more like plain soy sauce. Here's an example:

My 1911's aren't in my daily-carry battery anymore. To me, that means I must shoot 'em from time to time lest they become strangers to my hands. I picked up this drill from a guy who owned two Italian restaurants and had seven kids, so he didn't have much time to spend shooting the 1911 he packed every day. Once a week he stopped at my old PD range and bought a flat of 50 rounds of .45 ACP reloaded ball. At 25 yards, starting with a chambered round and seven in the mag, he methodically fired two mags right-handed, then two mags left-handed, doing both lefty and right-handed reloads. Next up were two mags rapid-fired 2-handed. He finished with one mag fired slowly and precisely, going for the tightest possible grouping. Fifty rounds, well invested in very little time.

It's a KISS thing. It works. Both your weapon and your basic skills are tested, and "muscle memory" refreshed, all in a measurable way. For me, it either reveals rusted reflexes, or provides reassurance; sometimes both.

My regular "default drills" are based on basics you can get from any number of books and videos. Then, I admit, I add a little salsa and spicy stir-fry sauce. This is both to challenge and entertain me, and also, certain aspects of it help keep looky-lous (looky-lice?) from milling around behind me, or worse — approaching me.

Adding The Salsa

A good but plain-Jane drill you prob'ly know pits the shooter against two to four standard IDPA/ USPSA cardboard torso targets. Using a shot-timer like the PACT Club Timer III, from the beep, put two rounds in each, slow enough to assure all hits are in top-scoring zones. Check your elapsed times. Push faster until you start dropping rounds outside the sweet spots, then back off, slow down and work your way up again. Maybe you integrate a reload. It's sound, but it lacks panache. Kick it up.

Between and around those full-size cardboards, add in half-size*, and some 10" and 5" mini-torsos**. Vary your drills; don't just shoot left-to-right and back again. Shoot the little guys first, then the larger ones or vice versa or "Connor-versa," which appears to onlookers to be a spazz-pattern. It is actually coldly calculated — by a spazz. Me.

The variety is healthy. You can snap-shoot the full and half-size targets, but the minis force you to concentrate, bear down and get squinty. Sure, program reloads in too, and switching from right to left hand. Now add more fun with malfunction drills: Say you have 10 identical 15-round magazines and six inert dry-fire rounds. In six mags, stagger placement of duds, like second round in one, sixth round in another, blah-blah. Then mix the mags up so you don't know where the surprises are. And on the timer, give yourself no slack for correcting your malf's. Now for the spicy stir-fry sauce:

Between sweeps of the targets, while gripping your pistol in one hand, bring your other hand back, touch your thumb to your nose, waggle your fingers vigorously, and shout as loudly as possible "O ye sinners, now shall ye repent! Let the Great Slaying begin!" or, "For freedom, Fritos and chicken-fried steak!" or, "Back awaaay from the bulgogi and nobody gets hurt!" Note: Never mess with my bulgogi. Never.

Or, try shouting "I love you and blood sausage too!" — but shout it in German; makes it confusing and terrifying. Ich liebe dich und blutwurst auch!

Exercising exemplary muzzle control and strictly observing all range safety protocols, slump your shoulders, hang your head and slowly turn around, looking dazed, lost, spaced-out ... Then, by degrees, "recover consciousness" and smile. It's unlikely anyone will be there by this point, so that smile can be very genuine. If any looky-lou's are still present, they'll prob'ly be frozen like deer caught in headlights. Perfecto!

If you see me at the range and I'm munchin' a sammich and sippin' coffee, stop and say howdy. But if I'm shooting drills, well ... Trouble not, etcetera. Connor OUT

*Available from MidwayUSA.com and other providers. **Go to BenStoegerProShop.com; see "Scaled Dry-Fire Targets."

DRAMATIS PERSONAE
Means "The guys from Bones in the Bearded Barley," okay?

November/December 2017

Climb in your 'Way-Back Machine and navigate to "Memories" in the July/ August Guncrank. Got it? I introduced you to 'Ank, mentioned "Bones in the Bearded Barley," and said there was no space to tell the story. Now envision me pulling up on the road, rolling down my window and sayin' "No time to explain. Get in the truck. Gonna go meet Collie." You in? There is a connection. Trust me.

Collie was quite simply the hairiest human being I have ever seen — ever — of any race, anyplace. We're talking "pelt" more so than hair, and it was all jet-black, coarse and curly, and grew at a furious rate. I've seen him in a loincloth — that's another story — and I can tell you it was "full coverage" hair. Adding to this, he was among the most muscular men I've ever seen, including Arnold in his prime and other professional body-builders. He was only about five-ten, but so densely slabbed with muscle it was cartoonish, and made him look like a meat locomotive.

Collie's father — we'll call him Ivan — was a huge, dark, hairy Slav from the remote Russian steppes. His big, slanted, half-lidded eyes, which he passed on to Collie, suggested when Genghis Khan swept through in the 13th century, he may have tarried a night or two. (Note: Genghis is credited with fathering up to 2,000 known children.)

As the Iron Curtain went up across Europe, Ivan was a young un-blooded Soviet soldier assigned to a lonely machinegun tower, where a minefield and barbed wire fronted a dirt road. His partner, described as a Stalin-worshipping drunken jerk, stayed smashed on samogon or sleeping it off, when he wasn't enthusiastically pretending to machinegun the West Germans on the road.

As time passed Ivan couldn't help noticing privately owned (!) trucks loaded with consumer goods, vegetables — even fruit and melons! — going by, and the clean clothes, real shoes and smiles worn by the people. According to his political officer they were miserable slaves of the capitalist swine, longing for Marxist progress and glory. Pretty happy, well-fed slaves, he thought.

One day a truck heaped over its rails with potatoes stopped on the road across from his tower. Three farm boys got out, loaded their arms with spuds, and commenced chuckin' 'em hard over the fence. "Why?" mused Ivan; "They can't hit my tower at that dista ... NO! They're trying to explode the mines!" They didn't succeed, which surprised Ivan. Sometimes the dang things detonated for no known reason. The boys finally drove away laughing. Gazing over the minefield, Ivan said it hit him like a thunderclap: POTATOES!

Thunderclapz X 2

Seconds later, while his partner snored, Ivan was creeping gingerly through the minefield, scared spitless but somehow simultaneously drooling, plucking potatoes off the ground and stuffing them into his belted blouse, expecting to be blown skyward at any second. Even the broken ones were the biggest, most beautiful potatoes he had ever seen, and as a former Russian farmboy, Ivan knew his spuds. Then, he said, as he crouched peering at a suspicious lump in the dirt beside and under a huge potato, the second thunderclap hit him.

"Here I am," he pondered, "Risking death by landmine or firing squad to pick up food thrown away by people said to be oppressed by greedy Western capitalists. If this is oppression, I want some!"

Ivan was almost at the fence. On the road, a man wearing a suit approached riding a bicycle. Ivan thought, "He could be a Chekist! NKVD? GRU? (The KGB was not formed until 1954.) I could be shot today, right here, for leaving my post, or for talking to this man." With his heart in his throat — and a load of potatoes bulging comically from his blouse — he hailed the man, who stopped, aghast. In broken German, with tears in his eyes, Ivan emptied out his story and a plea for help. Later, Ivan said only divine intervention could explain his meeting that particular man on that day.

The bicyclist was an escaped Russian-speaking Ukrainian, now a West German metalworks factory manager, and a huge fan of spy novels. He was exuberantly hooked — and a plot was joyously hatched. A few weeks later, Ivan added an extra bottle of samogon to his tower partner's libations. When the jerk was totally blotto, Ivan kindly fed him several ounces of "anti-hangover medicine" — actually, enough of a powerful laxative to keep a squad, umm ... "seated" for a week.

With his partner, minus boots and pants, securely "enthroned," semi-conscious and busily convulsing, Ivan moved briskly to the tower, where he disabled the machinegun, pocketed the bolts of their rifles, and for good measure, yanked the guts out of their rarely-operating field phone. Following his carefully, subtly marked path through the minefield, he found bolt cutters and

metal shears exactly where they were promised to be. Two minutes later he was in the ditch on the far side of the road, flinging off his tunic and donning a not-quite-big-enough long coat and a broad-brimmed hat. A new man strode due west, whistling, off to meet a friend.

The Instant Scot

The Brits granted him asylum, and a church sponsored his move to the highlands of Scotland. He immediately took a proper Scottish name and enrolled in English language classes. There he met the daughter of a Greek family who had fled the civil war in Greece. She was big, strong, dark, with eyes as black as her heavy, waist-length curly hair. Language barriers be damned; they knew true love when it gob-smacked 'em. Collie was their firstborn.

Our inside joke was "What do you get when you cross a big Greek girl with a big hairy Russian? Zorba the Bear!" (If you don't get it, Google-search "Zorba the" — you'll see.) He grew up speaking Russian, Greek, English and a smattering of local Gaelic, all with a heavy Scottish burr. "Collie," by the way, was not a diminutive for "Colin" or "Collier" as you might assume. No, his childhood nickname came from the "Rough Collie;" the shaggy, long-haired Scottish sheepdog. After 20 years in the army, he became a GLUD — a "Guy Like Us: Deniable" — and a superior mission planner and small-group operations leader.

Collie had his quirks. An example: Up on a riverbank in Africa, he stretched rope and canvas over an iron frame which once held a hefty irrigation pump and generator. This let him sleep 18" off the ground. He caught four big scorpions, held them down with a pencil, tied a loop of thread behind their cephalothoraxes, and hung one about 10" below each corner of his "cot." They dangled, seemingly enraged but helpless. A visitor, an annoying young US Army lieutenant saw one and screamed "There's a scorpion climbing up to your bed!" Phillips corrected him. "No, there are four, actually. Suspended, not climbing." He looked, he stuttered, and blurted "W-W-Why?"

Collie opened one baleful, goblin eye and growled, "To sarve as a warnin' t' others, ye daft booger."

Here's the scoop: Many stories — people and events — have lain untold for too long. I may have to tell them in episodes; in serial form. I will, if it flies with Roy, and with you. Connor OUT.

("IT FLIES." —-RH)MORE
DRAMATIS PERSONAE

Means more of "The guys from Bones in the Bearded Barley."

January/February 2018

"Collie in the Dark" — *Original artwork by Connor. Worth $Bajillionz$ when he's dead. Current appraisal: $1.37.*

The nine of you who actually read my scribbles know what's goin' on, right? I'm trying to tell a story called "Bones in the Bearded Barley," but it's problematic. First, it's too big, and I refuse to squash it down to roadkill, so I have to tell it piecemeal. Second, I won't tell it without talking about the people involved. I introduced you to 'Ank, a principal player (Guncrank, July/Aug 2017), and then to Collie in the Nov/Dec issue. If you read the latter, I ask you — How could I talk about Collie without telling you his father's story? Can't. Wouldn't.

"Bones" is a complex tale taken from what was supposed to be a four-hour truck ride followed by an easy 10–12 hour dress rehearsal/training refresher. Instead, it featured two days and nights marooned in floodwaters, a buncha stories shared among us, and a third "memorable" sorta-horrifying night. I 'splained some of it in Odd Angry Shot in the September and October issues of GUNS Magazine, plus the twisty-strange story of Milo, Ren and Isolde. If you don't get GUNS, you might want to read the story on the web site.

More On Collie & The Crew

Got a mental image of Collie? A big mobile knot of hairy muscle, with thick, curly black hair to his shoulders and a matching full beard ravens could hide in — if they dared. He was physically imposing, but by far his most striking features were his big, slanted, half-lidded eyes, with porcelain-like whites and jet-black irises. People often remarked his eyes appeared to be burning with rage. He was actually extremely even-tempered; he just looked like he was simmering on the edge of boiling all the time.

Collie never yelled, never cursed and never verbally flayed anybody. He didn't have to. He could burn you to the ground with a goblin-glance. If you fumbled some task or direction — as long as it wasn't repeated — he might call you "daft," or ask "Are ye daft, mon?" If you in any way shirked, tried to cut a corner, or did or said anything out of anger or meanness, he might say you were "actin' a booger," and say, like, "Doona be a booger; not ever again, lad." But if he even once pronounced anyone a "daft booger," they were toast; outta the unit or off the planet, whatever.

You could choose "work names" for the unit — I used John Connor, for "reasons" — but in addition to work names, Collie appointed "call tags," and when you got one from Collie, it stuck, and you didn't ask why. I don't know if it was another Collie quirk, or his obsession with double-blind security. He started calling me The Connor from the first. Some were easy to figure out, like "The Buckle," whose surname was Belt. "The Watcher" threw me at first. He was an Asian representing France, and I supposed, maybe a surveillance-and-observation specialist. That wasn't it. I inquired. He was amused.

"You do not know my work-name, do you?" he asked. I admitted I didn't. "It is Wa Ching." He waited a second, but I was still stumped. "I am Chinese. Wa Ching means some Chinese guy; like, a random Chinese man. It is clever, yes?" Yeah, I agreed; pretty clever. But why "The Watcher"? He explained that went back to the day he reported to the unit — to Collie. He knocked on the frame of the duty office door, and said a strange, earth-rumbling noise like "COOM!" boomed out. He saw a large, hulking, hairy something at a desk, head down, looking at a dossier The Watcher assumed was his. He entered and stood front and center. Collie looked up.

"Wah! Those EYES!" Watcher blurted, "Belong on a dragon boat, not on human, you know? If my grandmother saw him, she would run, hide, burn incense, call up ancestor spirits for protection." Watcher paused, looked up, added "My mother too, I think. I could not look into them; made me nervous. I am grown man, but he, those eyes, umm ... surprise me, okay? I looked out window to left, yes? He says You are? I still looking out window, and nervous I say fast, like, I-am-Wa-Ching." He says to me, I see. And so you are, with very small laugh. So he calls me The Watcher."

Runners & Dullards

Philip P. Phillips was called "The Runner," pronounced Rrroonerrr, in Collie's Scottish burr. He was the oldest of our mob, a marathoner, and could run us all into the ground over distances. P.P.P. was our quintessential Englishman; a Brit, sure, but pure Old School Englishman, with his fair hair, clear blue eyes, patrician nose and rangy frame — and his oh-so-English speech and mannerisms. All his "verys" were veddy-veddy; his "rathers" all raw-thuh, with the odd upper-crust English habit of chopping personal pronouns off the front of sentences. He used his briar pipe like an orchestra conductor's baton, or for pointing and poking, and often addressed comments to invisible third parties. That made for some interesting conversations, like, when I asked him about his work-name: Why the "Philips"? He poked his pipe at the air to his right.

"Boy is curious, eh? Sign of intelligence, p'raps?" Turning back to me, he said, "Of Macedon. Philip II. Overshadowed by his pup, Alexander the Great. Deserves better. Wrote thesis on him, un homage." I asked about the middle initial P — another Philip?

"Nay," he said. "Gift from Collie; raw-thuh insisted 'pon it. Knew I'd once run a marathon on historic ground." He looked at me quizzically, waiting for me to figure it out, but I was drawing blanks. "Historic ground? Eh? Eh?" My gears spun and clashed for a moment, then ... "Pheidippides!" I cried. "Marathon to Athens!" He was delighted; turned back smiling to his invisible friend, pipe poking. "Oh, bright boy!" he laughed. "Not the dullard he appears, eh? Yass."

And his droll, dry sense of humor: There was a base maintenance guy; good kid; not the brightest bulb, scared spitless of Collie and would scuttle out of sight when their paths crossed. Phillips always treated him with the kindest indulgence, but sometimes twisted his tail a bit, for fun. Among other peculiar pastimes, PPP was known to have been a professional hunter in Africa. The kid asked if Phillips and Collie had worked together there.

"Fabulous man on safari!" Phillips exclaimed. "Cape buffalo worship him as a deity, you know; rather a god of hate and murder. Respect that, they do. Lie down in the tall grass and avert their eyes 'pon his approach, they do, not wishing to attract his attention and p'raps offend him. Smashing, yass?" The kid's eyes saucered and goggled. His jaw dropped open. "Reeeaaalllyyy?" he breathed. Phillips patted him gently on the shoulder.

> Collie never yelled, never cursed and never verbally flayed anybody. He didn't have to. He could burn you to the ground with a goblin-glance.

"Off with you now, laddie. Work to do; be about it! That's the good boy!" The kid wandered away shaking his head. "True-hearted boy," Phillips said, "But," tapping his head with his pipe. "Insufficient bandwidth. Story of his life could be titled Gullible's Travels."

Note: I cut this by 1,000 words, but still maybe too much for you? Demand my expulsion NOW, or I swear, I'm gonna tell you more! Connor OUT.

Made in the USA
Monee, IL
15 April 2025

3642b1fa-0a72-4adb-ae38-ebddbaf7b124R01